— Awakening the —
CHAKRAS

"This remarkable volume is a groundbreaking integration of Western psychology and Eastern wisdom. The three authors are longtime intrepid explorers of faraway continents and spiritual mysteries. They bring a multidimensional understanding that will deepen the reader's appreciation of the chakra system. Moreover, contemplation of the magnificent color plates is likely to open new channels of intuitive insight into their power."

DAVID VAN NUYS, PH.D., PROFESSOR EMERITUS OF PSYCHOLOGY AT SONOMA STATE UNIVERSITY AND FOUNDER AND HOST OF *SHRINK RAP RADIO* PODCASTS

"*Awakening the Chakras* can provide a roadmap for navigating life's journey. The authors have presented their material in an engaging and interesting manner. Colorful artwork and inspirational messages help illuminate the reader's path and fulfill the authors' goal to rouse the inner spirit of those who accept their invitation."

STANLEY KRIPPNER, PH.D., COAUTHOR OF *THE SHAMANIC POWERS OF ROLLING THUNDER*

"The authors have collaborated powerfully to create a rich, poetic, and profound work of art as well as spiritual, psychological science. The collective wisdom and suggested practices are just what is needed for inspiration and balance in challenging times. Prepare to be led on a gentle, yet deep, expansive journey through the revelatory chakra system by the many masters the authors have gathered and generously shared."

SUSAN J. WRIGHT, AUTHOR OF *THE CHAKRAS IN SHAMANIC PRACTICE*

"*Awakening the Chakras* looks at the chakras directly from ancient sources and examines how to use them as a focal point for meditation and other inner work in a clear and concise way. It engages both sides of the brain through storytelling intertwined with historical information in a way that brings us to a place beyond usual perception. Victor, Kooch, and Pieter could not have written this book together without being an example of the harmony of the chakra practices mentioned."

MIRIAM JACOBS, AUTHOR OF *TAROT AND THE CHAKRAS*

"A multilayered perspective that enhances the information about the chakra system. Weltevrede's artwork brings the words to life. The authors' collective experience with this ancient system of spiritual development has enabled them to create a text that speaks equally to practitioners of all religious/spiritual traditions. This book rises to the top of the pile. It represents not only the most coherent explanation I have read to date but simultaneously the one that is most respectful of the ancient Vedic tradition from which it derives. Kudos to all three authors. It is a job well done!"

ANNA JEDRZIEWSKI, *RETAILING INSIGHT* MAGAZINE

"*Awakening the Chakras* is an exquisite book. Beautifully written and illustrated, it is personal, practical, and authoritative. Spiritual and wise, the book itself truly has the potential to help awaken the chakras."

ELEANOR CRISWELL HANNA, ED.D.,
PROFESSOR EMERITUS OF PSYCHOLOGY AT SONOMA STATE UNIVERSITY
AND AUTHOR OF *HOW YOGA WORKS*

"There is immense wisdom presented from both the Indian teachers and Western psychology. The synthesis of this remarkable material brought to you by extremely capable people is brilliant. This is not a minor work: It entices you in but demands more than a quick breeze through and can be used as an in-depth how-to manual for each chakra. A few words cannot do justice to this masterful presentation. This is a source you can trust."

JACK R. NEGGERMAN, MSSW, LISW, LICDC,
CERTIFIED GESTALT THERAPIST AND CLINICAL SOCIAL WORKER

"In this book Western psychology is informed by the power of Indian spiritual forms through a fuller understanding of the chakra system or hierarchy. The well-written narrative is easily accessible and an encouraging self-reflection at a deeper level than is usually possible in most Western systems of thought. This new work introduces the reader to a wisdom-centered view of self-awareness and consciousness."

CHARLES MERRILL, ED.D.,
PROFESSOR EMERITUS OF PSYCHOLOGY AT SONOMA STATE UNIVERSITY

"The authors are not only philosophers but have also given voice to divine guidance—a wisdom beyond ordinary reach."

RAMESH RASTOGI, LIFELONG ASSOCIATE OF HARISH JOHARI

— Awakening the —
CHAKRAS

The Seven Energy Centers in Your Daily Life

Victor Daniels,
Kooch N. Daniels,
and Pieter Weltevrede

Illustrated by Pieter Weltevrede

Destiny Books
Rochester, Vermont • Toronto, Canada

Destiny Books
One Park Street
Rochester, Vermont 05767
www.DestinyBooks.com

Destiny Books is a division of Inner Traditions International

Note to the reader: The authors and publisher make no claim nor take responsibility for treating any personal, interpersonal, family, or other physical or psychological disorder. When using any of the meditation, awareness, or other psychological or spiritual methods and practices described here, the authors advise all readers to work within the framework of their comfort zone.

Library of Congress Cataloging-in-Publication Data

Names: Daniels, Victor, 1941– author. | Daniels, Kooch, author. | Weltevrede, Pieter, author.

Title: Awakening the chakras : the seven energy centers in your daily life /Victor Daniels, Kooch N. Daniels, and Pieter Weltevrede ; illustrated by Pieter Weltevrede.

Description: Rochester, Vermont : Destiny Books, [2017] | Includes bibliographical references and index.

Identifiers: LCCN 2016031332 (print) | LCCN 2016035971 (e-book) | ISBN 9781620555873 (pbk.) | ISBN 9781620555880 (e-book)

Subjects: LCSH: Chakras.

Classification: LCC BF1442.C53 D356 2017 (print) | LCC BF1442.C53 (e-book) | DDC 131—dc23

LC record available at https://lccn.loc.gov/2016031332

Printed and bound in the United States by P.A. Hutchison Company

10 9 8 7 6 5 4 3 2

Text design and layout by Priscilla Baker
This book was typeset in Garamond Premier Pro with Gill Sans, Goudy Sans, and Grotesque used as display typefaces

To send correspondence to the author of this book, mail a first-class letter to the author c/o Inner Traditions • Bear & Company, One Park Street, Rochester, VT 05767, and we will forward the communication.

This book is dedicated to our teacher, guide, and friend
Sri Harish Johari,
one of the most remarkable people we have ever known.

AUM GANG GANAPATAYE NAMAH

Contents

Preface

How This Book Evolved

*And Grateful Acknowledgments to
Those Who Helped It Along*

In our travels along spiritual paths, it was a blessing to meet Sri Harish Johari, who introduced us to the chakra system. Dada, as his students called him, spent at least several weeks, and sometimes even months, of each year teaching in Europe and America before he left this mortal realm in 1999. When he traveled, he always carried a bag of gems that he sold along the way to help his students and pay for his journey. The Hindi name Johari means "jeweler" or "gemologist," just as the name Carpenter in English-speaking countries refers to those whose family history was lived out in the woodworking trade. Even though his family was not from a tradition of jewelers (they were rulers), he took his name seriously and became a knower of gems.

The most valuable jewels Johari carried were the gems of wisdom that he scattered among those who opened their hearts and minds to his teachings. He was a *jnana yogi* (a spiritual philosopher), a sculptor and painter, and a temple artist. He had deep knowledge of Vedic and Hindu teachings, ayurvedic (traditional Indian medicine) healing methods, and the philosophical traditions of India. He lived those wisdoms by example and sublime integrity in his daily life.

He was also a first-class cook. Rather than subject himself to the cooking of those with less knowledge of the healing properties of food and spices than his own, he spent a good deal of time in the kitchen, creating savory ayurvedic dishes (when he wasn't fasting). Before he ate with others, he always ensured that they were served first.

With unsurpassed charm, he shared soulful talks about various threads of yogic or tantric philosophy. As he did, followers and visitors would almost be transported to the realms of the mystic gurus, *sadhus, rishis,* and others whose knowledge he seamlessly stitched together.*

Besides the gems, the philosophy, and the cooking, he created sacred art depicting Indian mythology and philosophy. Each of his canvases and murals tells a story that waits patiently to be seen by all who are ready to receive it. One of the authors of this book, Pieter Weltevrede, was his principal art student, and Pieter's illustrations in these pages replicate the symbolic form of chakra wisdom taught by Johari.

The foundation for this work comes from Johari's thinking, writing, and his many discourses in Europe and America. After years of discussing the gems of knowledge he had left behind after his death, the authors came together to work on this project.

Even though Pieter spends part of every year in India, living and teaching at the Johari house and gathering insights from his long association with diverse gurus, not until 2001 did Victor and Kooch take advantage of an opportunity to spend time with Pieter in the world's largest spiritual festival, the Kumbh Mela in Allahabad, where millions of pilgrims assembled. Together with uncounted others, they plunged into the cool waters of the Ganges on one of the most auspicious bathing days, which is said to wash away all sins incurred up to that point. But since that experience was many moons ago, this writing project meant that it was time for them to return to India to seek out teachers and more knowledge about relevant sacred pathways to the inner self. And surely it would be valuable to revisit some of the ashrams and temples, fields, and forests that formed the cauldron of transformational experiences out of which the chakra system was born.

---

*Terms that may be unfamiliar to the reader, such as *sadhu* or *rishi,* are defined in the glossary at the end of the book.

When Victor and Kooch arrived back in India, they made their way to the Johari house in Haridwar, where they stayed with Harish's daughter Seema and her family. Seema herself is an important influence in this book, although quietly in the background. She offered food for the body and soul, never-ending cups of chai, and shared valuable insights into her culture and the time-honored traditions of her father and family. From the roof of her house one can look down on a branch of the great river Ganges that flows by just a few hundred feet away. Harish's granddaughter Anushree Agarwal helped in a multitude of ways, taking us places we would not otherwise have gone or known how to get to, and offering valuable information when we needed it. We also thank Seema's husband, Abhai Kumar, who helped facilitate our stay at their family home, took us to his wonderful rose farm and rosewater distillery in the countryside, and introduced us to his neighbors there whose farm allowed us to see what rural life in India was like perhaps hundreds or even thousands of years ago.

The day after returning from a side trip farther north to Rishikesh, Victor and Kooch had the good fortune to be in Haridwar at the same time as guruji Pilot Baba, who was at his ashram for just four days before needing to leave for Delhi. He had been a friend of Harish Johari, and the authors had met him in Europe, California, and Allahabad in the years after Johari passed on. He had been trained as a scientist and had a master's degree in organic chemistry; then from 1957 to 1972 was a pilot in the Indian Air Force, decorated for extraordinary feats of bravery. He became a pilot of Prime Minister Indira Gandhi's plane, India's equivalent of Air Force One. As Buddha taught, one of Pilot Baba's central attitudes is to *test every belief and everything told to you against your own personal experience, and accept only what proves true for you.* When he left the Air Force, he felt called to go into the Himalayas on foot, and spent sixteen years studying with the most accomplished swamis, yogis, and other spiritual teachers he could find. What a transition!

Since he was trained as a scientist before he became a pilot and later one of the world's most accomplished public yogis, he thinks critically and creatively about matters that many people take for granted and do not question. With this outlook of encouraging people to actually think for themselves rather than accept others' opinions, he was a perfect person to interview about the chakras. Numerous quotations and paraphrases of his comments found in these pages are taken from our discussions with him during three days of sitting and listening to his personal dialogues.

A longtime resident at the Johari house is Dada's student Heidi Rauhut. She took Victor and Kooch to the Santosh Puri Ashram in Saptarishi ("Seven Rishis") near Haridwar to interview Mataji Narmada Puri about her understanding of chakras. Those visits also profoundly influenced this book.

Another day Heidi took Kooch and Victor to the Shri Ram Orphanage in the foothills of the Himalayas, run by disciples of Baba Hari Dass, who now lives at his ashram in Santa Cruz, California. He is the only guru they've ever known who maintains a discipline of total silence. He communicates solely by writing messages on a chalkboard. Those messages sufficed to produce two books, from which you will find quotations in these pages. And sometimes Heidi would bring out a book from her personal library that she selected for the light it threw on the chakras. One of these was *Kundalini Tantra* by the founder of Bihar Yoga University in Munger, Swami Satyananda Saraswati, whose historic writings were first introduced to us by contemporary Swami Nityananda Saraswati. We have also included sayings and writings from other past and present yogis of the Indian subcontinent, including Anandamayi Ma, now long since passed away, who has a lovely glistening white marble temple in Haridwar, and Sri Aurobindo, who pulled together many threads of Indian thought into an integrated whole.

Although the three authors of this book each pursue a different life path, we are united in our love for Sri Harish Johari. Notably, Pieter shares his mystical illustrations from the viewpoint of a Dutch artist who has spent much of his life studying with Johari and other sages and gurus of India. Before severe storms closed the road, he had followed the rishis' route north from Rishikesh up into the Himalayas, where many ancient and modern gurus secretly lived and still live. Since the Kumbh Mela in Nasik (2004) he has had a close friendship with Avadh Behari Das Kathiababa, regarded by his order as a *jnana guru,* or "sadhu with knowledge." With him he could share and discuss his thoughts about Johari's work. Pieter has a degree in social science and is still using that outlook from time to time to look at the sometimes chaotic, but usually well-functioning, Indian society. Johari, and later Kathiababa, helped him to get a better understanding of this still-living ancient culture. The insights he gathered have profoundly affected this writing.

For inspiration, Pieter draws mainly on his personal experiences with Dada, on recordings of Johari's talks in Europe and America, and on his books *Chakras,*

Leela, and *Tools for Tantra*. Pieter's depth of knowledge of the visual tantric tradition offers a point of view that is time-honored yet unique. His words are directly tied into the visual Indian symbolic imagery of the deities that grace these pages. His artistic commentaries explain in detail the symbols and figures depicted in his sacred art and the tradition from which his art arose.

Kooch's contributions come from her intuitive and mystical inclinations, an experiential understanding that evolved from many special moments spent listening to Johari's remarkable teachings, her longtime studies with Sri Mata Amritanandamayi, and her studies and work in psychology, which emphasize Carl Jung's work and the powers of the subconscious mind.

Victor's Ph.D. in psychology, his expertise in scientific, academic, and therapeutic branches of that field, and forty years of university teaching motivated him to look deeply into the mental and emotional patterns associated with each chakra.

The authors' views are similar but not identical. Victor and Kooch draw more heavily on twentieth-century psychology, and Pieter emphasizes the historic spiritual traditions of India. The psychological perspective emphasizes a direct sharpening and more effective use of the senses, while the traditional Indian spiritual approach emphasizes withdrawing energy inward from the senses, in order to avoid being obsessed with them. If you come across this or some other apparent contradiction in the text, it will be a good time to remember the principle of "multiple perspectives"—that the same event may be viewed differently by different people, and the fullest understanding of it usually comes when the various views of it are taken into account.

A word about how we worked together on this book may be helpful. Although the largest share of the text was written by Victor and Kooch, Pieter also contributed text based on his understanding of the tantric tradition. All of the illustrations, both the colored paintings and the line drawings, are his work. We have all individually read and critiqued the entire manuscript, regardless of who was the principal author of any given section.

We wish to express our immense gratitude to Inner Traditions International and Destiny Books for backing this project, and especially to acquisitions editor Jon Graham and publisher Ehud Sperling. Since Destiny Books is the publisher of Johari's numerous works in the United States, this project as we have conceived of it and carried it out would simply not have been possible without their support. We were blessed with the remarkable good fortune of having Nancy

Yeilding as our copyeditor, who copyedited Sri Harish Johari's seminal book *Chakras: Energy Centers of Transformation*. Her painstaking work has brightened almost every page of this book. The discerning eye and judgement of project editor Meghan MacLean brought together and integrated the contributions of all of us who worked on this project. In early stages Inner Traditions's editor in chief, Jeanie Levitan, and her assistant, Patricia Rydle, offered wise guidance and direction along with Erica Robinson, who crafted the catalog description and cover copy for this book. Our publicist Manzanita Carpenter was also helpful. And we cannot fail to put in a good word for our late friend and literary agent, Bob Silverstein, who has passed over to the other side, for suggesting the title of chapter 3, "The Polarity Principle," and helping us conceptualize it. Philosopher Stan McDaniel also offered some useful suggestions for that chapter. Many thanks to all.

INTRODUCTION

When we talk about chakras, we talk about everything.

HARISH JOHARI

Why are you holding this book in your hands? Perhaps you think it will help you make personal changes you desire, or deepen your understanding of yourself and others. You may hope to awaken dormant potentials or discover what can make your life more than it is.

Harish Johari. Photo courtesy of Seema Agarwal, Harish Johari's daughter.

These are ancient as well as modern goals. Eons ago, in the dimly remembered beginnings of orally transmitted history, various people aspired to raise their consciousness. One outcome of their efforts was a set of answers that has been passed through the ages: the chakra system. As they sought to live a sacred life, some ancient philosophers found that wholehearted work with the chakras can light the path of awakening. They recognized that observing and meditating on your chakras can help you know your inner self, ignite latent abilities, and create fulfillment of and beyond worldly desires.

The chakra system, a vertical map of consciousness superimposed on points along the spine, underlies many yogic practices. Its study can help a student, or a sadhu or you, to tread a path that leads to lasting happiness and a connection with the universal spirit of creation.

WHAT ARE THE CHAKRAS?

Just when and where the chakra system originated may never be known. Its oldest written records date from a thousand-year period of forest-dwelling rishis' teachings, as chronicled in the *Kundalini Upanishad*.[1]

Whatever its origins and age, knowledge of the chakra system has been passed down through generations by sage after sage. Sri Harish Johari openly transmitted its essence to Western culture. His classic work *Chakras: Energy Centers of Transformation* is one of the most valuable resources on this subject.[2] Johari taught that the chakra system is a representation of creation from top to bottom, from the highest to the lowest qualities of consciousness.

The Sanskrit word *chakra* means "wheel of light." Each chakra has a dominant function or quality and several secondary qualities. Expressively portrayed as vortices of swirling energy, each chakra is connected with specific patterns and potentials of thinking, feeling, sensing, and acting. Each one is aligned with a different consecutive point on the spine, with the first (root) chakra at the base of the spine and the seventh (crown) chakra at the top of the head.

See an overview in the table "The Seven Chakras in Brief" on the opposite page.

Chakras are an ancient system of inner awareness and reflection that belongs to yoga. The aim of yoga is union with the source, or cosmic consciousness. It is a pathway to *dhyana* or deep meditation that can lead from finite to infinite

THE SEVEN CHAKRAS IN BRIEF

CHAKRA	NAME	TITLE	ELEMENT	FACULTY
1	Muladhara	root chakra	earth	smell
2	Svadhishthana	passion chakra	water	taste
3	Manipura	power chakra	fire	sight
4	Anahata	heart chakra	air	touch
5	Vishuddha	throat chakra	akasha (space)	speech, sound
6	Ajna	the third eye	mahat (all)	mind
7	Sahasrara	crown chakra	beyond elements	consciousness

consciousness. We all have a spark of this eternal flame inside us. For the yogi, chakras are a system to realize this Self. The goal of yoga is to be free of the tyranny of the desires of the lower chakras. For those who persevere in following a yogic path, at the end of *leela,* the great game of life, it is said that ultimately just one desire remains: union with all people, beings, and other entities in the cosmos, but, most important, union with the One where everything originates. By opening oneself to the world of the chakras a person begins to consciously convert mental energies into spiritual energies, like a phoenix rising from the smoldering ashes of an obsolete state of mind.

Pilot Baba compares the energy fields of the chakras to gravitation. "Gravitation is one of the most powerful energies in this universe," he says. "To which chakra is your personal gravitation pulling you? That's probably where you need to work."[3]

He states that a self-realized person's life force moves freely through all the chakras, so that their energies flow together in a harmonious way in accord with whatever a situation requires. Most of us, however, have at least a few stumbling blocks related to the workings of our chakras. Learning about the chakras helps us on our way to self-realization. And there are many obstacles on the way. Knowledge of how these centers affect us can help us move past them.

The sages who spread the knowledge of the chakra system established a systematic path for "waking up" to greater consciousness and freedom. They were inspired to help humanity remove the mental filters and blinders that trap the mind in restrictive boundaries and other time-bound illusions that society's dominant belief system labels reality. As we remove misperceptions, we become able to perceive what truly *is* real, both within and outside us. Our personal quest begins to follow a psychologically and spiritually sophisticated path for transforming our inner spirit and our relationships with the world. As our insight deepens we can become more inwardly whole, outwardly wise, and mentally free.

Every account of chakras and how to work with them reflects the philosophical context within which it arose. A person who practices a spiritual discipline may talk about the chakras in a different way than one who follows a psychological path. This book presents beneficial ways of using the chakra system that are accessible to people who follow any religious, philosophical, or psychological approach.

CHAKRAS AND PSYCHOLOGY

In the mid-twentieth century, psychologist Abraham Maslow described a hierarchy of needs, a map of consciousness not so very different from the chakra system. Maslow's hierarchy includes "physiological and safety needs," which he also calls "deficiency needs." It also includes "belongingness and love needs" and "self-actualization needs," which he collectively labels "being needs."[4]

Of course, no such map is reality itself—it merely represents inner states of being. As semanticist Alfred Korzybski pointed out, a map is not the territory it depicts, nor is a word, idea, or thought the thing it represents.[5] But even if we know that, we may forget it and get caught in *samsara* or *maya*—the world of illusion in which we mistake our ideas for the realities they represent.

Western psychotherapy's dominant goal has been to make people sane, in the sense of being able to feel all right within themselves and to function in the world. Some psychologists, like Maslow, go further. They want people to feel truly healed and whole, in deep contact with themselves, and in satisfying relationships with others.

The sages who created the chakra system had an even more ambitious goal. They saw society itself as crazy in certain ways, and what we typically call normal as part of that craziness. *Normal* does not mean "sane." It means "the norm, the average." To be "lost in illusion" means that we often act in ways that are a result of mistaking our ideas and socially conditioned responses for reality itself. We legalize ways for some people to become incredibly wealthy while others stalk the streets in hope of avoiding starvation. Some of us are inwardly turned against ourselves and outwardly antagonistic toward others. We forget that living in inner and outer clarity, kindness, and harmony is possible. Since both psychological insights and chakra work can offer greater understanding of our personal hierachy of needs, their truths can overlap.

Each of us is surrounded by forces that dominate our minds and lives. As long as people have been on Earth we have been calling these forces *deities*. It is a way to express our amazement and admiration for the mysteriously beautiful creation of this universe. When we can experience this as filled with love and care, we call it divine. We try to express with this word our awareness of some transcendent consciousness that is behind the game of life. We created forms for these divine forces to express their different characters. These forms are made by humans to get more understanding of the forces that are present in nature. When we can see the divine in them we can more easily free ourselves from desires that try to push us in harmful directions, away from desires that we identify with so fully that they become the central motivating forces that create the psychodramas of our lives.

Developing the full positive potentials of the chakras leads toward more understanding of supreme consciousness and the Divine. The *Divine* can also be translated as "the inexplicable." It can only be experienced. It is the most profound of all experiences.

CHAKRA IMAGERY

The images found in these pages come from an ancient tradition. They seem to belong to a common dream world, open to everyone, like a collective unconscious. It was part of Johari's contribution that he created a coherent system from a very complex tradition. To make the spiritual content of the chakras clear, he drew and painted visual images for each chakra, based on ancient Vedic traditions. Much of the imagery here is based on his work.

Talking about the chakras as a concept is food for the left brain, which likes abstract thinking. We also have a right brain that needs something concrete, such as a percept. A percept without a concept is empty, and a concept without a percept is blind. Words like *chair, computer, airplane,* and so on have meaning only when there is a concrete object or percept to which they correspond. If the visual depictions of the chakras in these pages are combined with conceptual study, the chakras will become more meaningful and valuable.

The descriptions of the illustrations are actually a story of a spiritual journey where deities play their roles in explaining how to use the chakras effectively. Chakras are not tantric or Hindu property, although they come out of these traditions. They don't belong to any cult or religion. They are the result of a thorough study of human nature, which is universal.

Each percept or symbol has its own story. For example, even in the West, the seductive charm of Venus, the Roman goddess of love and beauty, never dies. Many believe that such deities live in the substratum of our existence. Even if we don't know some of the history of the ancient deities, we still pay heed to lessons that they offer, such as preferring to get married in the lucky month of June since the Roman goddess Juno gives a special blessing to the bride who marries in her favored month. Or we can be misled if we misinterpret their messages.

The deities and other items in the chakra imagery represent forces in us that we need to recognize. They represent things like the breath, the gases in our body, the nerves, the sense organs, being awake, dreaming, or sleeping, mind, ego or intellect, and so on. Sometimes these are easy to perceive. Sometimes they are more subtle. We cannot see but still feel them, or we can only hear them like music. And there are even those that go beyond sensory perception and can only be experienced. As when we peel an onion layer by layer, at a certain point we will reach the center, where it all came from.

In the chakras the forms of the deities can be seen as an ABC of the alphabet. Once we understand that, we don't see letters anymore, but words with meanings. And they convey a message, a teaching. Once Dada took us to the Daxsh Mandir in Haridwar. He guided us through the temple, which was filled with images of Shiva and the ten Mahavidyas. At a certain point he explained to us how Indians see these images. When they see an image of Shiva, they also see all the little symbols used in that image, such as the items the deity is holding or the animal depicted with him. All these symbols are connected to stories. In a flash of a second the viewer is connected to all these elaborate stories. For Western people that is not easy. It takes time to see and understand the different symbols that are used.

In this book we try to explain the different deities and their symbols. They tell a story that brings us to a place beyond sensory perception, words, thoughts, or images. The images represent concepts. Studying them tells us more about the depth of Indian or yogic or Vedantic spiritual knowledge. Through these connections we can more easily understand and enjoy the path that the chakras are showing us. Once the message is understood and experienced, the images are not needed anymore.

Indian philosophy puts creation in a cyclic form, not in a linear one. It tells us where we come from and where we are going. Chakras are a story of the elements (earth, water, fire, air, and void) that are connected to our world of sensory perception. It tells us how the sense organs originated, and how we can find our way back to what is beyond the senses.

HOW THIS BOOK IS STRUCTURED

Three introductory chapters describe processes and perspectives to guide our inner journey.

Each of the seven chapters from four through ten deals with a specific chakra. They share a common structure. Each one starts with a sentence that sums up that chakra's central qualities and a relevant quotation from Sri Harish Johari. This is followed by "Correspondences," an outline that includes the physical location of the chakra, key phrases related to its influence, links to astrology, days of the week, elements, and sense organs.

Then a descriptive section, "Essence," tells what the chakra is all about. Next a unique "Table of Possibilities" shows forms that each chakra's energies can take. After the table, a section called "The Bright Side" starts with a three- or four-line comment on gifts and strengths, followed by supporting text. Then "The Dark Side," which begins with a few lines about issues and challenges, offers a parallel description of difficulties that can emerge in that chakra. "Past Roots" explains how problems related to a specific chakra may begin.

The next major section is titled "The Body and Emotions Pathway: Feeling Tones in the [respective] Chakra." Its first section, called "Personal Transformation," suggests methods to realize the power of a chakra's opportunities and reduce that of its obstacles. The second section, "Relational Transformation," offers ways to improve your relationships with friends, family, lovers, and others.

Then comes a section titled "The Pathway of Spirit: Imagery in the [respective] Chakra," in which Pieter describes in detail the meaning of each of the principal images in the beautiful painting of that chakra given in the color insert and the line drawing that corresponds to it. At that point, when you look at the pictures, they tell a story and you know what the pictures mean.

The last major section of each chakra's chapter, "Practical Tools For [respective] Chakra Work" includes ways of using your understanding of the chakras to benefit your everyday life. These encourage self-discovery and meaningful connections with your chakras.

After the chapters on each of the seven chakras is a chapter on removing obstacles and then a concluding chapter. The book also includes a glossary of important terms.

With open minds, we honor your own path and way of looking at the world. We realize that you are unique, with your own religious, secular, spiritual, agnostic, or atheistic outlook, and that your own chakra work begins where it begins for you, not where it begins for anyone else. Mataji Narmada Puri points out that you can only start from where you are: "We only know as much as we know now. We have to take whatever time it takes. Go on doing what you can do at this point because you can't do anything else. Enjoy yourself as you are, and enjoy life."[6]

As we three worked together, we tried to illuminate a pathway that leads toward a fuller, more authentic and contented life. As you connect with each chakra, you can develop your beneficial qualities and deeper understandings of your true self. We invite you to rouse your inner spirit to live more harmoniously and happily as you move toward fulfilling your personal yet unpredictable destiny. You might even see the sacred mystery in your life. But now it's simply time to turn the page.

1

AN INWARD EYE

Meditation on the flame of a lamp produces a state of mind called witness consciousness. This witness of the self is ageless and timeless, that essence which survives all transformations of personality, all emotional storms, all changes of thought, all experience. . . . The witness is centered in the region of the third eye.

HARISH JOHARI, *DHANWANTARI*

SANTOSH PURI'S ISLAND AND NARMADA PURI

The ancient Indian city of Haridwar is called the gateway to the gods. Not far from it the Ganges River, Mother Ganga, splits into seven fingers that spread over a vast flat expanse of the North Indian plain. A few miles north of the city, not far from Seven Rishis Road, heavily populated with meandering orange-garbed sadhus, you can stand beneath a strip of trees on the west side of the river and look northward at the front range of the majestic Himalayas in the distance. When you look east, you see the nearest channel of the river and then an island, a vast expanse of rock, gravel, and driftwood that has floated downriver and found a calm resting place. When you sit by the bank to take in the spectacle of that vast landscape, from time to time someone might walk past you along the dirt footpath that runs alongside the river.

Just downstream, the nearest channel flows wide and shallow and you can cross through it onto the island. Until some years ago a slender sadhu named Santosh Puri lived on the island. Naked except for a covering of ash on his body, he was a *naga baba,* an ascetic renunciate who milked his cows for food, and depended on "what the Ganga brings" for his firewood and other necessities of life. *The Ganga* was an expansive term that meant not only the river but also anything brought to him by divine fortune. A naga baba makes the ultimate non-materialistic statement. He possesses nothing but a container that can serve to carry water, milk, or food or be used as a begging bowl; a loincloth to tie around his waist when he goes into town; and perhaps a blanket to protect against cold or rain. In the naga baba's view, all material desires are futile distractions that come between himself and God.

On the island near Seven Rishis Road, a small collection of naga babas lived for short or longer periods. In 1969, a twenty-four-year old German woman went to India on a spiritual quest and ultimately found her way to that island. She instantly perceived Santosh Puri to be her guru, and devoted herself to following his path of austerity. For an entire year there was no conversation, no discussion, no eating together. Her only words in his presence were the mantra *Om Namah Shivaya.* They communicated nonverbally, slept next to the river, and cared for Santosh Puri's holy cows. Often he sat up meditating in the middle of the night. At 2:00 a.m. every day he rose in the darkness and carried out religious observances. Again and again he tried to send his self-declared disciple away, for a woman was not part of his plan for a life of celibacy and austerity. Although she experienced many daunting challenges and nearly died several times, the woman's spiritual energy did not waver. Eventually Santosh Puri stopped objecting to her presence, acknowledged his love for her, and gave up his vow of celibacy. They married and had three children. As the years went by she became the venerated Narmada Puri, or "Mataji," mentioned in the preface and the introduction. Her book *Tears of Bliss: A Guru-Disciple Mystery* is a heart-moving testimony describing the dedication and austerities of a spiritual renunciant.[1]

Many of Mataji's struggles during her early years on the island were at the first-chakra level: sheer physical survival, life or death. She seems to have willingly accepted her hardships such as living on her own in caves and going without food for long periods. Perhaps in a sense, Mataji's choices were soulfully linked with her guru's name, Santosh, which means "contentment; self-sufficiency." Usually (but not always) he modeled contentment with a shield of wisdom for almost every circumstance. In his complete surrender to God's will, a humble and ego-freeing pathway was etched into the depths of his character. We can only surmise that he was awake in higher-chakra consciousness, as he possessed a remarkable acceptance of difficult circumstances that could not be changed, and an overall spirit of peace or contentment even in the face of great hardships.

Another female guru, Gurumayi Chidvilasananda, claims that "It's when you are free from selfishness . . . when you are not thinking about yourself in a selfish way, that you experience the tender shoots of contentment growing inside your heart."[2] Her understanding is like a magnifying glass that enables us to contemplate Santosh Puri's brave choices and our own selfish or selfless, worldly or spiritual nature.

THE SEVEN CHAKRAS ON THE ISLAND

"When you go to India to discover more about chakras, be sure to talk with Mataji," Pieter told Kooch and Victor in late 2013 before they boarded an airplane for Delhi. Following his advice, they went to her ashram just north of the ancient holy city of Haridwar, and conversed with her in its flower-laden outdoor pagoda built on top of Sri Santosh Puri's last resting place, where he was buried sitting upright in a full lotus position.

Mataji taught that chakras are the five elements in action, teachings that are beautifully represented in plate 1: Seven Cosmic Energy Centers. Muladhara, the first chakra, is connected to earth, the sense of smell, and the importance of security (food, shelter, and work). Svadhisthana, the second chakra, is connected to the water element, the life-giving forces, and the sense of taste. Meditating on the second chakra teaches us about the importance of family and the emotional web of our own life. Manipura, the third chakra, relates to the fire element and sense of sight. It is the seat of ego. Name, recognition, and honor are important here. Anahata is the fourth chakra and it is linked to the element of air and the sense of touch. It is located in the heart region, where we can feel unselfish love and compassion.

Vishuddha, or the fifth chakra, is connected with the *akasha* (or space) element and the sense of sound. Higher teachings such as discipline and self-control are linked with this center. In the Ajna, or sixth, chakra, one goes beyond ordinary thinking, and can enter into deep states of meditation. When someone (mostly yogis or people on an spiritual path) opens the Sahasrara, or seventh, chakra, self-realization and communion with the divine spirit is said to be attained.

When we go back in time and look closely at life on Santosh Puri's island, we can envision the higher workings of the chakras. Santosh Puri disdained the glamour- and celebrity-consciousness of the second chakra. He seldom left the island. Indeed, one year when the Ganges flooded, everyone else evacuated the island but he found a perch high in a tree and watched the flood waters sweep past him below. He never allowed any honor or reverence to be shown to him. His vow of celibacy was a second-chakra event, and so too was giving up the vow, marrying Narmada, and raising a family. As for the third and sixth chakras, he expressed a gentle yet fierce strength by living a life of radical renunciation with his third eye wide open to see beyond worldly understanding.

The fourth chakra is visible in his and Narmada's selfless care for each other, their family, and their cows. But it went further. They cultivated a loving attitude toward everyone. Despite possessing almost nothing, their ideal was to eat only after they had fed the cows and at least ten other people. They did not congratulate themselves on being spiritually minded—it was their humble life.

"Everyone was welcome at Babaji's duni," says ashtanga yoga teacher Narayan Puri. (*Babaji* is a term of respect used for those whom others consider great gurus. A *duni* is a sacred firepit in which the flame is never allowed to go completely out.) Narayan Puri continues:

> People of all religions, races, castes and creeds came to be in his presence; Sadhus from different . . . orders, high-ranked Pandits sitting next to low or out-caste workers, criminals beside policemen and merchants . . . Muslims, Hindus and Christians, as well as the dogs and the cows. All enjoyed being near Babaji. . . . One time a Brahmin priest asked Babaji, "Why do you let all these strange people stay at your duni? You are a Hindu, a Sannyasin." Babaji just smiled and said, "I am no Hindu, no Muslim, no Christian. I am a fakir, a yogi. I have no temple; the Ganga is my temple." . . . He lived in Atman consciousness, All is ONE.[3]

Though at first glance it may seem paradoxical, the fifth chakra can be seen in Santosh Puri's and Narmada Puri's discipline of silence during her first year on the island. Santosh Puri taught by example. He showed that we can hold back the flood of trivia that makes up most everyday speech, and communicate what truly counts through gratitude and action.

The sixth chakra is apparent in Santosh Puri's ability to see deeply into other people, and occasionally to be the apparent cause of events that to others seemed miraculous. He and Narmada Puri both seem to have succeeded in perceiving the divine spirit in all (or at least most) people and beings.

Of the seventh chakra, or at least touching a trace of it, Narayan Puri writes,

Being in his [Santosh Puri's] presence during meditation, the veil of thoughts melted away like fog in the coming daylight. The essence of "I" melted into the pulsation of the present moment. . . . After experiencing this Grace, Babaji often just smiled or sent me off to do seva (selfless service). Always . . . his grace continued flowing and surrounding me as if it had always been there. . . . [This] lean fakir [was] a being of Truth, a yogi beyond words, beyond facades, a Self-realized soul.[4]

Now let's consider some reflections that provide a context for our present work.

"WHAT'S IN IT FOR ME?": EXPLORING YOUR CHAKRAS

Checking out what's happening in each of your chakras requires examining your internal energies. This reflective process can help you better handle both problems and opportunities. Speaking of his personal experience, Pieter says, "When we first got confronted with learning about our chakras, we had no clue about our inner world. It was just one big fog. From social sciences we got some concepts like ego, superego, subconscious, and also learned names for mental problems like schizophrenia, psychosis, neurosis, and now ADHD and autism. But the inner world still remained a mystery. There were no stories and no teachers. Sri Harish Johari helped us to understand that the main contribution of the chakras is that they help give meaning to the world we are living in."

Meditation enables you to dive within your inner being, where meaningful dialogue with chakras begins. When you make a point of noticing how your energy moves through various situations, you're likely to become aware of your chakras and the polarities that exist within them. Many of us think primarily about the positive aspects of chakras, but when we have troubles or worries, their opposite qualities can come into focus. When that happens, you may be wise to reflect on a troubling issue and do your best to work it through, or you might conclude that you're not quite ready to deal with that issue yet. Either way, viewing your situation through the consciousness-expanding lens of chakra meditation can help you strengthen and regain your inner balance. Even if at present you're not ready to do inner work on a given issue, when the challenges of your situation or your reactions are less intense, you may feel differently. Then you can dive into inner space and connect with the force field of subtle chakra energy that relates to your experience and the feelings you hold.

When you decide to work with your chakras, consider following these four steps:

First, select a situation and a *chakra that corresponds with qualities related to it. In this book you'll learn more about chakra correspondences.*

Second, be willing to be in the present moment and perceive what you are actually doing, even if it contradicts your self-image. This can be tough. It may require facing and acknowledging a less-than-admirable trait. For example, it feels good to think that we're offering open hearted love from our fourth chakra. However, we may be in complete denial that we're passively acting in a selfishly controlling way in order to get what we want, rather than acknowledging our partner's needs, which is a third-chakra motivation. This particular kind of self-deception is widespread.

Third, work to consciously evolve meaningful connections with your chakras through greater awareness of mind, body, breath, and spirit—or even through sacred dance and movement or creating rituals that use the elements of chakra correspondences. By connecting with their obvious and subtle energies you can act intentionally to create a more thoughtful, stronger you.

Your fourth step is to commit to doing the inner work required to free or unstress your energy and balance your chakras. You can do this by learning to use the potentials of each chakra that best fit a given place and time, and meditating on the center that's most important in regard to what you're doing at a given moment.

For most of us, these four steps take time and effort. They require motivation, dedication, and perseverance. Are you willing to give them a try?

Several lanterns of perception can increase your ability to work with chakras. As you move through the chapters on the specific chakras, besides focused meditations, other methods for working with each chakra are offered. Don't imagine that you have to use all the methods mentioned. Use those that appeal to you. Different approaches work for different people. Use what you find useful.

BALANCING YOUR CHAKRAS TO UNLOCK POTENTIAL

Developing our chakras means awakening and expanding possibilities within ourselves. "We are going beyond the previous limitations of our inner nature, and awakening our higher sense of who we can be," says Mataji. She goes on,

> In this process, when you open your chakras there is a union of the high and low. The chakras are all connected. As a result, when you awaken the chakras at the top you also awaken those at the bottom. The energy that is working in the higher chakras becomes active in the lower ones as well. With more understanding of upper levels of consciousness that you're trying to climb to, you can work more effectively in the lower chakras.[5]

As we work to connect with the energy of our higher chakras, it is easy to fall into the trap of thinking, "Oh, my energy is higher than another person's." When we do that, we slide right into self-centered ego. Philosopher Ken Wilber sidesteps that tendency by speaking of *deepening* rather than *raising* our consciousness.[6] Here he echoes psychologists Carl Jung and Sigmund Freud. *Deepening* refers to becoming able to perceive the deeper thoughts, feelings, motives, and impulses that lie hidden in our subconscious. We may suddenly remember past events we have forgotten that show us in a less-than-favorable light. We become more aware of how we are responding at deeper levels in the present moment.

In this sense, *deeper* and *higher* are part of the same path toward greater realization of our potential. They are part of the process of finding our inner self that helps us move beyond an egotistical view of ourselves and others. As we do this, we move away from being forever trapped in aspects of our personality that we dislike, or that are counterproductive for us. We create less bad *karma* (the helpful or harmful effects of our actions). As we discover how our chakras are connected, we illuminate inner truths and open doorways to constructive change.

Pilot Baba's view of connections among the chakras is similar to Mataji's. "As you use each one, you are drawing from the energies of others as well. You want to be able to see *which wave you are riding,* and also what it is drawing from other chakras. How is the way you are going to think, speak, or act connected with your past and/or with your present state of mind and feeling? In your meditation you have to go deep, deep into your inner silence to perceive these things, to know your mind." He continues:

> Your energy can get stopped at any point, stuck in destructive ways of being. When that happens, you are crossing the river looking back, thinking and acting as you have done in the past. Instead, if you are on the path, cross and keep going. Higher consciousness can raise lower consciousness. That opens the window to do something different. You don't have to just plod along. There are points at which you can *make a jump,* like a monkey that jumps from branch to branch. That is part of what "transcendental" means. You transcend your old way and move on in a new way. It is possible. I have seen it many times. But don't think that you get wise in one jump. You have to jump into something new again and again. Cross the river and keep going. It is a process. You grow into it.[7]

The term *balancing the chakras* is widely used. It is analogous to balancing the left, analytical, "masculine" hemisphere of our brain with the right, creative, "feminine" side. We need both sides working together to function optimally. Anyone who gets stuck in using just one side of the brain, or just one chakra, cannot develop their full potential.

Part of balancing the chakras is using them in complementary ways. Then you can draw on the positive energy of the chakra that offers most in a given situation. When Pilot Baba says, "Which wave are you riding?" he's asking which chakra energy is dominant for you, or dominant at a given time and place. Knowing what empowers you gives you the freedom to choose whether to meet a situation directly, or step out of it if that's possible and appropriate. The fourth chakra is central when we speak of balancing the chakras because it exists at the midpoint, with three chakras above and three below it. Because so many people are afraid to open their heart, it is where most people get stopped, so that they live out most of their lives in their first three chakras without ever developing the potentials of the fourth, fifth, and perhaps even sixth and seventh chakras.

WORKING WITH WHAT YOU CAN DO NOW

In response to a question about the best way for someone to work on developing the positive potentials of their own chakras, Mataji replied, "You have to do things when the time is right for you. You can't make springtime in winter. Some people, once they begin searching, have a fairly easy time of it. Others have to struggle. Some even go in absolutely the wrong direction until they find the right one. The awkward attempt to understand something that we don't yet understand is all part of the path."[8] Even when you meet difficulty, facing it resolutely can help you evolve on your personal and spiritual path.

Pilot Baba adds, "We all have different kinds of energy. Your chakra work begins where it begins for you; not where it begins for someone else. If you're an alcoholic and you need a drink, for instance, accept that. Then you can begin to make choices about what you're willing to let go of, and strive to improve the actions you take."[9] You begin your journey from where you are standing now.

A spiritual teacher from Nepal, Milk Baba, says simply, "How can anyone learn about chakras unless they do the work to awaken their chakras?"[10]

Some people like to work with one chakra until they get it "right." Others prefer to move back and forth between different chakras and their respective qualities. If you're in the latter group, you might even decide to focus on a different chakra during each day of the week. You can use the correspondence charts to see which chakra is linked with which day of the week and do the work and meditations connected with it. For example, on Sunday, the day linked with the third chakra, you could focus on your solar plexus. You might chant the seed sound *RANG* for several minutes, then chant the associated mantra, *ahimsa* (ahheemsuh), several times for peace of mind before meditating on your inner experience of third-chakra qualities. Then notice how you do and don't express its qualities during the day.

Focusing on a different chakra each day of the week might feel like too much "jumping around" for you. An alternative way to work, suggests Mataji, is to select one chakra and meditate on it every day for a month. As you do, focus on awakening a particular positive potential until you feel it in your daily life. Or you might focus on a negative quality connected with a chakra that your witness consciousness tells you is causing you trouble and work on letting it go. When you focus on one chakra daily in your meditation for a month, you'll learn about it through direct experience. After focusing on a different chakra each month for seven months, you'll have a fuller understanding of them all.

DO YOU NEED A GURU TO WORK WITH YOUR CHAKRAS?

Pilot Baba and Mataji Narmada Puri both say, "Not necessarily." Mataji says simply, "You can work with the chakras comfortably by yourself. Your guru is already inside."[11] This does not mean that a guru or teacher is not useful—just that at a certain point it is important to find your own internal teacher who will awaken your understanding of your unique path to your own liberation. Pilot Baba explained to us:

> Everything is a gate. You yourself can choose which gates you want to walk through. One gate will take you to this [He opens his hand, palm upward]. . . . The other will take you to this [He shows a closed fist]. . . . Which life do you choose? Are you going for the light? Focus on the best thing that seems possible for you. Surrender everything that keeps you from following that path. Just be there.
>
> When I went into the mountains, I had a feeling of someone forcing me to go higher and higher, in the Himalayas and in myself. It was my own impulse, not what anyone else was saying I should do. I am saying, trust your

own experiences. Do not trust what other people are telling you, or telling you to do. That is true freedom, true liberation. As long as you are following others' agendas, you are not free. In our schools and our society we do not teach freedom. We give it only lip service. We need to truly teach it.[12]

His words share several points in common with Western existential philosophy, such as the emphasis on our personal responsibility for what we do and what we perceive, and even for the language we choose to describe our experience and the events around us. "You create your own language," he said. "You can't understand the meaning of the words without having the experience."[13] Only through direct experience does so-called information become real knowledge.

Likewise, French philosopher Jean-Paul Sartre declared that each of us is responsible for everything we do. Even if we seek advice from others, we choose our adviser and have some idea of the course he or she will recommend. Not choosing is still a choice for which we are responsible. If faced with inevitable circumstances, we still choose *how we are* in those circumstances.

Baba Hari Dass adds succinctly, "If you want to collect pearls, you have to dive deep. So don't confuse your mind by sitting on the beach and expecting pearls to come sit in your basket."[14]

Johari shared a similar view:

One who is responsible for all he does doesn't have to blame anyone else for his problems. When you learn that independence, and gain the confidence in yourself, then you can work most effectively on your chakras. . . . You don't need somebody to come and guide you at every step. Learn not to depend on a teacher, not to depend on anybody, not even to depend on God, and then you will depend on you. Then you will grow up and be responsible for all that you do.[15]

This view parallels that of analyst Carl Jung, who distinguished between individualism and individuation.[16] *Individuation* is realizing our own unique potentialities. It is coming to know, giving expression to, and harmonizing the various components of our psyche. He found that through listening to the messages of our imagination and dreams, we can contact and reintegrate our different parts. *Individualism,* widely misunderstood and misused, all too often actually means a *lack* of individuality, in that we are expected to mouth the same slogans, act the same ways, and buy the same products as others, while looking down on those who are different. Or it can mean identifying with our self-centered ego, thereby getting lost in illusions about who we are instead of actually discovering our inner selves.

Movement from *individualism* to *individuation* in which we draw out our full potential is a major step in becoming whole. As we come to know our uniqueness, we are no longer slaves to others' beliefs, in contrast to the pseudo-individualism of following others' views of who and how we ought to be.

Jung pointed to a "universal individuation"—a community of realized selves. On such a path we see and hear how we share the common spirit of the world, at the same time that we are becoming more fully ourselves. In so doing, we awaken to becoming our own guru.

On the other hand, if we have the chance to spend time with a truly self-realized person (of whom there is not an oversupply), we'll probably find value in doing so. After all, imitation is one of the major ways we learn. That includes imitating the actions and attitudes of others whose consciousness and behavior we admire.

Now let's consider some reflections about how to work or play with your chakras. Through moment-to-moment exploration, unknown mysteries about yourself and your surroundings can become known. Are you ready to go from learning about your chakras toward personally experiencing their qualities?

2

SOLVING YOUR PERSONAL MYSTERIES

As there are moments when sunlight momentarily illuminates the patterns of waves and flows in a river, so too there are moments when the clear light of consciousness reveals the patterns in the [person's] life role. At those moments the [person] loses . . . attachment to a role and begins to see his [or her] life as part of a larger whole

HARISH JOHARI,
LEELA: THE GAME OF SELF-KNOWLEDGE

Harish Johari had a comfortable childhood. His father was a judge, stationed in several places in India. He was a yogi and had very few expectations. He lived in the here and now, where he performed his duty. When Harish decided to become an artist, the father said: "Now you have to study everything, because an artist has to know everything." In a 1999 interview about Harish's life and work, Amritha Sivanand tells this story:

As a young man he worked as a factory manager. However, upon getting married he asked his new wife if she was "prepared to starve." He explained to her that he wanted to pursue a career in art, "and that almost certainly meant they would be poor for a long period of time, but in the end both happy and rich." The alternative for her, he said, might likely be a miserable husband with years in a boring job. She agreed, and Johari quit his promising job the next day. . . . He then took up art projects not for money, but for payment in kind—clothes, rice, spices, and so on—and that way avoided even having to shop. "We had no money to spend, but we had food to eat, clothes to wear, and everything I needed was there."[1]

Quitting his job as a factory manager to be an artist and ultimately a jnana yogi and guru was a challenge for his family. He left the world of expectations. He chose to follow the path to which he felt called. His wife came from a poor family and always lived a simple life. She let go of her expectations and supported his aspirations to follow the star that beckoned to him.

FROM EXPECTATION TO REALITY:
LIFE UNFOLDS

On a large island northwest of Europe, another young man grew up where few people had material luxuries. "Life was very simple," says Roger Bannister, the world's first athlete to run a four-minute mile. "My parents had come from the north, which is a fairly rugged, bleak, hard-working part of England, and so there was not the expectation of luxury." Without such expectations, he says, most people were not unhappy that they did not have luxuries.[2]

For many, Bannister put his finger on the devil in our desires. *We make ourselves happy or unhappy not about what happens, but by comparing what happens to what we expect.* Johari claimed that problems most often come when we expect something. If we don't expect something there is no problem.

Of course, some kinds of expectation are essential to life. Learning to do almost anything involves a cause-and-effect expectation: "If I do *this,* then *that* is likely to happen." Moreover, major achievements may occur when we expect much from ourselves. And much of life can occur only in the context of shared expectations. When we drop a letter in the slot or send an e-mail, we expect that it will reach its destination.

But such simple cause-and-effect relationships are the lesser part of our lives. So are the expectations connected to them. The more complex webs of interactions often cause us trouble, because so much of life consists of multiple feedback loops rather than simple cause-and-effect relationships. That's what karma is all about. I don't just speak or act in a certain way toward you. Rather, often my actions affect you in ways that cause you to react toward me in ways that I may or may not like—and perhaps affect many others too. In a sense, much of this book is about expectations, the actions connected to them, and their effects on our relationships, on our world, and on inner or outer events that engage the energetic components of the different chakras.

We all also *hope* that certain life events will turn out to our advantage. Or we *fear* the opposite. Such hopes and fears are anticipations in the face of uncertainty, but they don't have quite the status of an expectation. But whether we're expecting or hopefully anticipating, many of our thoughts and actions are arrows pointing toward the future. Will I get the job? Will the project turn out well? Will I pass the course? Will my true love and I live happily ever after? We anticipate success, failure, something in between, or even something totally unexpected. *Life unfolds,* giving up its secrets as we go along.

Uncertainty may be active or passive. It's active when my decisions will affect what happens. It's passive when I'm a spectator—when nothing I do will make a difference or I choose to do nothing. When I watch my favorite team, I can hope that they will win, but my thoughts and expectations have no effect on how the game goes.

But when anticipation or hope is masking a fervent desire that something will turn out a certain way, my response is likely to be stronger and less flexible when my expectations aren't met. My joy or grief may be so great that I can't think straight or act wisely. Or something may turn out okay, but it's not quite what I wanted. Western guru Ram Dass, a student of Indian guru Neem Karoli Baba (who was also a friend of Harish Johari) writes,

There's this Chinese boatman, and he hits another boat in the fog. He starts swearing at the other boatman. "You SOB! Why didn't you look where you were going?" Then the fog lifts for a moment, and he sees there is nobody in the other boat. And he feels like a fool.

[Self-]righteousness is roughly the same thing. . . . The journey of consciousness is about arriving at a balance in life where you are open to the mystery of it all. Indeed, uncertainty and expectation can be among the great delights of life. Vocalist Emmylou Harris sums it up in an interview. "There's a certain grace in accepting what your life is and embracing all the good things that have been—but there's still an expectation of good things to come. Not necessarily what you expected." . . . In my own consciousness, I watch how long it takes, when an expectation isn't fulfilled, before I come back again to . . . just be with what is . . . in the presence of the great mystery.[3]

The Great Mystery. Everything that hasn't happened yet is part of it. We can be fairly confident that what actually happens will differ at least a little from our expectations. Life unfolds.

Nonetheless, for most of us, unfulfilled expectations can lead to needless anger. Ram Dass pointedly says, "When I start to get angry, I see my predicament and how I'm getting caught in expectations and righteousness. . . . Being peaceful yourself is the first step if you want to live in a peaceful universe." And then he adds a line that is very useful in working with chakras: "Spiritual practices can themselves become obstacles if you become too attached to them. Use these methods as consciously as you can, knowing that if they are truly working, eventually they will self-destruct."[4]

What you may need to work on tomorrow or next week, and which method will work for you then might be different from what is most useful to you today. In a sense much inner work is like a spiral. Each time you revisit the work you've done in a given chakra, or a given polarity within a chakra, you return with greater consciousness gained from whatever else you've been doing in the meantime.

There's also the point highlighted in the old bumper sticker about "random acts of kindness." When we perform such acts, we expect nothing in return. Doing something for another or giving something needed without expecting any return is an elixir for the soul. We feel better inside, and kinder, more compassionate, and richly connected with others. In that sense, releasing an expectation of "getting" becomes its own reward.

FROM DAILY DESIRES TO DIVINE LAWS

Getting upset when something doesn't go as we expect is almost always the result of wanting something to happen, but it doesn't. To avoid feeling bad at such times, some Vedic philosophers suggest that we overcome desires and become desireless. That perspective overlooks the insights of philosopher Adi Shankara (788–820 CE), who pointed out in *The Crest Jewel of Discrimination* that not all desires are created equal. Renouncing all desires, he noted, would quickly bring on big problems, such as death. We all desire food, water, and conditions that meet other basic needs. Problems arise both when real needs go unmet, and when we think we need much more than we actually do. The desires we do well to let go of are those that in cause some kind of pain, injury, or damage when we try to fulfill them.

Shankara may have read or heard Buddha's Second Noble Truth, articulated some 2,500 years ago. It holds that much unnecessary suffering is caused by selfish desires that cause others harm or keep them from getting what they need when we try to fulfill them. Desire for what we are unlikely to get is not so useful either. We can become slaves to our expectations and attachments.

EXPECTATION, EGO, AND DESIRE

Spending some time assessing which of your desires are rooted in deep needs has great value. You may want to let go of some of the others. Desire creates attachment. Attachment often creates bondage. Chakra awakening is a step-by-step process of overcoming, sacrifice, renunciation, and letting go. It's not a process of getting all the stuff you want and doing whatever you wish regardless of the effects. To release a desire that's not good for you, look at how to make it a better desire.

To be a self-realized sadhu like Santosh Puri requires complete surrender of ego, of letting go of almost all attachments to material goods, worldly accomplishments, and sometimes other people. By comparison, most people's desires for companionship and attachments to others are an integral part of their lives. But even some sadhus feel attachments to their religious order or their friends.

For a person who is not a sadhu, a good starting point in balancing your chakras is to discover and accept where your energy most often lies. Watch your mind, feelings, and attachments carefully. During witnessing or contemplative meditation, reflect consciously and carefully on what is no longer serving your sense of what is best for you. Are you willing to let it go? Look at what may really be better for you, others, or both. Don't worry about what you wanted in the past. In this moment, what feels right for you?

Quite a few people want to think of themselves as enlightened or more self-realized than they actually are. Mataji remarked,

It's horrible to see someone who wants to be spiritual and thinks they're spiritual but they're not—they're just talking the talk. But it's equally bad for the yogi who goes to the jungle and sits there to meditate and find God, because God is a unity between worldliness and spirituality. Since both exist, we have to honor both. For example, business life should also be the beginning of a divine life and respect for other people and beings, not a rejection of spiritual values. My own way is humility and complete acceptance of the divine spirit, however that may manifest itself in life.[5]

Pilot Baba adds,

Chakra work is not for those who think they are highly spiritual and realized. They are pretending to do much but do not know it. And you find only one person in a hundred who is not pretending. A central objective is to attain a clear mind. *You can't do that if you are pretending you already have it, because then you're blind to the ways your mind is not clear.* It is common among intellectual people who have a great deal of knowledge to be egotistical about how much they know. They are confusing knowledge with realization and wisdom in living.[6]

Such people are stuck in "spiritual ego" or "intellectual ego" without realizing it. The word *ego* has several distinctly different meanings. At a primary level, the drive toward self-preservation, and a feeling of self-respect, confidence, and being a worthwhile person are often woven together and called *ego*. These are first-chakra ego needs.

Another meaning of *ego* is the "me" that we identify as ourself. This is our sense of ourself as a separate person. This includes what we think and feel and sense and do.

Let's take an example of somebody we all know, a boss of a small company with hardworking, loyal employees. As boss he is everywhere, working for the creation of honest product and the welfare of his workers. His work consumes eighty to ninety hours a week. He loves his work and everybody respects him. He allows himself a holiday to recover and reflect. He has no time for the outside world, unless it is connected to his work. When there is entertainment, he selects carefully.

We all have this kind of ego in some form. And most of us extend it beyond ourselves, at the same time we recognize that there's a difference between the me that's defined by the boundaries of our body and our larger Self. Our sense of ourself might include our favorite sports team or school or political party or religion—or our car, house, or bank account. Our ego in this sense can also exclude whoever or whatever we define as "not like me." This makes it easy to act in hurtful and destructive ways toward whomever or whatever is outside our ego sense, whether it's our ex-partner or "those others." Family therapist Lyman Wynne coined the term *rubber fence* for this sense in which the ego can expand or contract.[7]

Third, ego can refer to that mental function that deals with getting our needs met in our physical and social environment. This ability helps us survive, find purpose, and act effectively in the world. It's pretty much what Sigmund Freud meant by *ego*. (Except that he did not actually use that term at all! The first person to translate much of Freud's work from German into English, A. A. Brill, incorrectly translated Freud's basic German words *I, It,* and *Over-I—Ich, Es,* and *Uber-ich*— as "Ego," "Id," and "Superego." Despite later translations by others that corrected the mistakes, the original mistranslations and concepts are still widespread in English.)[8]

A fourth meaning of *ego* is our self-image. Most of us want to think well of ourselves. When our acts conflict with who and what we think we are, our ego morphs into accepting whatever we do and think as being right. It's easy to lie to ourselves in ways that paint our self-image as being more admirable than we really are. Vanity and narcissism are part of this. The Vedic philosophers saw this kind of ego as a false identification of the self, combined with attachments to the desires of the chakras.

In yet another meaning of *ego*, *egotism* and *egotistical* mean "thinking that we are better than others." Such egotism can get mixed up with one aspect or another of any chakra. For example, first-chakra insecurity often has its roots in a flawed sense of self. Somehow, somewhere, even the dictator who crushes others feels crushed inside. So does the person who imagines him- or herself to be "better or more spiritual than others." *Real spirituality involves mutual respect, a sense of basic equality,* and, as Mataji noted, *humility.*

Whether in the realm of religion, romance, politics, commerce, or any other aspect of daily life, those who imagine themselves to be better than others (and as a result may feel entitled to make decisions about what others can or cannot do) are not only self-centered, but also usually self-righteous. Few things blind us more than self-righteousness. Sometimes people intentionally inflict the most despicable kinds of cruelty on others while self-righteously convincing themselves that they are justified in doing so. It's all egotism. Ugly, destructive egotism. Fortunately, it's behavior one can change.

BEYOND WORDS: REALITY AND ILLUSION

Truth is a perfect correspondence between our perception and an event itself. Such truth can be elusive, since our concepts, preconceptions, prejudices, beliefs, ideologies, attitudes, metaphors, and other mental filters usually transform the messages our senses send to our conscious mind. Most people usually think their perceptions are accurate, but often they're not even close. Our perceptions are seldom actually objective, but usually are at least partly subjective. Even in science all "objective" research is carried out and interpreted by a subjective researcher. In traditional Indian philosophy there is no objectivity, only subjective reality.

Fortunately, knowledge of the chakras, and our honest observation of ourselves and others can thin the mind-mists of illusion. Many of our problems can be resolved with sincere effort to understand how we are affected by them. This chapter and those that follow offer tools to help awaken a personal sensitivity to inward truths. These can liberate our mind, body, emotions, and spirit. We suggest the following meditation as a good starting place to dive into the ocean of swirling waves of chakra energy.

TRATAK MEDITATION: A FOUNDATION FOR DEVELOPING CONCENTRATION

One of the most ancient, formal meditative methods that can transform our inner self is called Tratak. It includes:

1. Developing the ability to focus your attention where you wish, when you wish.
2. Developing the ability to know what your attention is doing at any given moment.
3. Noticing, moment by moment, what is occurring in you and around you. (This is called witnessing or witness consciousness in yogic traditions and mindfulness in Buddhist traditions.)

How to Handle the Impact of Past Trauma on Meditation

Very occasionally a person gets stuck in their meditation if the deep breaths awaken the memory of an early life event in which they were afraid and held their breath. If this happens to you, stay with that recollection for as long as needed, running it through your mind again and again, letting yourself physically relax a little more each time you review it, until you develop your ability to breathe deeply and freely. This may require several sessions. If you continue to feel tense when recalling the event and it stops your ability to meditate, you may be wise to see a counselor or psychotherapist who is experienced in working with and releasing memories of past traumas.

 Tratak Meditation, Step by Step

If you are already skilled in this technique, you might want to skip ahead to chapter 3. If not, there is no better place to start learning to meditate and enjoying its advantages than right here and now.

✶ Preparation

Choose a place to sit, whether cross-legged on the floor or upright on a chair. If on the floor, use a meditation cushion or doubled over pillow or other object to raise the base of your spine a few inches off the ground so you can sit up straight. If there's a wall behind you, sit far enough forward that your back is not touching it. (Or, if you have not previously meditated and your back muscles are not strong, you can sit with your back against the wall for support.) If you're on a chair, sit a few inches forward from the chair back. (If you have back pain when you sit up straight, find whatever position works for you. Some of our students have meditated while lying down. That tends to make it harder to maintain mental focus, but they report good results and it's better than no meditation at all.)

Before you get started, place a distinctive visual object six feet or more in front of you. In a dark room a candle flame is ideal. (You will want to put it on a flameproof tray, far enough from you that you can't knock it over.) In a lighted room, a flower in a vase works well. Or a statue of Jesus, or Buddha, or Kwan Yin (Kannon) if you wish. You could use the painting of the meditating yogini in plate 2: Spiritual Alignment = Natural Harmony. Or, if you prefer, you can meditate outdoors and let a tree or flower or even a fencepost be your focus.

✶ Starting Sequence

Each meditation should begin with this Starting Sequence of four steps to shift from ordinary into meditative consciousness. It doesn't take long; usually just three or four minutes. When you're finished, you'll probably already have more of a sense of inner calmness.

First, sense your breath. Then move your body from the waist upward, around and around in a circle. Inhale during the back half of the circle and exhale during the front half. As you stay with that breathing pattern, let the rotation of your torso's circle shrink until you stop at a point where you're perfectly centered in relation to gravity.

Next, take five full breaths in which you do no more than pay attention to your breathing.

After five deep, slow breaths, continue with five more breaths in which you do a mental and sensory body scan from head to toe to find any places where you're holding even a little tension. Determine whether any such place has a message for you. Then let go. Relax completely except for the energy needed to sit up.

With awareness of your breath, count to ten on your inhalations (one number on each inhalation), and empty your mind on the exhalations. Or repeat a mantra you've selected on your inhalations and empty your mind on the exhalations. Continue this focus for about ten breaths. You can choose one of the mantras for a chakra you may be working on, which you will find listed in the "Sound Healing" section of the "Practical Tools" given for each of the seven chakras. Or you can choose any mantra that you wish. If you would like to, you can let your eyes move to a different visual object during each breath, or let your ears listen to a different sound during each breath. This can help you move from everyday consciousness into meditation. Doing it again at the end of your session can help you move out of meditation and back into everyday consciousness.

Focusing Your Attention

Focus your attention on the visual object you previously placed some distance in front of you—or on some visually distinctive object you've already selected. Intently watch the flickering of the candle flame, the flower, or whatever other object you choose. Notice its every detail. Imagine that in a moment you will have to look away and draw a picture of it from memory, making it as accurate as possible.

Then, you will notice that your mind has drifted to something else—and you are thinking (whether in words or by visualizing a mental picture or playing a mind-movie) about a presentation you have to give tomorrow, or about what your friend told you yesterday, or whatever—and you've forgotten all about watching your candle flame or your chosen object. (To be concise, we'll just say *candle flame* from here on and it will represent whatever object you're using as a point of focus.)

Notice whether the place where your attention has drifted has any message you need to remember (and if so, if it isn't too distracting, jot down a word or two to remind you of it on a notepad you keep handy during meditation). Then bring your mind back to the candle flame.

Each time you notice that your attention has wandered away, as it will time and time again, just bring it back to that candle flame. That's Tratak. You are learning to notice where your mind goes, where it is, and what it's doing. You are also learning how to concentrate and focus your mind. You're not trying to push anything out of your mind, but rather to focus it where you wish. This ability is essential in order to be able to be mindful. It is also valuable to learn to maintain attentive focus because it is a key to success in a whole spectrum of life tasks.

Sounds simple, doesn't it? But actually, most people you meet on the street have only a minimal ability to control and focus their attention. Here you are learning, in a sense, to "stand behind your mind" and notice what it's doing. That's why this faculty is called the witness or witness consciousness. You become the witness of your own mind in action. That often gives you the choice to let it continue what it's doing or to direct it to do something else.

You've probably experienced one-pointed attention at least a few times, or perhaps many. For example, if you're singing and your attention is totally focused on the song and the melody, that's one-pointed attention. When other things take part of your attention so that you're paying only partial attention to your singing, that's many-pointed attention. If you assign a small part of your attention to the task of noticing what your mind is doing and bring it back to the singing, that's two-pointed attention, or "witness consciousness." Mastering this skill is essential for developing the positive potentials of the chakras and to understanding their flow into the inner river of your life.

Meditation with a Mantra

If you wish, you can use a mantra in your meditation. For each chakra we suggest several possible one-word mantras. If you're inclined to use a mantra, select one you like and will feel good repeating. Or choose one from a source other than this book (perhaps from your chosen religious tradition). Swami Rama says a spiritual master gave him the mantra "Always be cheerful" and that for years it served him well. A mantra can be one word, several words (such as *Om Namah Shivayah*), or even be several lines long and also be useful for chanting. Some mantras are in Sanskrit, the most ancient of written languages, some in English, and some in other tongues.

> Repeat your chosen mantra to yourself as you inhale, and empty your mind of it and everything else as much as you can as you exhale. Continue this for at least ten breaths. (You can do it for many more breaths if you please, with an empty breath between each set of ten.)
>
> You can also use your mantra in the midst of your everyday life—especially when you feel mentally or emotionally drained or down.
>
> Some people recite their mantra with a string of beads called a *mala*, which resembles a rosary, repeating their chosen mantra as they move from bead to bead. If you don't have a mala, or don't care to use one, just chant (silently or out loud, as appropriate) in a way that feels right to you.

If Mantras Are Not Your Thing, Count Your Breaths

Some spiritual traditions suggest counting your breaths to focus your meditation. This method parallels the method of using mantras described above.

> As you inhale, count the number 1 in your mind. Then, as you exhale, try to empty your mind of all thoughts and just be aware of your internal and external sensations in the immediate present.
>
> Next, mentally count the number 2. Again, as you exhale, empty your mind as completely as you can. Continue in this same way until you reach the number 10.
>
> Then take one "empty breath" in which you do not count.
>
> After that, start again with the number 1, and repeat the same procedure. Continue counting up to ten, in rhythm with your breathing, until you feel like your mind is calm, clear, and focused. (If you prefer to do this counting meditation with your eyes closed, then you can *visualize*

each number as you inhale. If you can't visualize the entire number, visualize whatever piece of it you can.)

When you repeat a mantra or count your breaths, it gives your mind something to hold on to as you learn to focus your attention. This makes it easier to learn how to direct your attention more effectively in daily tasks and conversations.

Ram Dass offers a few words that add to our perspective here:

While a practice is a discipline, it's better to be gentle with yourself. . . . It's just a matter of timing. . . . Our mind conceives the next level of consciousness before we're ready to go there. . . The result is we're always a little ahead of ourselves in our thoughts. We don't slow down enough to be fully in our being. . . . We're constantly creating new models of ourselves before we're fully here with what is. . . . Don't figure you're going to get enlightened yesterday. Relax. Just start to tune yourself to the spirit within. . . . A practice that was appropriate for you initially may not be useful further down the line. Keep staying open and hearing these delicate shifts and balances as they go on inside you.[9]

Enhancing Your Ability to Focus

Drawing or painting a *yantra* (a mystical geometric diagram) or painting one of the line drawings in this book can be a tool to develop your ability to focus. (You might want to make a photocopy of the drawings and paint your copy rather than paint in the book itself.) This is a concentration exercise with sacred geometry that can keep you involved for hours. Whenever you paint onto the line of the drawing, your thoughts are somewhere else. Slowly you can get control over your thoughts by doing such painting more often. After your drawings are complete they can also be used for Tratak. Also, painting a mandala as a centering device is a good exercise.

In the next chapter we describe how to use Tratak as the first step in a Polarity-Balancing Meditation that helps you explore the inner chambers of your mind in relation to each chakra. The suggested meditations bring greater self-knowledge and connection with the predominant movement or stillness of your inner energy.

And if by chance you manage to go beyond the fifth chakra and move into the higher conscious states that reach beyond words and logic, you may have a chance to stimulate the opening of the lotus petals of divine awakening.

First, however, we'll take a few pages to explain the nature of polarity-based thinking and how it differs from the dualisms that sometimes dominate our thinking. In an important sense we're offering you tools to step into a different world. Are you ready, as Pilot Baba says, to make the jump from dualistic thinking to polarity-based thinking?

3

THE POLARITY PRINCIPLE

Qualities such as fear, passion, anger, greed, malice, jealousy, envy, selfishness, and sloth constantly spoil body chemistry. When . . . these negative qualities begin to influence the cells of the body, the spine becomes tense and the body's natural radiance is lost.

HARISH JOHARI,
AYURVEDIC MASSAGE

Not many people can be buried underground or in an airtight compartment underwater for two weeks and live to tell the tale. Fewer yet have done so while being hooked up to a battery of medical biofeedback instruments that show heart rate, breathing, and other vital signs.

Pilot Baba is one of those few. When voluntarily buried, he goes into *nirvikalpa samadhi* (a state of dissolution of the self-conscious self) and the medical instruments flatline as if he were dead. When he comes out of that state, the instruments return to normal, and he continues to walk among the living.

One of Pilot Baba's insights echoes that of the Western psychoanalyst and sociologist Erich Fromm. Both noted that many aspects of who we are can take either positive or negative forms. We may choose to live in ways that are either caring or careless. We may act in ways that encourage our growth and development, or ways that are harmful to our self, others, or our communities. Since we can't do much about our genetic makeup, it's vital to treat both ourselves and those around us in ways that encourage our—and their—positive potentials. Which potentials we develop affect the directions in which our lives unfold.

Tantra yoga and the study of chakras encourages us to look deeply at both the positive and negative aspects of ourselves. When we label some thoughts, attitudes, and actions negative because they bring some kind of harm to us or others, that's basic ethics. But most of us also think of many qualities as negative that harm no one—except for the harm we do to ourselves by thinking of them that way. Sometimes they are a source of useful energy. In *Awakening Shakti,* author Sally Kempton explains:

> The word *tantra* [has] two roots. *Tan* means "to expand or develop." *Tra* means . . . "to save, liberate, or redeem." . . . Tantra is a series of practices and teachings that help us realize that the world is filled with divine energy. . . . It is also a series of tools . . . that we can use both to liberate ourselves from illusion and to make our worldly lives more beautiful, abundant, and skillful.[1]

Tantra is a spiritual path that embodies the principles of the chakras that will unfold in these pages. It teaches the discrimination and discipline required to comprehend and maintain the delicate balance between the poles of positive and negative energy needed to harness the will to awaken in higher awareness. Johari gave this advice to help us understand how to take the better road: "When you are judging an action yourself, you have to ask yourself if the action is good for you, good for the people around you, good for humanity in general, and good for planet Earth. If it is, then go ahead; otherwise refrain from the action."[2] Of course, you can only really know whether something is good for you, others, or the Earth if you are a keen observer of your own motives and inclinations. In Johari's words,

> To live in constant awareness means that one should know what is happening inside, because the world outside is viewed by an individual according to

his or her state of mind. When one is sad, the world outside appears to be quite different than when one is happy. Every individual is restricted by many individual strings, which comprise one's frame of reference. One's state of body chemistry provides the mood, feeling-tones, or emotional nuances with which to view the world outside.[3]

Swami Muktananda adds, "Simply witness the different thoughts as they arise and subside . . . no matter how many worlds of desires, wishes, and positive and negative thoughts your mind creates, you should realize that they are all a play of consciousness. . . . Your goal is not to battle with the mind, but to witness the mind."[4]

BEYOND THE WORLD OF BLACK AND WHITE

Simple cause-and-effect thinking—*THIS* action *HERE* causes *THAT* effect *THERE*—usually leaves many things out. Often the omissions are far more important than we realize. Swami Prajnapad claims, "In nature, action and reaction are continuous. Everything is connected to everything else. No one part, nothing, is isolated. Everything is linked, and interdependent."[5]

Undulating waves of causes and effects infuence each other and react back on us. Everything from a single action to an entire life, in both its essence and details, is a complex fabric for which Viennese psychologist Max Wertheimer used the term *gestalt,* described in English as meaning a "pattern, whole, or configuration."[6]

So-called knowledge comes in at least four forms: accurate, inaccurate, confused, and irrelevant. In practical terms, knowledge is *accurate* (true) to the degree that action based on it has the results that we think it will. It is *inaccurate* (false) to the degree that such action has results different from those that we expect. In that case we think we know what's going on but our thoughts are wrong. Knowledge is *confused* to the degree that it is a more or less tangled mixture of the accurate, inaccurate, and irrelevant. Big problems result from the fact that most people think their knowledge is true when much of it is actually confused, false, irrelevant, or all of the above.

When we act in a way that helps or harms someone or something, our mind stores memory traces or impressions of that event as a collection of neural impulses—or in yogic language, *sanskaras* (also called *samskaras*). Then often our mind and spirit meddle creatively with those memory traces. We might remember and acknowledge what we did. Or we might remember a hurtful act but deny that it harmed anyone or anything. Or we might even push it out of our awareness completely, using one of the mind's many tricks for avoiding uncomfortable thoughts and feelings. Such mental tactics spotlight a major challenge: the need to distinguish between actual events and our mental representations and interpretations of them. The tendency to get trapped in false thinking most often occurs when we view our world through the lens of dualistic black-and-white thinking.

Such thinking has its uses. One is that it helps us make quick decisions when necessary. Another is that it points to ways we might act to bring about a better outcome as it warns us not to act in other ways. It may help tell us who to trust and who to be wary of. Such distinctions simplify our lives. But many dualisms are framed as good or bad, right or wrong, where such terms don't reasonably apply. Framing events that way and then trying to wipe out the side of the dualism that we don't like can lead to regrettable mistakes—or even horrendous ones.

Figure 3.1 shows a starting point: a simple diagram of a dualism (or duality, as you prefer).

Figure 3.1. Black and white form, a representative dualism.

In the realm of opinions, beliefs, and attitudes, however, not much is so straightforward. When faced with an apparent black-or-white fact that contradicts what a person thought was so, he or she may try to investigate what's actually going on, or may deny that the fact is real or relevant. We can label the former inquirers and the latter deniers. A denier is most concerned about preserving his or her self-image as "right," or about maintaining social ties with others who think the same way he or she does. Fortunately, it's possible for a denier to learn to let go of that habit. A friend's observation explains this well: "I learned that lesson decades ago in the middle of a discussion/argument with someone I respected on the top deck of a ferry crossing Puget Sound. She said, 'You really don't like to be contradicted, do you?' I

Figure 3.2. The yin-yang symbol.

was dumbstruck. In that situation she was so obviously right! And my self-image had been that I was so open-minded." That incident was the start of his quest to become truly open-minded—to transform himself from a denier to an inquirer.

How can we move beyond the rigidity that dualism breeds? One step is to apply the polarity principle, a way of thinking that helps us climb out of unconscious ego traps. This can help us avoid getting caught in webs of mistaken or confusing thoughts that we ourselves have spun.

What is the polarity principle? We find the beginnings of an answer in ancient China. With their conceptions of yin and yang, sages of antiquity were already trying to avoid the pitfalls of dualism. In the yin-yang symbol shown in figure 3.2, the white dot in the black circle reminds us that there is always some yin in the yang. Likewise, the black dot in the white circle tells us that there is always some yang in the yin.

Yang often refers to qualities typically thought of as masculine, like assertiveness and action, while yin often refers to qualities widely thought of as feminine, like nurturing and passivity.

The same principle applies in countless matters unrelated to gender. With almost any person or group there is something about *them* that somehow resembles *us,* and some quality in *us* that closely resembles *them*—even if we don't like it and won't admit it. To acknowledge our similarities as well as our differences is part of basic polarity-based thinking. This insight can help us avoid some of the worst pitfalls of dualism. It can help us avoid a common mistake that often torpedoes relationships: projection.

If I am projecting, I see you as the living incarnation of whatever qualities I dislike and won't recognize in myself. *I* am good and righteous and *you* are bad and mean. I am generous and you are selfish. Whether in religion, politics, or everyday relationships, this usually leaves whatever sense of shared community we might have had in shreds. We end up alienated from each other, even when we are trying to do the right thing.

But if I know that what I dislike in you exists in me at least in some small degree, I'm less likely to be so antagonistic. And if I acknowledge that the qualities I like in myself also exist to some degree in you, I'm likely to feel friendlier toward you.

Now let's go one step farther. We can stretch the black and white rectangle (figure 3.1, page 39) across the page, and gradually shade it from white at one end to black at the other, as shown in figure 3.3. The left end of the continuum represents the absence of a specified quality or the smallest possible amount of it, and the right end represents 100 percent of the quality or the greatest possible amount.

All points in between represent different degrees of the quality. For instance, the left end might reflect a very peaceful person while the right end represents someone ready to punch the wall. Or the left end reflects a neglectful parent

Figure 3.3. The gradual shading of a quality from 0 to 100 percent.

who shrugs off a baby's cries, while the right end reflects an attentive parent who cares for the infant well. The left end might be a greedy miser who cares only for himself while the right end represents a saint who consistently puts others' needs first. With anyone, we can look at a single quality represented by one such line, or a profile of the person reflected in many such lines, each referring to a somewhat different but somehow related quality. Within the grouping of possibilities found in each of the seven chakras, this principle can be very useful.

With most personal qualities, the majority of people are not at either extreme, but somewhere along the line between them. We can move in one direction or the other, toward having more or less of a specific quality.

Another key insight is that *normal* need not mean virtuous, sane, or good in any identifiable way. It refers to the *norm,* to what is most common in a given culture. It means *average*—the way most people are. We might be part of a community, a political party, a church, or a nation in which most members of that group often think that others who think, feel, or act differently are *evil* or *crazy,* even when the truth is just the opposite and they themselves are the nutty ones and fruitcakes. Fortunately, we can learn to trust our own inner guide even when it contradicts what everyone around us is saying. We can move toward sanity even in an insane society. Chakra work can help with this.

PERCEIVING REALITY THROUGH A NEW LENS

Most events in our minds and emotions include two or even several elements mixed up together. As we acknowledge such complexities, we become less likely to make Big Mistakes that make bad situations worse, or good situations bad. Venn diagrams offer a step toward clearer awareness and reflection. A simple one is shown in figure 3.4.

We can label all elements that are present only in circle A As. All elements only in circle B are called Bs. And elements only in circle C are called Cs. So far, that's just dualistic category making. Then things become more interesting. Everywhere circle A overlaps circle B we have ABs. Where circle B overlaps C we have BCs.

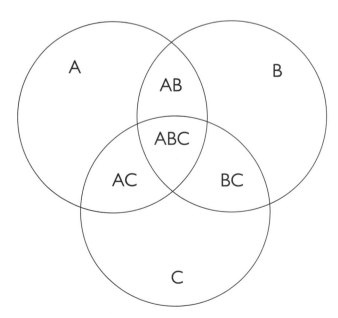

Figure 3.4. A Venn diagram offers a clear way to understand complexity.

Where circle A overlaps C we have ACs. And in the middle, where circles A, B, and C all overlap, we have ABCs.

This is how most of life really is, only more so. In psychology, social relationships, politics, economics, religion, and many other realms, a Venn diagram gives us a richer picture of what's occurring than a simple dualism like the black and white rectangle on page 39.

But there's a catch. Most of us not only have dualistic thinking deeply embedded in our neural circuits, but also emotional attachments to our well-worn dualisms that make it hard for us to let go of our mistaken ideas so that we can instead perceive our lives and worlds more accurately.

INSIDE EACH CHAKRA

Each of the seven chapters on the chakras has a table showing the possibilities of that chakra, containing about a dozen lines. Each line describes opportunities on one side and obstacles at the other. Although they're shown in a table with just those two sides, they're actually more like the line made up of fifteen squares shown in figure 3.3. The personal qualities on both the opportunities and obstacles sides are expressed more strongly as you move toward the left and right ends of the line of polarity, and not very strongly in the middle. Taking small mental steps toward the left can stimulate movement toward functioning more effectively in that particular dimension of thinking, feeling, and acting, and toward the next higher chakra. Or if you lean in the direction of obstacles on the polarity line, the movement of chakra energy may be stagnant or downward flowing.

Our ideas about any real thing, condition, or event are always just a representation of it. They are never the reality itself. Often they're no more than symbols or metaphors. Reality just IS. The closer our thoughts come to the way it really is, the truer they are. But for the most part we live in a world of maya or samsara, a wispy fog of illusions through which we often only dimly apprehend inner and outer reality. All too often, someone who is certain that he knows the absolute truth about something is actually dead wrong, yet refuses to hear or see anything that calls his belief into question.

We make fewer mistakes as we learn to recognize stories, metaphors, and symbols as such, rather than confusing them with the realities they represent. We can also watch out for our ego attachments to particular stories, metaphors, and symbols. Noticing and releasing such attachments helps us come closer to the truths of our own soul.

BALANCING THE CHAKRAS

Inner balance is usually helpful. People who are crazy are often called unbalanced. When I am balanced, I am mentally present in this moment. I am free to think, feel, and act as I choose from my poised, centered place. In regard to chakras, the term *balance* is most often used to indicate the attainment of a sense of inner equilibrium so that we act wisely in our present situation. It also means working to move from the obstacles end of a chakra's continuum of possibility toward the opportunities at the other end.

Italian psychologist Roberto Assagioli suggests four ways to balance apparently opposite poles.[7] (We write *apparently* because most people define many things as opposites when they are merely different from each other, and not actually opposite at all.)

One is developing the habit of *appreciating* instead of negatively judging others (people, perspectives, or ways of life). This neutralizes the negative energy charge between the poles—and also happens to make life generally more cheerful for the person who gives up being judgmental.

A second means of balancing involves finding a transcendent principle "which transforms, sublimates, and reabsorbs the two poles into a higher reality."[8] We come to see how the differences are part of a greater unity—like followers of two religions discovering that most of their moral and ethical principles are similar.

Assagioli's third approach is "by consciously and wisely directing the alternations . . . between the two extremes . . . so that the result is harmonious and constructive."[9] Since there are cycles in the seasons and the heavens, it makes sense for there to be cycles in human affairs. He offers the example in which "oscillation between excessive authority and uncontrolled freedom" can lead to developing a balanced attitude.

This has more than a little in common with Buddha's Middle Way, which advises us to find a middle path out of our extremes, a path that avoids attachment to the worldliness of possessions, power, and reputation on one hand,

and the painful, vain, and unprofitable extreme of excessive asceticism on the other. Buddha was unusual in Indian tradition in that he renounced not only worldly ways but also extreme asceticism. He realized that instead of mental clarity and inner peace, his extreme ascetic practices had ruined his health and dulled his mind. He formulated the Middle Way after having been brought back to health from a near-death experience and hearing a story of a lyre strung too loosely, too tightly, and just right. In many matters you can find your own Middle Way. Avoid being too extreme even in espousing the Middle Way itself.

Tibetan Lama Tarthang Tulku offers a useful clarification: "There are two kinds of 'giving up' or 'letting go.' There is giving up attachments, and there is giving up because of difficulties and disappointments. The person who has inner strength and openness does not 'give up'—but gives up grasping and attachment, and consequently gains freedom and confidence."[10]

Finally, Assagioli's fourth approach is "creation of a new being, a new reality." We move beyond what we knew before, keeping the best elements of our past while creating something new and better.[11] This voyage of discovery can occur as we move toward greater inner development by gaining awareness of the energy movements in our chakras.

POLARITIES AND SHADOWS

Strolling along a sidewalk on a sunny day as we go about our business, few of us notice the shadows that we cast. Psychiatrist Carl Jung used the metaphor of the Shadow for the sides of ourselves that lurk in our unconscious, sides that we pay little or no attention to and may not even know exist. A whole world of feelings, thoughts, impulses, and "characters" moves and speaks in every person's shadow. They may be negative aspects of our personality that we don't want to recognize because they unmask a false view of how we see ourselves. Or they may be positive qualities that could serve us well if we opened the door to inner strengths and possibilities that we've kept under wraps.

Each polarity in each table of Chakra Possibilities exists along a continuum that runs from the demonic to the divine, from the destructive and deadly to the spiritual and godly. The chakra qualities express polarities rather than dualities; shades of gray rather than black and white. With many polarities in the chakra qualities tables, obstacles point to shadow sides of the opportunities. Likewise, opportunities point to possible shadow sides of the obstacles.

Why does this matter? For one thing, it keeps us from getting stuck in one-sided viewpoints or being too egotistical. We can look over at the shadow we cast and realize that it too is part of us. This is a good antidote for self-deception in which we think that we're better than others. By contrast, if we feel stuck in a negative possibility, looking at the strengths and good feelings on the positive side of that polarity can show us how to let more of our positive qualities emerge.

The vision granted us in plate 3: *Ardhanarishvara: Perfect Balance* can inspire our aspirations to achieve the beauty and serenity of greater balance.

WORKING WITH YOUR POLARITIES

Now let's look at a way of working with your polarities that involves a meditation that you can use with every chakra. If you want to change anything you're saying or doing, and act or think or feel differently, you have to be able to see and hear and feel what you're saying and doing *now—at the very moment when you're doing it.* That's the case in working with your chakras just as in working with anything else.

The starting point for this method is to practice Tratak meditation as described on page 29. Once you've developed the ability to do Tratak, which helps you to be aware of what your mind is doing moment by moment (rather than being completely identified with what you're saying or doing), then you'll be ready to continue most effectively with this exercise.

Some people find that continuing to silently recite their mantra or count their breaths throughout the session helps them maintain focus on the subject they're contemplating rather than interfering with it. Do what works for you.

 Polarity-Balancing Meditation

Select a chakra that embodies a concern you'd like to work on. One approach is to start reading about the first chakra and keep on working with it until you feel finished. Then go on to the second chakra. And so on. Or follow Narmada Puri's suggestion of spending one month getting to know each chakra. Or if there is a particular chakra that calls out to you, go right to it. For instance, if you're struggling with dominance or powerlessness issues you can go straight to the third chakra.

Next, choose a line from the "Possibilities" table of that chakra. If several qualities hit home, choose the one that feels most important to you now. (Later you can repeat this meditation with other attributes from the table.) Remember to keep both the opportunities and the obstacles of the polarity in mind.

Then set a candle, flower, or other object several feet in front of you (or farther) to provide an object for your visual focus.

Go through the "Starting Sequence" described on page 30 as a part of the Tratak meditation. Imagine that you are sitting behind yourself as a witness of whatever thoughts, feelings, and sensations occur in your mind and body.

Center your attention on the polarity you selected and the situation or pattern in your life that is related to it. Let your visual focus on the object in front of you remind you to keep your mind focused on that polarity. When you notice that your mind has drifted away from the object, bring it back into visual focus, and also refocus on the chakra and polarity you're concerned about.

Notice whatever thoughts, feelings, sensations, memories, or mental pictures, mind-movies, or sentences come up in your mind. One or more of these might be uncomfortable, disturbing, or anxiety arousing. One or more of them might be pleasant, cheering, hopeful, or emotionally neutral. And perhaps one thought, feeling, memory, or sensation may dominate your mind so that you can't stop thinking about it.

Throughout your meditation session, notice any physical sensation, such as tightening a muscle, holding your breath, your heartbeat speeding up, or physical relaxation. First simply sense and witness it. Then notice whether you're talking to yourself about your experience. Is there any message for you in what your mind, emotions, or body are doing? If so, record it so you won't forget.

Then if anywhere in your body has tightened up, release and relax that tightness—or notice what it's trying to tell you that you haven't been hearing or seeing. (You could even tighten it more to see if some message emerges from doing that.) Be open to insights or messages from your deeper self about how you can move away from the obstacles toward the opportunities side of the polarity—or about how to handle an obstacle. Do so in a receptive manner. If you try to "think it through," you may lose the meditative state of consciousness. During this meditative time, you want to encourage your brain to generate alpha waves, not beta waves.

When you feel done, be done. You might take a few minutes for unstructured witnessing, or just do ten breaths of mantra or counting meditation to end your session.

Alpha and Beta Waves and Biofeedback

Alpha waves are a form of neural activity in the brain associated with relaxation, imagery, artistic creativity, meditation, and comfort. Beta waves are a form of neural activity associated with conceptual thinking and problem-solving such as working out mathematical problems. If you attach electroencephalogram (EEG) biofeedback electrodes to designated points on your skull using a conductive ointment, you can actually watch these and other brain waves on a video screen placed in front of you.

One of the authors finds it interesting to begin a biofeedback session with high beta and low alpha levels and then move into a meditation practice. Usually the somewhat looser colored line that has been programmed to show alpha waves gradually rises and the tighter contrasting line that shows beta waves gradually falls until an alpha-beta cross occurs. At that point the alpha activity level is higher than the beta level, a reversal of where they were at the start of the session. Alternatively, monitors can be programmed to emit a high-pitched sound with beta activity and a low-pitched sound with alpha activity. In that case, the loudness of the sounds changes with your mental state. (With appropriate electrode placement, you can also observe or listen to other neural activity, such as theta and delta waves.)

If you have a hard time learning to meditate, supervised biofeedback training can serve as an instructional aid. It can also be very useful in psychotherapy, such as in treating chronic tension, and with health problems, since clients can learn to regulate such functions as heart rate and blood pressure by watching representations of them on the video screen.

If you like, you can come back to that same polarity and contemplate it another day if you feel a need to do so. Or perhaps you feel finished with it, at least for now. Your inner path is yours to explore in rhythm with your inclinations, desires, and commitments to know your deeper self.

With a better understanding of polarities, it's now time to explore the first chakra and your basic connections with earthly forces, to enter the dwelling place of the sleeping Kundalini energy.

4

FIRST OR MULADHARA CHAKRA

The Root Chakra

In the first chakra we learn to be and feel more secure as we integrate the forces of thinking and doing, mind and body.

A person who is dominated by the Muladhara Chakra is obsessed by the desire to find security. . . . Like the element earth they are solid and strong, endure all kinds of hardships, and are productive.

HARISH JOHARI AND WILL GERAETS,
*THE WISDOM TEACHINGS OF HARISH JOHARI
ON THE MAHABHARATA*

First or Muladhara Chakra Correspondences

Key phrases: Security, survival needs, root of inner being

Physical location: Near base of the spine/tailbone area

Endocrine gland: Adrenals

Astrological link: Mars

Day of the week: Tuesday

Element: Earth

Sense: Smell

Sanskrit Derivation: mula (root); *adhara* (support)

Massage: Feet, calves

Leela Game of Self-Knowledge: First row—Genesis, Maya, Anger, Greed, Physical Plane, Delusion, Conceit, Avarice, Sensual Plane*

THE ESSENCE OF THE FIRST CHAKRA: LAIR OF THE COILED SERPENT OF KUNDALINI

The core of the first chakra is physical survival. Physiological needs for breathable air, water, and food are primary. Located near the tailbone of the spine, the Muladhara Chakra is also connected with bodily comfort and psychological development. It is where we awaken to a basic sense of ourselves as separate individuals and to our connections with others. Paiently and persistently, its energy enlivens our desire to be in this world. On good days, it sharpens the zest for life that keeps us yearning to smell the roses, mobilizing our willpower, determination, and willingness to reach out and accomplish. On bad days, our insecurities, fears, and defenses may dominate. Ruled by down-to-earth, practical concerns, this chakra, like the underground forces that sustain a tree, is linked with the element earth. For all these reasons, it is called the root chakra.

Embracing life is a first-chakra anchor. We start by finding food and shelter. We go on to meeting psychological needs such as feeling secure and confident. As these transient and eternal desires become aligned and fulfilled, we try to balance our animal and spiritual nature. With perseverance, this can help us find harmony in a sometimes alienating and disharmonious world.

When you quiet your mind and guide your root chakra's energies wisely, it can harness internal forces needed to tap into the energies of the higher

---

*Leela, The Game of Self-Knowledge, a game played with dice, has a game board that takes players row by row and by upward arrows and downward snakes through seventy-two squares from lower to higher states of consciousness with each throw of the dice. The first row and its nine squares, for example, correspond with qualities of the first chakra. This ancient game and an accompanying book with the same title were extensively researched and then produced by Harish Johari through Inner Traditions International publishers. (The children's game Chutes and Ladders is a deteriorated form of this ancient tool for expanding consciousness.)

chakras. Whether you are an idealist, a skeptic, a visionary on a transcendent journey, or just trying to make it through each day as best you can, this chakra is allied with powerful forces that can inspire you to overcome obstacles. Naturally aligned with soul purpose, it can support a quest to take tangible steps to fulfill your deeper potential and accelerate your personal evolution. But when this chakra is discordant, it can incite needless frustrations, anger, mental stagnation, fear, obliviousness to mind-body connections, and problems in relating to others.

All this may sound like the effects of an unpredictable throw of the cosmic dice, but for the most part you can choose to take charge of the directions in which you move, mature, and evolve. After all, the rousing forces associated with the first chakra, symbolized in myth and legend by the planet Mars, are like a double-edged sword that symbolizes your power to fight for right or wrong, honor or disgrace, compassion or cruelty. Whether you face a physical, verbal, emotional, or financial threat, your first-chakra survival reactions are triggered. When you reach for the sword, you may win or lose, bludgeon or be bludgeoned, stand or fall. A major task is learning to meet an attack of any kind intelligently rather than ignorantly. If you are secure in your first-chakra energies, when you are insulted, ridiculed, or slighted by others, you'll know that they, not you, are the ones with problems. Waking up this chakra's positive potentials helps enhance confidence, inward strength, and self-awareness. These qualities, points out Swami Satyananda Saraswati, can lead to "awakening of things from the unconscious field of existence which one may not have had prior conscious knowledge of."[1]

India's spiritual masters claim that in the first chakra a psychospiritual energy called Kundalini lies dormant, sleeping coiled like a snake at the base of the spine. Believed by yogi Gopi Krishna to be the driving force behind inspiration and genius, Kundalini energy is said to flow through our bodies in spiritual channels or lines called *nadis*. Each chakra is believed to be an intersection point where many nadis come together. Working with these conduits of the life force (especially the two nadis that are said to originate in the first chakra, the lunar channel, cool like the moon, called the Ida Nadi, and the solar channel, hot like the sun, called the Pingala Nadi) stimulates the Kundalini force. Also, balancing these contrasting feminine and masculine energies creates a strong inner foundation that is said to strengthen each of the higher chakras' potency. But when we asked spiritual master Pilot Baba if it was necessary to understand the nadis to work effectively with one's own chakras, he shook his head. "If your focus is on how to work in practical, useful ways with your own chakras," he replied, "it is not necessary."[2]

In tantra yoga, Kundalini is viewed as a form of cosmic energy that is present in some form in all living beings. When we work on ourselves through meditation, breath work, and yoga, our first-chakra energies naturally activate the awakening of our Kundalini. Then as we work with each of the remaining six chakras, we increase the potential for Kundalini energy to rise up the spine. As this occurs, our abilities and inclinations usually become infused with a spiritual dimension. Moving our energies away from the first chakra's obstacles toward its opportunities is a gentle way to stir the movement of our Kundalini and illuminate our consciousness. At its best, when the sleeping Kundalini force rises, it produces an alchemical transformation in our mind that turns base earthly elements (or you could call them "tendencies" or "inclinations") into a golden key that opens inner doors to more spiritual consciousness.

FIRST-CHAKRA POSSIBILITIES

OPPORTUNITIES	OBSTACLES
Awakening Kundalini	Ignorant, lacking attentiveness
Grounded	Distracted, flighty
Comfortable in your body	Defensive
Secure, self-sufficient	Needy, insecure
Friendly disposition	Anxious disposition
Uninhibited, straightforward	Inhibited, indirect
Sense of self-worth and value	Low self-esteem
Self-determining	Dependent on others
Courageous	Fearful, timid
Able to let go when appropriate	Grasping, hoarding
Responsible	Blames others, irresponsible
Does what is needed, perseveres	Puts off action, gives up easily

THE MENTAL PATHWAY FOR WORKING WITH
FIRST-CHAKRA ENERGIES

The Bright Side of the First Chakra

> **Gifts and Strengths:** Responsible, confident, with the ability to get what one needs and to help others do the same.

As your first-chakra qualities develop in positive ways, you feel increasingly worthy, self-reliant, grounded, connected with your body, and happy to help others. You enjoy the challenge of new adventures and alternatives, and are comfortable either alone or in a crowd. You are open to hearing the opinions and attitudes of others, including their political and religious beliefs, yet you think for yourself (or you feel good with the leader of your choice). All things considered, life feels good and you look forward to the future. Comfortable with your worldly reality, you hold on to outlooks and opinions that are truly valuable to you and let go of those that are not. Confident and self-determining, on the whole your life feels fairly uncomplicated except when inherently complex situations present themselves. When that occurs, you usually meet them head on.

Gurumayi provides a valuable insight about self-confidence.

Confidence is a delicate term. It is one of those qualities that cannot be understood without humility. The right amount of the right kind of confidence strengthens you. You move forward in your endeavors; you are not afraid to develop your abilities. . . . But overconfidence weakens you; it makes you a laughingstock. In effective first chakra work, you become confident . . . but not overconfident.[3]

The Dark Side of the First Chakra

> **Issues and Challenges:** You search for ways to feel safe, secure, worthy, and relaxed, and strive to follow your own preferences rather than others' designs.

Food, water, physical safety, clothing, shelter, work—when these essentials are lacking, most of us find life to be a challenge (or focusing on chakras to be a challenge). Even when these basic needs are met, few people completely escape the problems and complexes that impede first-chakra development. Insecurities are widespread. Knowing how to live free from hang-ups about our body and emotions is rare.

Fear is the most basic and pervasive first-chakra issue. People and groups who want to take advantage of you in some way are experts at triggering your fears about the terrible things that will happen if you don't join them, do as they want, or send them money that will go to reducing this or that threat. First come fears of not getting your survival needs met; then come fears related to everything else you care deeply about.

In a more general sense, if root-chakra energy is discordant, a person may be self-doubting, timid, anxious, or exhausted. Or may be stuck in the reptilian brain or animal nature and be selfish, greedy, or violent. Tasks, responsibilities, deadlines, and actions needed to make it through each day can seem overwhelming. Even the physically strong can get stuck in limitations. They may look for someone to tell them what to do and easily accept others as authorities over their choices.

A person with basic needs that went unmet at some earlier point in life may be insecure and afraid that their needs will never be met. As a result, for some people ethics and decency go out the window. Actions are accompanied by selfish thoughts such as "I'll do whatever I have to do to survive. I don't care whether I hurt others to get what I want." This attitude can be conscious or unconscious. Other people with significant unmet needs will maintain decent and ethical behavior in most matters, but still consider it a wild dream to imagine moving energies beyond the work that occurs within the first chakra.

Although it's tempting to think that in modern times we should always be able to find ways to fulfill basic needs, it may or may not happen. As people strive to survive, they may become stressed and distressed, and then knowingly or unknowingly make choices that misuse their energies. The pressures of society have increased so much that psychological insecurity is now a common problem.

Past Roots of First-Chakra Problems

Every infant needs to be fed, held, and comforted. Physical and emotional affection are essential to a sense of security in the body and the world.

Viennese psychiatrist Alfred Adler identified two patterns of childhood experience that can lead to insecurity, a widespread first-chakra problem. He labeled these *the abused child* and *the neglected child*.[4] Abuse may be physical violence by parents, siblings, or others who repeatedly hit or spank the child. The child learns that the world is dangerous, and develops tactics of protection that become embedded in the psyche. Often these involve chronic and unquestioning compliance, and giving in to whatever parents or other authority figures demand. The results may include giving up any sense of autonomy and self-direction. One young adult who was often severely beaten with his father's belt, for instance, becomes defensive about any comment regarding his actions whether or not it is intended to be critical. His inner child is stuck, afraid and crying.

Alternatively, physical abuse during childhood (often euphemistically justified as "teaching a lesson" by its practitioners) may lead to chronic rebellion and refusal to accept any kind of authority. In outwardly violent and dangerous circumstances this may have value. More often, however, it does more harm than good. Children who bully other children often come from families in which they themselves were bullied, either by their elders or their siblings. This can lead to insecurity in which a person considers him or herself defective, finds no way to be right, and has trouble accomplishing almost anything constructive.

Sometimes a child may feel abused or neglected even in the absence of real abuse or neglect. For instance, a child who receives a wealth of nurturing, care, and even material things may feel neglected if he or she perceives that a sibling gets more. This can happen when an older child is "dethroned" by a new baby in the family who needs and receives more care. A sense of *relative deprivation* occurs when a person feels deprived by comparison with others. If such incidents are intense enough, they can cause an inferiority complex or similar hang-up that is carried into adulthood. Peace at home (one's inner foundation) becomes an unattainable goal.

We all have our memories about our childhood. And it is not always easy. Harish Johari himself did not have an easy youth. He was extreme in his searches in every direction to find the reason behind everything. He used his childhood problems and other experiences, however, as the motivating forces that made him as he became: confident and established in himself. He never saw them as a complex. In many instances we can view our difficulties as a source of psychological disorders or use them as inspiration and motivation for the rest of our life.

THE BODY AND EMOTIONS PATHWAY: FEELING TONES IN THE FIRST CHAKRA

Personal Transformation in the First Chakra

A master key to awakening first-chakra powers is learning to listen to your inner self. Only with awareness in the moment can you notice what you are actually feeling and thinking, and realistically consider your best options. At that point you can truly ask yourself how to be the best person you can be and how to be a good friend to yourself. This means becoming more conscious of messages from your own body, mind, and emotions, and acting intelligently in response to them. It also means learning to live with life's mysteries and uncertainties rather than imagining or insisting that you know all the answers. And it includes realizing that when you don't know which choice to make, you can remain within the still point of waiting and watching until clarity bubbles to the surface. Through inner exploration, you invoke the freedom to move away from rigid preconceptions, vulnerabilities, and early programming toward becoming more conscious, centered, and able to make your own best choices.

Relational Transformation in the First Chakra

As the inner wheel of the first chakra revolves, your understanding of the world expands. You become more in tune with others, including family, friends, and lovers. With greater emotional maturity, you're more likely to do what's useful, to choose to act in ways that benefit others as well as yourself, and to take responsibility for your own actions. With personal growth comes the realization that self-improvement includes vigilant responsiveness to both challenges and opportunities.

As your sense of inner security grows, you give up blaming others when events do not go as you wish. You begin to understand that your relational problems and attainments are usually as much your doing as the other person's. You start to recognize that your own attitude and actions affect everyone around you, that whatever you do to another you also do to yourself in some way. Becoming more sensitive to inner and outer emotional signals guides your understanding of how to build healthy relationships and clear communications.

Doing these things may mean fighting strong unconscious impulses. "With the Muladhara chakra we have to work hard," says Pilot Baba. "It is so difficult to get free of this chakra's limiting tendencies, and work toward the higher chakras."[5] But with hope, faith, and dedication to the expansion of your consciousness, such growth can occur.

THE PATHWAY OF SPIRIT: IMAGERY IN THE FIRST CHAKRA

The Square, the Lotus Petals, and the Seed Sounds

Looking at the picture of the first chakra (plate 4 and figure 4.1) we find an abstract symbol representing the element of this chakra: earth, where it all starts. And that is the square with four directions: north, south, east, west. Since ancient times we have needed maps to travel on Earth. Most are composed of many squares. They are not the reality they supposedly represent, since the Earth is round. But we only use the flat square form when traveling. In a new place, one of the first things that we have to check is the different directions: where the sun is coming up and where it is going down.

The first step is to realize that Earth provides all that we need. Earth is like a foundation on which everything happens. That is why contemplative meditation on this chakra can help us to become more grounded. In India it is also said that sleeping with feet toward the south or sitting facing south should be avoided. This has to do with the magnetic field of the Earth.

The seed sound of the element earth is LANG (lahhhnggg). When pronounced correctly it will cause energy to inwardly flow in an upward movement and vibrate the two hemispheres of the brain. It also affects nerve endings in the area of the first chakra. *LA* represents the Earth and *NG* is the mind. When chanted together they can bring the energy up.

The pillars for life on Earth are air, water, food, sleep, and sex. Our body and mind are running on these forces. To attain a balanced and harmonious life we need to get them under control. This strengthens our willpower—our ability to set a goal and persevere until we attain it. In the first chakra the main concentration is on food. Food fasting in whatever way can help us get more control of our eating habits (for more information see *Dhanwantari* by Harish Johari).

The four lotus petals around the square at the center of plate 4 and figure 4.1 represent the four mental modifications that belong to this chakra.

Figure 4.1. This drawing depicts the deities—Brahma, Ganesha, and Dakini Devi—and core imagery shown in the painting of this chakra (plate 4: First or Muladhara Chakra).

These are: state of great joy, state of natural pleasure, satisfaction with the control of passions, and blissfulness in concentration. These are the energies of the divinities connected to each petal. Opening the petals and connecting with their energy provides a strong foundation for continuing our journey through the chakras. In the other chakras we will confront many more mental modifications. We will need a firm foundation when we face them. Then the four lotus petals will nudge us upward toward a higher plane of consciousness.

Each of the lotus petals also has a seed sound. They are: VANG, SHANG, KSHANG, and SANG, starting with the petal pointing to the right and moving clockwise.

 ## Seed-Sound Breathing

Inhale deeply and then let the seed sound emerge as you exhale. Do this quietly in your mind. With your next breath, carry the resonance of the seed sound to the root of your spine. Listen with your inner ear to hear its tone and feel its vibration.

Now take an empty breath.

Then verbally repeat the seed sound, loud enough to hear it with your outer ears.

Do this again and again, with an empty breath between each repetition, until you feel the sound vibrating through your entire body. When you feel finished, you are.

 ## First-Chakra Visualization with Seed Sounds

1. Start by visualizing the four lotus petals around the small central square. After looking at the four lotus petals in the painting, close your eyes and try to see them in your mind. Then you can add the square that they surround.

2. While you are doing this visualization, you can also chant the seed sound of the element earth, LANG.

3. Then chant the seed sounds of the lotus petals: VANG, SHANG, KSHANG, and SANG. Utter each sound while visualizing its petal, moving clockwise, starting with the one pointing to the right. Do you feel different as you utter each one, in contrast to the others?

The Elephant with Seven Trunks

After you have visualized the basic image, more symbols can be added. First is the elephant with seven trunks, which correspond to the desires of the seven chakras, represented by the seven colors of the rainbow. The name of the elephant is Airavata; he is one of the fourteen gems that we receive from the deities when we start our life on Earth. His gift is our sense organs and work organs. With the sense organs we can experience the world outside us. With our work organs we can act in it. With these instruments the mind can collect the information that can help fulfill our needs and desires and act accordingly.

The sense organ for the first chakra is the nose with which we smell. Here we become more aware of the information behind the smell. It tells us about the condition of our body, food, and environment. The work organ associated with the first chakra is the anus.

The elephant, always looking for survival and food, also stands for strength. When we work on our physical strength, which is nourished by the element earth, we can learn from the elephant to be humble under all conditions. Humility and simple living are two important conditions for spiritual growth. The aim is to become more aware of our habits and develop more self-control and patience.

Ganesha

The next figure we meet is Ganesha with his elephant head. He is sitting in a full-lotus pose at the bottom of the square, with the tip of his crown in the small square. Ganesha is sometimes referred to as the lord of all existing beings. Once he was asked to go around the universe as fast as he could. He said that was a very simple request. Then he went around his parents, Shiva and Shakti. They are the essence of all existence, which is the truth. Here Ganesha showed that he is not distracted by the outside world and sees only truth. "Even if one does not see the Truth and acts against it, the Truth remains the Truth!"—so goes an Indian saying.

By accepting the form of Ganesha, who also symbolizes teaching and learning, our artistic right brain gets more freedom, which can start moving our energy upward. Ganesha is very approachable, but at the same time has this quality of wisdom. He is invoked at the beginning of any undertaking, worldly or spiritual. If we cooperate, he will remove some of the obstacles on our path to truth.

To see this short, pot-bellied figure with elephant head as a deity is a challenge to our rational, analytical left brain. Children have no problem with him and just love him. But for the rational mind of many adults he seems difficult to accept. Meditation on him will give us the firmness we need on our journey. With one of his four hands he is blessing us and grants us fearlessness in whatever we undertake. With his second hand he holds the hatchet with which he can control our elephant of desires (our sense and work organs). With the lasso in another hand he frees us from our bondage to worldly attachments. With the *laddu* (a sweet made of chickpea flour) he shows his sattvic (pure, clear) nature.

Brahma

Then we face Brahma, the lord of creation and main deity of the first chakra. He is the creator of the physical plane (Bhu Loka). He created beautiful forms, colors, smells, tastes, and sounds. Yet in so doing, he also created a big problem for us. We become so attached to this outer beauty of the world that we can lose our connection with our inner or spiritual Self (*atman*). In the first chakra there are often so many problems that we have little time for any thing else.

But besides beauty, Brahma is also filled with goodness and truth. These are three qualities by which we can recognize the presence of the Divine. To help us Brahma gave us a manual in the form of the four Vedas that teach us the art of living. His four heads represent these four Vedas.

Brahma is sattvic in nature. That means he is at peace and content within himself. He is not carrying any weapons! By right understanding we can understand the sattvic state of the universe. For that he holds the scriptures (Vedas) in one of his hands. In another hand he holds the sacred water (Ganga) or elixir, representing the purifying power of water, the element of the second chakra. Yet another hand holds a lotus flower, symbolizing the purity of creation. With the remaining hand, like Ganesha, he grants us fearlessness. To experience the sattvic nature of Brahma most fully we should meditate during the twilight hours of dawn and dusk.

Dakini Devi

In the images of this chakra the male (left brain) is always accompanied by the female (right brain). Since the first chakra is the storehouse of our lower brain or our animal instincts, it is important that the two cerebral hemispheres learn to work together. Only then do they have a chance to convince the lower brain, our will, and our body to act together and behave better.

The Shakti or female deity in the first chakra is called Dakini. Brahma is the abstract principle; Dakini is concrete energy or power. In the philosophy of the chakras, everything that moves is Shakti, or the pervasive energy of the universe, our world, and ourselves. Without pleasing the woman, the ancient Vedic sages told us, we cannot enter into the spiritual path that leads toward cosmic consciousness. Dakini invites us into the first chakra. In the picture she sits opposite Brahma, on the right-hand side.

What kind of woman is Dakini? One so beautiful that we lose ourselves. As we gaze at her, she shows us the beauty inside ourselves. Beauty is not in the form, but in consciousness, which is eternal and free from death. Fear of death is the most basic psychological block of the first chakra. The skull in her lower left hand symbolizes the detachment from outside beauty and form.

As the personification of nature, Dakini guides us through this chakra, sometimes gently, sometimes with turmoil. She can become fearsome and angry when we disobey the laws of nature. She becomes very pleasant and loving when we live according to these laws. When we are in tune with nature she will become the mother of wealth and will offer the security we need to continue.

Dakini's single head shows the concentration that is needed to live in harmony. When there is concentration, there is less ego and more space for the Self, or atman, in us. She holds a sword to destroy fear and ignorance and a shield to protect us. The trident represents the oneness in creation. Creator, preserver, and destroyer are working together as one to create this cosmic game within which we live that is hidden in the chakras.

We might think that should be enough in the way of symbolism and hidden meanings for one chakra. But we would be mistaken. There is more.

The Triangle, the Lingam, and the Snake
In the center of the picture is an inverted triangle with a *lingam* (a stylized representation of the male sexual organ that looks like a cylinder standing on end

with a rounded top, widely used as a symbol of Shiva), and a snake coiled around the lingam. In India the lingam is more than just a male sexual organ; it is also a symbol. Some even say that everything that comes out of the Earth (or yoni, a stylized representation of a female sexual organ) can be viewed as a lingam—a mountain, stone, church with a tower, temple, tree, and even us. Not everyone agrees.

The downward-pointing triangle is a symbol for female energy and is called the seat of Kundalini Shakti, who here has the form of a snake. The triangle contains the vital life force in the form of pleasurable desires. These make us feel alive. In the first chakra we find these desires in a basic and primitive form without any cultivation. They keep us so busy that we may not know, do, or feel anything else.

In this field of seemingly uncontrollable desires the lingam appears. The lingam symbolizes Shiva as the male energy. Right in the beginning the first spark of the spiritual Self (our true nature) is present, but does not yet have a face. This true nature can only been seen after deep concentration. Even a brief glimpse of it can illuminate the path that extends beyond physical and psychological existence.

But we are just starting here. Kundalini Shakti as a snake also does not yet have a face. The snake represents energy and wants complete union with Shiva or the lingam. With her mouth open she is directed toward the upward-going canal of spiritual energy called Sushumna Nadi. When she moves up to the fourth chakra, both Shiva and Shakti will get their faces. In the sixth chakra, they will be as one, finally to unite in the seventh. Now they are still in their basic forms with the strong desire to become one.

In short, in the first chakra we have to learn to survive on the physical plane. We must take care of our physical earthly needs and the basic security of safety, food, and shelter. We don't get this with abundance, but with restraint and free will. This is what the ancient sage Patanjali called *yama*. Yama is a process to get body and mind under control. And that can most easily be done in a disciplined life. The *Yoga Sutras* compiled by Patanjali sometime between 200 and 500 B.C.E. (according to different sources) offers ethical principles for living that are rooted in the first chakra and extend into the higher chakras. The yamas include nonviolence toward all, unswerving truthfulness and honesty, sexual continence as much as we are able, not stealing (more broadly, not taking that which is not freely given), and noncoveting (which means letting go of that with we to do not truly need). Following these disciplines, Patanjali said, quiets our mind and helps us function better.

 ## Visualization of the Triangle, Lingam, and Snake

Visualizing the details of the image can help you keep them in mind and work to realize the qualities they represent.

> First visualize the petals and the square in the illustration of the first chakra.
>
> Then visualize the triangle with the lingam and the snake as Shiva and Shakti—here Shiva represents the path of a meditating yogi and Shakti represents your life energy and the energies around you. Visualize the two energies moving through you and eventually joining as your awareness rises through the chakras.

 ## Visualization of the Complete Illustration

In his book *Chakras,* Johari introduced a visualization technique that can help develop deep concentration. It involves placing a piece of paper over the line drawing for a particular chakra and carefully tracing it (or drawing it by eye, or first tracing until you feel confident enough to try drawing it on your own). Then if you wish you can color it as carefully and precisely as you can, using whatever color painting or drawing medium you prefer. If a color goes onto a line, your thoughts were somewhere else. Maintaining your concentration while coloring will improve concentration in other daily activities. After coloring the image, you then look at it very carefully, at some length. As you spend time on every detail, an imprint is made in the brain. This is helpful when you paint the image again mentally.

In the visualizations of art in these pages, you can trace the drawing, you can paint it, or you can look at it very carefully and then close your eyes and try to see a picture of each detail and the whole drawing or painting inside your mind. People differ in this ability. Some can see something inside their mind while others have a hard time doing that and contact the work more easily through hearing or their kinesthetic sense (touch). Likewise, some people love the tasks of tracing or painting it. Find a discipline that you can enjoy, one that will keep your mind engaged with the image.

The instructions given here refer to the imagery for the first chakra shown in figure 4.1 and plate 4, but the same technique can be used with the line drawings and paintings of each of the chakras.

Do the coloring (and then the visualization) in the particular order given.

1. Start with coloring the four lotus petals around the circle in the center of the drawing in a vermilion red color. Go clockwise, starting with the one pointing to the right. If possible, articulate the seed sound of each petal as you color it. They are: VANG, SHANG, KSHANG, and SANG.

2. Then put the yellow square inside the circle.

3. Now add the animal that carries the seed sound of the element. In the first chakra that is Airavata, the elephant with the seven trunks in the colors of the rainbow. At the same time add the seed sound LANG.

4. In front of the elephant's blanket put orange-colored Ganesha with all his attributes.

5. Before we go to the male energy, we first have to pay respect to the female. If one wants to have something done by the male, it is best to ask the female. At the right side, place Dakini with all her attributes.

6. Then place Brahma with all his attributes at the left side.

7. In the center color the red, downward-pointing triangle.

8. Inside the triangle comes the grey lingam.

9. Finally, conclude with the snake coiled around the lingam with face up and mouth opened toward the canal that carries the energy up (Sushumna Nadi).

10. Now visualize the image, step by step, in the same order, along with articulating the appropriate seed sounds.

If this visualization is done properly, you may feel the Kundalini energy moving softly upward in your spine and energizing the brain. If possible, do this process under guidance of a teacher. Personal instructions will save time in figuring out exactly what is meant.

Reflections

Our journey toward greater wisdom can begin and then we can return to our daily life with all its traps and tests. With the study of our first chakra we are now more aware of the multifaceted background of the world in which we live. We start understanding more of the forces that surround us and express themselves in nature. When we feel security regarding our food and shelter and our physical nature, we can move on to the second chakra.

PRACTICAL TOOLS FOR
FIRST CHAKRA WORK

Choose which of the following approaches work best to aid you in working with your first chakra energies. Don't feel like you have to do everything or use them all. Different methods work for different people. However, we do recommend that you include some form of breath control (*pranayama*), relaxation, and meditation with each chakra.

Relaxation

Purpose: Feeling inwardly calm.

When you're firmly committed to your goals (even if it's your commitment to meditate regularly), you might realize that you want a break from your work to do something more relaxing. Unless you have to meet a demanding deadline, go ahead and give yourself permission to take a relaxation break. Obvious? It seems so. But it may require a new commitment or a break with a well-entrenched work-ethic routine to realize that you can do it.

Taking good care of your physical body by practicing hatha yoga or tai chi, or going dancing, or doing martial arts or other sports are ways to heighten your increasing sense of well-being. With greater self-control and awareness, you naturally set in motion a self-care plan and consciously or subconsciously begin to dialogue with a nurturing inner voice or guide who can help you explore your first chakra in relation to taking better care of yourself.

Breath Control or Pranayama

Purpose: Improved presence, somatic awareness, and relaxation.

Prana or air connects us with our outside world and gives us the vital life force. Since prana is connected to our nervous system, we can control our mind by controlling our breathing. Slow breathing calms the mind. Some forms of pranayama are best done under guidance of a kind guru. There are many variations.

> Take three breaths in which you do no more than sense your breath moving in through your nose, down into and then back up out of your lungs, and out of your mouth. Slowly inhale and exhale.
>
> Now close your eyes, and center yourself by moving your upper body in a circle, inhaling during the back half of each rotation and exhaling during the front half. (If you read about this in chapter 2, in the "Starting Sequence" for Tratak, but did not try it, we suggest that you actually do it now, at this very moment, and see how it feels.)
>
> Once you feel complete physical balance, do no more than sense your breath for five inhalations and exhalations. Then for the next five breaths, scan for tensions in your body, and let go of any tension not needed to sit erect. Relax as completely as you can while keeping an erect sitting posture.

When you feel upset and off-balance during your everyday life, taking just a minute or two to go though this breathing, balancing, and releasing tension process can be beneficial and help move you into a different mental and emotional state. Once you have done it and know how total physical balance feels, you can probably move into it almost immediately without going through the entire sequence. This also gives you a moment to pause, be aware of yourself and your surroundings, and think before you make your next move. Similarly, a martial arts master strives to maintain perfect balance in order to be able to respond instantly to any move an opponent makes. The same principle can apply in verbal exchanges in which you are tempted to act or speak unwisely.

Concentration: Witness Consciousness (Yogic term) or Mindfulness (Buddhist term)

Purpose: Observing and sharpening your mind.

Concentration and mindfulness or witness consciousness are closely related. Don't be confused by these different terms. Both witness consciousness and mindfulness refer to noticing what your mind is doing as it occurs moment by moment. It's as if you slide around to stand behind yourself and then watch yourself in action. This includes noticing not only your mental activity but also your physical sensations, like tension and relaxation, and your emotional reactions. It can also include noticing what's happening around you. It exists within the broader category of staying in the here and now. Concentration involves focusing your mind on what's important to you and where you want to be.

You notice when you are being big minded, and when you are small-minded; when you are kind and when disdainful, when you are truly listening and when you are just waiting for a chance to say your own thing. Zen teachers speak of one-pointed awareness. Here we are describing two-pointed awareness. It involves your doing-thinking-feeling-sensing-self and your witness, who watches and listens to your doing-thinking-feeling-sensing-self.

Think of your mind as a circle. If you're like most people, there is a line drawn down the middle. One part of your mind (the part of the circle on one side of the line) is here and present, available to enjoy and cope effectively with the world. The other part of your mind is filled with thoughts about the future, memories, hopes, worries, and expectations, plus TV commercials and magazine ads and your favorite celebrities, and a motley collection of mental and emotional fascinations.

Your witness consciousness allows you to detach and watch what the rest of your mind is doing. A concentrative discipline allows you to move the line in the circle to enlarge the amount of your consciousness that is available and attentive to what's truly important. For example, a mother might have one-third of her attention on a telephone call, one-third on a soap opera, and the remaining third watching her children doing their homework. With mindfulness, this mother could notice how her attention is divided. She may then turn away from the television, end her call, and place her complete focus on her main priority, being more present with her children. Conversely, premier musicians will have almost their whole mind on the musical piece and on hearing the rest of the musicians and how they blend together. Witness consciousness occupies just a tiny bit of mental capacity, alerting them to get back into the music when attention wanders.

The combination of concentration and witness consciousness working together helps a person gain more mind control, which results in making better choices. Every chakra demands a different kind of concentration. In the first chakra, concentration emphasizes awareness of the physical body and its demands.

Polarity-Balancing Meditation

Purpose: Deepening your first-chakra work.

"The greatest mistake mankind has been making for thousands of years," writes Swami Satyananda Saraswati, "is that he has been fighting with himself.... All the passions are stored in Muladhara, all the guilt, every complex, and every agony."[6] On the other hand, concentration on the first chakra is said to remove ignorance and fear and increase harmony and calmness.

For this meditation, you will need between ten minutes and half an hour so you can include balancing, breathing, releasing tension, and at least a little Tratak.

First look through the table of First-Chakra Possibilities found earlier in this chapter. Scan through its polarities. Which seem most salient for you? Be sensitive to what feels important for you now. If an item feels too heavy and you're not ready to delve into its implications in your life at present, then leave it alone and select a subject with which you feel a more comfortable connection. Or perhaps a topic may feel heavy, but you have a sense that you need to deal with it now and can manage that. Or can you think of something else related to the first chakra that is more relevant to your situation?

Then set the table down and turn to Tratak, concentration on a candle flame or flower or other object. As you take ten slow breaths, recall the quality you have chosen to focus on and let that come to the forefront of your mind. Picture it as an image, or hear it as a silent spoken word.

Then let the item or polarity you chose "merge" with the candle flame or flower, so that when you focus on your chosen object you are connecting it with impressions related to your first chakra.

When you notice that your attention has drifted to something other than the polarity and images or words related to it, notice whether it holds any important message for you. Then return your mental focus to the candle flame or other object you selected to remind you of the polarity you've chosen to contemplate.

Allow whatever occurs in your mind or body to arise and simply notice it. Perhaps memories of situations in which you felt insecure will reveal themselves. Or possibly an insight, accompanied by a change in your feelings and your breathing, will shine a light on how to treat yourself or others better. Be your own witness to whatever occurs within you, noticing when your mind has drifted, then bringing your mental focus back to your chosen polarity.

As you do this, continue to be subliminally aware of your posture, balance, breathing, and body sensations. Don't try to think in a problem-solving way. Stay with your focal image or word(s), and continue to let your witnessing self mindfully notice what occurs in your mind-emotions-body. Items may bubble up from your subconscious, such as memories from long ago. As your field of consciousness around this first-chakra polarity expands, you may even choose to include thoughts, feelings, or sensations that you've been actively working to avoid. If this happens, the key is to witness or notice your thoughts. Do not actively justify or rationalize them. If you think there's something bad about them, then "step around behind yourself" and notice your process of judging yourself.

When you feel finished with your meditation, be finished. Take ten long, deep breaths to transition back to everyday consciousness. With each breath, look at or listen to something different in the environment around you.

If you'd like some words of inspiration to help you plunge into this inner work, try this: "While meditating don't concentrate on the results of meditation," says Paramahansa Yogananda. "If you seek results, you will be disappointed if they don't come."[7] Trust your observations; trust your process.

Affirming Your Sense of Security

Purpose: Feeling secure and confident.

Get into a comfortable position, take a few relaxing breaths, close your eyes, and look inward. Ask yourself: What words and feelings do you personally associate with the first chakra? How can you use your understanding to inspire and guide your life?

Find the spot near the base of your spine that is linked with your root or first chakra. How do you experience this force? Connect the energy you hold in that part of your body with thoughts of unconditional self-love (whether you think you deserve it or not!). Once your mind is centered in harmonious thoughts, imagine your inner spirit as being strong like a tree that sends its roots deep into the earth. Acknowledge your feelings as being like expanding branches of confidence and security, and visualize your will to succeed in your own way as being deeply rooted in the fertile energy of your first chakra.

From this point of feeling grounded and connected to your strength and vitality, let your mind visualize yourself doing what you need to do to move toward the attainment of your most important goals. Let your inner guide, muse, or voice help you find the best practical steps you can take toward inner contentment and outer fulfillment. In your mind's eye, see yourself confident, optimistic, successful, and appreciating the richness of your moment.

If you hear an inner voice say, "I can't do that!" then move into your witness consciousness, notice your self-defeating inner talk, and try moving your attention into repeating your mantra or smelling a flower instead.

Sound Healing

Purpose: Raising energy and strengthening mental focus and desired qualities.

 Mantra Chanting

Mantra work can clear hazy mental states and help you align with the energy of the thoughts and feelings they represent. They are special sounds that can create needed vibrations that fill the mind after long practice, and keep it more and more calm.

Choose a mantra or word of power that you like, either in Sanskrit or English, from the following list. Or select another related word that fits you better if you prefer.

Practice chanting your mantra or word of power for several minutes or longer. Experiment with closing your eyes while you chant and feeling its sound vibrate within you.

FIRST-CHAKRA MANTRAS

MANTRA	PRONUNCIATION	MEANING
shanti	SHAWN-tee	peace
ksema	k'SAYmah	safe, secure, comfortable, at ease
anirveda	aneerVAYdah	self-reliance, self-confidence
svatantra	svahTAHNtrah	autonomy, self-reliance, freedom

 Music

Begin to consciously notice how the music you most often play makes you feel. Play only music you truly enjoy. Many people (especially young people) think they should like the same music their friends and in-group like, even when they really don't. Seek music for the backdrop of your life that helps you feel inspired, healed, and refreshed.

Taking Action

Purpose: Using meditative awareness to affect your words and actions.

During your meditation, what actions did you imagine taking in regard to your chosen polarity? Did you realize that you want to start doing something differently in your daily life? Meditative awareness gives you a chance to see that you're acting a certain way, or are about to act a certain way. With such awareness, you can choose to act deliberately rather than reactively.

> After you've noticed a thought, feeling, or impulse that you want to change, *stop right at that moment, before you actually do it,* then choose to do something more beneficial.
>
> Then compliment yourself for your new behavior. Pair your statements of appreciation with specific actions.
>
> Make a commitment to this beneficial change in your everyday self-talk and you will probably start to feel a positive change.
>
> During your daily activities (that is, not during meditation), when you notice that you wish you had just done something differently, make a note of it. Next time, when you notice that you're in the middle of speaking or acting of feeling that way, *notice that.* In the future, when you notice that you're about to speak or act or feel that way, STOP! Then choose to do something else instead, and act in that new way. Having practiced this sequence in your mind's eye during meditation, now you can actually carry it out in your everyday life.

Here's an example: You choose to meditate on your first chakra in relation to inner balance. As you meditate, you find that you'd like to let go of some habitual way of responding. For instance, you might notice a mental habit of silently—or even out loud—telling yourself that you did something poorly and that it means you are "not okay" and something is wrong. In your meditation, you may have realized that you really are okay. Reflecting further, you may note that your ongoing negative self-talk is part of an old mental pattern, and you want to stop making such comments to and about yourself. Right now, start your transformation by verbally appreciating yourself throughout the day. Remind yourself to frequently say, "I did that pretty well." (When you've done this in meditation and reach the step of integrating it into your daily life, you can notice yourself standing on the brink of your old pattern, stop, tell yourself something like "I can do that!" and then go ahead and do so.)

Understanding the first chakra is a starting point for studying our basic tendencies and inclinations, the root of our self-concepts, and further self-inquiry. Next we look at how to create a better relationship with our inner self and with others through the possibilities of the second chakra, sometimes called the dwelling place of the self.

 **5**

Second or Svadhisthana Chakra

The Passion Chakra

In the second chakra imagination is stimulated. You seek entertainment and sensory pleasure, enjoy family and friends, and express creativity.

Since Tantra accepts desire as the prime motivating force of the universe, it does not ask its aspirants to renounce desire. Other spiritual sciences advise the avoidance of desire. . . .Yet one is left with the paradox that to achieve desirelessness, one must have a strong desire—to be desireless! . . . A person's psyche is strongly influenced and conditioned by the quality of the object of his or her desire.

HARISH JOHARI, *TOOLS FOR TANTRA*

Second or Svadhisthana Chakra Correspondences

Key phrases: Procreation, sensuality, sexuality, emotion, pleasure, family, fantasies

Physical location: Pelvis, genital region

Endocrine gland: Testicles or ovaries

Astrological link: Mercury

Day of the week: Wednesday

Element: Water

Sense: Taste

Sanskrit Derivation: *sva* (self); *adhisthana* (dwelling place)

Massage: Thighs, buttocks, pelvis

Leela Game of Self-Knowledge: Second row: Purification, Entertainment, Envy, Nullity, Astral Plane, Plane of Fantasy, Jealousy, Mercy, and Plane of Joy

THE ESSENCE OF THE SECOND CHAKRA: JOY, FANTASY, AND DESIRE

Located in the pelvic region, this chakra is most often linked with sexual energy and fantastic, cosmic lovemaking! At least in the West that's the widespread stereotype of second-chakra energy, and tantra yoga is commonly regarded as the art of sacred sexuality. Within narrowly defined limits this perception is accurate, but it is also just one aspect of a larger picture. In *Living with the Himalayan Masters,* Swami Rama writes,

> According to the science of Tantra, male and female are two principles of the universe called Shiva and Shakti. These two principles exist within each individual. There are three main schools of Tantra: Kaula, Mishra, and Samaya. The *Kaulists,* or left-handed tantrists, worship Shakti, and their way of worship involves external rituals, including sexual practices. . . . Laymen often misuse this path. In the *Mishra* (mixed or combined) school, inner worship is combined with external practices. The latent . . . kundalini . . . force is awakened and led to the *anahata* chakra (heart center), where it is worshipped. The . . . *Samaya* or the right-hand path . . . is purely yoga; it has nothing to do with any ritual or any form of worship involving sex. Meditation is the key.[1]

Both the right-handed and left-handed tantric paths acknowledge the spark of the universal life force, the divine presence, in every person and living being, but the "left-handed path of Tantra" also includes making meditative and yogic practices central components of lovemaking. This means overcoming the traps of fantasies and physical desires of the second chakra that may spark feelings of envy, jealousy, and possessiveness that deplete emotional energy. It also means striving to develop joy, seeing the divine in human and other living forms, and devoting yourself to realizing the oneness of humanity. Viewed through this lens, the second chakra becomes a temple for honoring the purity of sensual desires, creative thinking, and a channel for moving energy toward higher states of consciousness. In *Tantric Quest* Daniel Odier, who was taught by a *tantriki* (a devotee of this path) for some time in India, writes,

> In Tantrism, we throw our entire beings in, endlessly, without distinguishing between pure and impure, beauty and ugliness, good and bad. . . . All the pairs of opposites are dissolved in the divine. The deepest urges, the most sublime capacities—no one lacks them. . . . We accept the complete spectrum of our thoughts and our emotions. . . . When one sees nothing but a singular and shared divine energy in all things, the consciousness can no longer go astray.[2]

The right-hand path of Tantra emphasizes discipline, austerity, and worship. A right-handed tantriki might use sex only for having children, or might even become a *brahmachari,* one who abstains from sex entirely. This tradition sees avoiding second-chakra sensory pleasures and worldly entertainment as a way to avoid the overpowering carnal desires that can distract us from waking up our spiritual energies.

We are not choosing sides among left-hand, middle, and right-hand tantrism. Different paths suit different people. We do need to point out, however, that there is more to the second chakra than sensuality and sex—or abstention from sex, as you prefer. Think showbiz, Hollywood, Bollywood, glitz, glamour, and fame. Almost every movie, TV show, and article in the tabloids that concerns entertainers and celebrities, portraying love and romance, families, betrayal, and divorce involves this chakra's energy. Shifting moods, imaginings, desires, and fantasies can cause feelings at the second-chakra level to suddenly change like dancing shadows.

For most people, it is the chakra of the joys and sorrows of family life. The family is usually an ideal place to learn to live with others, although there are always exceptions and no family is ideal. And when we interact with people in our family, problems will come, but living together offers us the chance to work through them. In India the belief is widespread that we select our parents. In any case we have little choice but to accept them as they are.

Appreciation of physical beauty and the creative and expressive arts, notes Johari, is also linked with the second chakra. These are good ways to express second-chakra inclinations and energies. He adds that it is also the chakra of business, selling, advertising, and commerce. In the second chakra, as in the first, much of what we do is guided or driven by the subconscious. Some of these underlying influences manipulate us like puppets on a string, due to the emotional and mental conditioning of our personal history, while others are part of the collective unconscious and a component of human nature. One attribute that has both personal and collective roots is the attempt to avoid or hide thoughts, feelings, and actions that portray us in an unfavorable light. This refusal to look at and listen or admit to what we are actually doing often leads to making mistakes in our choices and getting our soul "stuck" while presumably on the journey toward higher consciousness.

Below are some second-chakra possibilities. As with the first chakra, these are not dualisms. Each exists along a continuum of expression from the left to the right side. (Imagine working with a slider that you can position anywhere from extreme left to extreme right.) Looking at this table, what influences are likely to be most useful for you to consider now?

SECOND-CHAKRA POSSIBILITIES

OPPORTUNITIES	OBSTACLES
Sensitivity	Indifference, disinterest
Harmony	Confusion, disharmony
Respect	Exploitation
Self-reliance	Dependence
Courteousness, graciousness	Inconsiderateness, unpleasantness
Fosters autonomy of self and others	Possessiveness
Initiative and enthusiasm	Dullness and listlessness

SECOND-CHAKRA POSSIBILITIES (cont'd)

OPPORTUNITIES	OBSTACLES
Mercifulness	Imperviousness
Appreciation and contentment	Envy and jealousy
Creativity	Sloth (or inactivity)
Joyful lovemaking	Energy-draining sex
Austerity, purification	Indulgence
Humility	Self-glorification

THE MENTAL PATHWAY FOR WORKING WITH SECOND-CHAKRA ENERGIES

The Bright Side of the Second Chakra

Gifts and Strengths: Enjoyment of life; being guided by appropriate emotion; maintaining positive relationships; being one's true self.

The Svadhisthana Chakra is connected with the element water and fluid emotions. It energizes the mind with fluctuating waves of feelings that can illuminate the self and soul, and provides a kind of sanctuary in which human consciousness can arise like a butterfly emerging from a caterpillar's cocoon. Through upward and downward flows of arousing energies, it balances feminine and masculine instincts—passive yin energy and active yang forces, and enables the mind to develop wings to soar far above duality-bound qualities.

Connected with feelings, moods, and hormonal ups and down of the body's sexual thermometer, it opens or closes the door of opportunities for birthing personal and family connections. Linked equally with marriage and divorce, joy and jealousy, fantasy and nullity, second-chakra energy can bring the best of life's joys and pleasures or drive us to flee its challenging sorrows and pains. Relishing whatever forms of glitz, glamour, and celebrity consciousness we find enticing can sometimes make us forget that most of life can go on just as well without them.

When this chakra is balanced, you seek a pathway to experience the intangible gifts of love, and naturally strive to keep your relationships mutually respectful. You do your best to find and share happiness, especially with those closest to you.

Useful expressions of second-chakra energy can include creativity and originality, encouragement of others' uniqueness, and a willingness to build harmonious relationships. You hear and respond to the essence of another person's words, thoughts, and feelings in a kind way without trying to remake the other to fit your own wishes and expectations. Compassion, mercy, and kindness come more easily when you realize that you are one with the greater family of humanity, and not just with those who gave you birth. You are special and extraordinary, one unique spark in the unfathomable flame of cosmic mysteries.

In daily life, secure second-chakra energy contributes to your sense of being high-spirited and feeling attractive. While you may be passionate in your pursuit of pleasures, enjoyments, and entertainments, you can also appreciate what is good in your present situation just as it is. When you feel connected with the life-giving forces of this chakra, you're likely to create positive realities and come up with dynamic approaches and strategies to make your life vibrant and meaningful. Johari claims, "This awareness of possibilities creates excitement, and we begin to take a more active interest in life."[3] Fantasy, creativity, and possibility are hallmarks of the second chakra.

The Dark Side of the Second Chakra

Issues and Challenges: Fear of engaging people; giving up your own desires and inclinations in order to please others; excessive need for validation or adulation; lacking purpose; jealousy and envy.

When second chakra energies go astray, its shadow side can appear in guises such as addiction, betrayal, revenge, or aggression. Aggressive sex, which some people associate with the second chakra, actually takes place in the first, where it is animal behavior, and in the third, the realm of domination and control. There can be possessiveness mixed with passion that shackles someone in the chains of another's desires and expectations regardless of their own feelings, wishes, and inclinations. A potential danger of the second chakra is clinging so tightly to another, or one's image or expectations of another, that it stifles their chance to develop their own individuality.

Somewhere in the middle of the continuum between opportunities and obstacles related to the second chakra are the many people who are simply shy or anxious about initiating contact with others. Great ease or difficulty in reaching out are opposite ends of one of the second chakra polarities, while mildly shy or uneasy feelings about dating and mating are somewhere in the middle.

The interest or disinterest of romantic partners or potential lovers can bring the validation that "I'm hot stuff" or the invalidation that "I'm not much." If the golden guy or gal that everyone desires goes off with someone else, you may go into a distressing tailspin. Or slump into a dark corner so that no one can see your feelings of disappointment. Out of your unfulfilled expectations, or jealousy or envy, you might dive into a pit of hopelessness, where revenge, depression, self-pity, or other dysfunctional thoughts, feelings, and actions and reactions sabotage your ability to find happiness. When you look within yourself and can't see anyone other than a reflection of the external person on whom you feel dependent for validation, you are trapped. Addiction, sloth, torpor, dullness, and listlessness can result. Your sense of self-worth falls into dark cracks of unhappiness.

In everyday matters, toxic second-chakra interaction includes thoughtlessness and expressions of critical or hostile feelings, often with little or no sensitivity to the other's intentions or motives. This is especially hurtful when one person acts from a desire to do something helpful and the other takes it the wrong way and replies in a cross, angry, or otherwise inconsiderate manner.

Most love relationships are second-chakra events. But because this is the chakra of "wine, women, and song," we easily confuse the word *love* with several very different phenomena. Some are almost opposites. Most of us sometimes experience *object-centered love,* a focus on the concrete satisfactions of being loved. In a sense, we treat another person as an object who exists to fulfill our desires. (An infant's love for the mother's milk-giving breast is object-centered.) We might try to keep our lover in a role that meets our needs without paying much attention to taking care of his or hers. Our focus is mainly on our own interests, and the possibilities are legion.

Projective love is a special variety of object-centered love. It exists when you have fixed ideas about what you want in another person and you perceive them through the template of your preconceptions. It's as if you have a stencil and observe them only by what you can see through the cut-out letters. As you spend time together, you discover ways in which they differ from what you wanted. As you come to see the other as they are, your love for them mysteriously fades.

Related to projective love is the *good material pattern* in which you see them more or less as they are, but with notable flaws. However, you think the flaws can be remedied, and find them satisfactory enough that you are willing to undertake the job of fixing them. However, if you keep trying to repair what you think is wrong with them, they may go from loving to hating you, as you rob them of their capacity to be true to themselves. Many marriages in which the partners look perfect for each other start out in this pattern, and then end up crashing like waves against a rocky shore when the partners realize that they can't remake each other.

Romantic love, which everyone knows from story and song, may or may not include conscious love, a fourth-chakra quality in which you truly desire the other person's well-being. When you can feel love and consciously express desire for the other person's growth and welfare as they envision it, you experience the arrow of Eros joining you together in a mutually enriching way. Both of your second chakras burst with excitement as the flame of love ignites.

Often, when we first fall in love, it is object-centered, second-chakra love. Then we start to see the imperfections in the other and feel antagonistic and begin battling, which takes our love to the third chakra. Only after working through that can we experience the real love of the higher chakras.

Past Roots of Second-Chakra Problems

One childhood source of second-chakra problems is lack of love, appreciation, and validation. Infants need to be physically held and comforted. If Mom and Dad (or Auntie or Nanny) are too busy with their own interests, even if their infants or children play an important role in their thoughts, they may fail to give them the comfort and affection they need. Those other interests might be preoccupation with a career at one extreme, or spending evenings getting drunk at the corner bar at the other. An example is a woman who, even though showered with an abundance of material gifts from her parents, feels empty inside because they never took time to truly share their hearts. "I'm giving my child everything," the parents tell themselves, while not realizing that they're failing to provide some of what their child needs most. Pioneer psychiatrist Alfred Adler's term for this pattern is *the neglected child.*[4]

Such patterns often are passed down through the generations. But their chain of pain can be broken. Giving a child the sensitive physical, emotional, and intellectual care he or she needs provides a foundation for building inner confidence, faith in love, and solid moral fiber.

A different source of second-chakra problems occurs when a child gets whatever he or she wants without having to do anything to receive it. This is the classical pattern of *the spoiled* or *pampered child*. Often this lucky yet unlucky person fails to develop a sense of responsibility or learn the vital elements for achieving success in life.

Second-chakra impulses are naturally most active at the age of seven to fourteen for boys and six to twelve for girls. (But they can continue for years after that—especially sexual desire and validation or invalidation.) This is the period when in a playful way we discover our peers. And we are confronted with emotional turmoil in our contacts with others in our age group. Guidance from parents to help their children develop a sense of fair play and to become acquainted with the arts is valuable.

THE BODY AND EMOTIONS PATHWAY: FEELING TONES IN THE SECOND CHAKRA

Personal Transformation in the Second Chakra

Self-reliance, self-determination, and following your free will may seem like clichés, but that misses the point. Reliance on others, liking whatever they suggest that you like (whether explicitly or implicitly), and being addicted to following the latest trends are common. Watching, reading, or listening and accepting whatever the media beams at you instead of making your own choices is often the norm. And many mass-media messages intentionally inhibit a connection with deeper feelings that can help you align with your inner truths and advance on your personal path. That can be the case whether those messages come directly from the media or secondhand from your friends, family, or social group.

One key to becoming more truly yourself, more self-reliant, and more in touch with the choices you want to make is to become deeply aware of your very own feelings—even when these are barely perceptible inclinations and impulses—rather than accepting others' demands, attitudes, or outlooks. Ask yourself: Do you or don't you take the initiative in moving forward with what you truly want to achieve? Are you free to be the person who you truly are inside? Do you trust your intuitive sense? Are you willing to work on developing the emotional qualities you hope to make part of your daily life?

Relational Transformation in the Second Chakra

Encouraging others to become more truly themselves cleans and clears the metaphoric mirror that shows you how to do that same thing for yourself. Being receptive to hearing and encouraging others' genuine preferences, especially about their own feelings, opens the potential for greater trust and happiness. Relationships between two or more people tend to evolve in positive directions when each appreciates and accepts the other as they really are.

Central to harmonious relations is sharing uncritical space for the other's initiative, interests, and creativity. Whether platonic or romantic, appreciating others' choices about their ideas, feelings, and actions, even if you don't understand them or are bemused that their choices differ from your own, lets a person know you acknowledge and respect them. How many handcuffed prisoners, when asked why they maimed or killed another person, reply, "He didn't show me no respect!"?

Jumping over boundaries of solitude can be easy when another's smile or attitude contains a green light that invites friendship or lovemaking. When the waters of sexual energy flow, if they are contained in a chalice of mutual sensitivity, deep feelings rise effortlessly into the cup of love. The uplifting energy of body and soul receptivity to another's emotionally loaded glance or touch clarifies the heart's declarations.

A step toward uniting lovers' separate flames of spirit during lovemaking is for partners to harmonize their breathing. Sensing the rhythm of each other's breath, breathing in and out together, can weave separate life forces together in the lovers' blissful movement toward sacred union.

"Sexual awareness and desires can manifest at any stage of evolution," says Satyananda Saraswati. "Sexual awareness never really dies because it is fueled by the primal energy which is present all throughout. Sex can manifest at any stage and one should never think that one has transcended it."[5]

In the system of the chakras we end at the seventh chakra with the lord of sex, Kameshvara, and his wife Kameshvari. In the first three chakras the sex is physical. In the fourth too, but just touch is enough. In the fifth only the voice is enough. And in the sixth just the presence of the other can give sexual pleasure. In the seventh the partners are in total balance and are one. In India they say that you don't start there, but you end there. Chakras place sex in a broader context, which brings us to love for the other and finally to love for all, which can lead to universal love.

THE PATHWAY OF SPIRIT: IMAGERY IN THE SECOND CHAKRA

The Circle, the Lotus Petals, and the Seed Sounds

The abstract form of the second chakra is the circle and the crescent. The circle is a symbol for the element water and the crescent for the moon. The first thing we see is the relationship between water and the moon. Emotions are entering the game! The moon is also related to procreation or the power to give life. That makes the genitals and the womb the work organs of the second chakra.

Without water no life is possible. Water is the essence of life. Both our planet's surface and our bodies are three quarters water. After we discovered traces of water on Mars, we started believing that life may be possible there.

When we study the circle further, we see that it is an expansion of a point, which is the source of all symbolism. It is the *bindi*, the still point around which everything evolves. The radius of desires makes the point move around itself. As such it gets the shape of the zero, which represents infinity.

As our emotional mind develops, our world and our personality start to expand. Looking at those around us creates all kind of emotions. We come to know family and friends, and we are attracted sexually to others. At first the circle of people we meet is small—only whoever is in our immediate environment. In the first chakra our personality was preoccupied with the security of food and shelter. The world was very basic. In the second we get food for our desires, sexual fantasies, and creativity. Security now includes our personal sense of self, our beauty and youth. Since water is connected to taste (tongue is the sense organ linked with this chakra), for most people not only our food, but also our lives become more tasteful.

The mental phenomena connected to one of each of the six lotus petals are: affection, careless indulgence, suspicion, disdain, delusion, destructiveness, and pitilessness. They can all generate negative thoughts that have a downward whirlpool effect on our psyche. In this chakra we can become aware of them and

Figure 5.1. This drawing depicts the deities—Vishnu and Rakini Devi—and
the core imagery shown in the painting of this chakra
(plate 5: Second or Svadhisthana Chakra).

discover where they are coming from. We will study them more when we meet the
crocodile, a symbol of our animal nature (see next page). But family life with all
its responsibilities can be helpful in controlling our emotional fluctuations. Our
interactions with our direct environment and our small circle of family and friends
function as a school to correct our wrong choices. After we gain some understanding of how to balance our emotions, we can more easily go into the larger world of
the third chakra.

The seed sound of the water element is VANG. *VA* represents the power of Varuna, the deity of water and ocean. The *NG* sound moves energy upward. With this sound we can vibrate our brains. When you produce this sound, put your hand on your skull and feel how it vibrates. Nothing else can make the brain vibrate like that.

 ### Turning the Inner Sound on with Visualization

1. Visualize the six red lotus petals, starting with the one to the right of the one on top. As you visualize each petal, moving clockwise, utter its seed sound: BANG, BHANG, MANG, YANG, RANG, and LANG.
2. Then visualize the silver crescent moon.
3. End with the seed sound of the element: VANG.

The Crocodile

With the crocodile (the carrier of the seed sound VANG), we meet the monster hidden in the second chakra. It can be seen as a dragon. In India they call it *makara* (the source of the English word *mugger,* which implies a stealthy approach before a vicious attack). Other habits of this animal are sunbathing, floating, and fantasizing. And we all know the power of crocodile tears.

It is not difficult to imagine that crocodile energy can create a chaotic state of mind in which we run from here to there and constantly change. In such a state we cannot find rest. To ground ourselves we can focus again on the pillars of life: food, sleep, and sex. Food fasting—such as not eating food one or two days a week—is beneficial and it also has a good effect on the development of the sense of taste.

Once we get a little control of this tendency by grounding and centering ourselves we can more confidently work on the other obstacles. We work with our crocodile by understanding it. Since its energies are inevitably part of us, we would do well to experience and understand them. This is a tricky task. We have to satisfy our urges, learn to play with our body, and discover the pleasures connected to it. Sexually, for spiritual growth it is best to stay with one partner. Concessions are unavoidable and we learn that one cannot do everything one desires. Love for the physical body might change to love for the person and spirit that inhabit the body.

Vishnu

After Brahma created the physical universe made from the five elements, he needed a force to preserve this creation and keep it in a harmonious and balanced form. That force or principle is called Vishnu, which means the "Pervader" or "Preserver." Vishnu pervades everything in this universe. He maintains the balance between creation (Brahma) and destruction (Shiva). It is said that whenever there is a dominance of demonic forces on Earth that disturb the balance, Vishnu will come to save us in a new incarnation. As such he is the eternal hero of the second chakra. His most famous incarnations are Rama and Krishna in the great Indian epics of Ramayana and Mahabharata, respectively. The romantic nature of these stories is very beneficial in this chakra.

With Vishnu we enter the mental realm, which can overpower the physical beauty of Brahma's creation. This is the world of dreams, where extraordinary creation occurs. Dreams occur not only in our sleep. We can also dream with our eyes open! The realm of deep sleep corresponds with Shiva, who reminds us of the emptiness behind all creation. In that way death belongs to Shiva, whereas life belongs to Vishnu. They exist together and cannot be separated.

With Brahma we get science, where we use sensory perception. With Shiva we gain transcendent knowledge, with the help of the yogas. Vishnu gives us religion, where we can use all of our mental and intellectual faculties. It can be quite helpful to pay attention to what religions have in common. Major religions have a theology and a moral code. Theology answers the questions of where we come from and where we go and why we experience all this. It deals with karma and *dharma* (our duty in being one with nature). But since a religion can all too easily get stuck in false dogmas, we must think very clearly so that we can see through them, follow what is of value, and let go of what is not.

Just as Brahma offered the yamas, the first part of the moral code or ethics that we need to live with ourselves and each other in a balanced and harmonious manner, Vishnu offers the second part. These *niyamas* or ethical duties and positive attitudes and habits, systematized in detail by Patanjali, are beneficial for our spiritual journey. They are self-purification, contentment (accepting ourselves, others, and whatever life has brought us—which usually brings happiness), self-discipline, self-study that leads to self-awareness, and self-surrender, or giving ourselves to a purpose greater than ourselves. Vishnu offers these rules of conduct to help us purify our worldly practices.

Vishnu can be seen as the key to realizing the plan or ultimate goal or dream of life. One of the names of Vishnu is Hari, which means the "Remover." He removes the ignorance that makes us believe we are a separate entity. But nothing can exist apart from him. By removing our ignorance he also removes our sorrows. The Vishnu depicted in figure 5.1 and plate 5 is just one symbolic representation of this energy created by human beings.

In the picture Vishnu has four arms representing the four aims in life that give us full enjoyment. The mace or club in his lower right hand represents wealth (*artha*) or the earthly security of the first chakra. The enjoyment of beauty (*kama*) is symbolized by the lotus flower in his lower left hand. We have the right to enjoy, but also the spiritual ability to detach and let go. The discipline of surrendering to the law of nature (*dharma*), where we can find harmony and balance, is symbolized by the chakra wheel. The last and final aim is liberation (*moksha*) or becoming one with the source. The conch shell in the upper left hand represents the sound of the mantra, regarded in the yogic tradition as an indispensable tool for liberation. The second chakra is also the place where purification is needed. Humming or chanting to reset the brain waves can be a powerful tool.

One last thing that needs to be explained is the nature of Vishnu. As lord of maya he creates a mental illusion of reality, where it is very difficult to find him. He hides inside this game of life (called leela) and we have to find him. He plays with us and challenges us with earthly tests, through which we slowly learn the truth. In *Leela: Game of Self-Knowledge* Harish Johari offers us a playful way to become more aware of the path that we are following. Everybody has a different path, but many of us are going to the same place. Surrendering to this playful nature may help us to reach the fourth chakra, where we can experience conscious love. With Vishnu, in this second chakra the desire for love begins to have a spiritual content.

Rakini Devi

The picture also includes Rakini, who helps us to understand and work with the split energy of the second chakra. This split energy is represented by her two heads. Rakini opens the way to enter the second chakra. The realization of the presence of another person in our lives and the encountering of this other wakes up our crocodile with all his hunting emotions, which can so easily create negative feelings.

Rakini forces us to find a balance between the world inside and outside. The arrow in one of her hands represents the concentration on an object or objective needed to fulfill a desire. Once it hits the target the concentration is gone again. It is not permanent yet. But there is also an upward movement in the symbol of the arrow. The upward-pointing arrow is mercy or compassion for the suffering of the other. Mercy can be so intense that ego disappears and we feel cosmic love, not only for a specific other (or the beloved one), but for all sentient beings of the creation of Brahma. Then we are able to see the real inner beauty of creation. Without such compassion, dharma or following the laws of nature is not possible. Mercy is the arrow that brings us almost to our goal of becoming one with our source. To do so we have to live what we just realized. Understanding the pain the other causes us helps us understand that which we cause the other.

The skull represents nonattachment to the body and mind and reminds us to overcome the fear of death. Through such nonattachment the real romantic hero of the second chakra, who is ready to sacrifice his life for his beloved, can awake. The romantic hero stories of Vishnu help to bring this impulse to a higher level, and we can experience a divine love starting to stir somewhere within us. Through love, the fourth chakra is closely related to the second!

With a drum, sound and rhythm are introduced. Dance is a great way to relieve tensions created by the emotions of meeting others. But not only dance: All arts have sources in the sexual energy of the second chakra. To achieve our desired art piece we learn to concentrate. We learn to play, and lose the concept of time. We can experience moments of deep concentration, where the I dissolves and only playful art remains. This art can become spiritual and bring one to a higher level.

The romantic hero or heroine who sacrifices him or herself for divine love exemplifies the ultimate emotion in the second chakra. It can carry one along the path of *bhakti* or spiritual devotion, one of the principal yogas, which is comparable to an arrow that flies straight toward our cosmic source.

Rakini holds an ax, one of the oldest tools. With that she can remove our nonspiritual qualities that are created by our crocodile. In the battle with this animal in us we have to use our ax of discipline, also a very old inner tool. Only then can the practicing of ethics, the absorption in art, and the preservation of family life have their purifying effect on us.

Reflections

In this chakra we face our crocodile. Emotions can become too overwhelming. But when the beloved becomes our world and makes the outside world less important, slowly the word *truth* is understood as "love." Not as the lust of the crocodile, but as deep compassion for all that lives. This way this chakra can transform our energy and bring us to higher levels, and even the highest! Then it is truly Svadhisthana Chakra, the dwelling place of the most realized Self. Thanks to Vishnu we can enjoy the Divine in the game of life.

PRACTICAL TOOLS
FOR SECOND-CHAKRA WORK

Relaxation

Purpose: Relaxing the nervous system and increasing prana.

Since chronic muscular tension contributes to several kinds of physical problems, we tend to be healthier and more effective in our relationships and in most kinds of work when we are relaxed. Some physical and mental tensions cannot be fully released by meditative relaxation alone.

Johari used to say that we would all be better off if everyone got a massage each day. "Every day?" You might think. "I can't spare time for that." Nor can most people. But you can probably find time for a half hour or hour massage once a week, or at the very least twice a month. (If you can't afford regular visits to a massage professional, taking even a one-day basic massage workshop, and getting your partner or a friend do likewise, will teach you enough to trade massages regularly.)

The results? You'll probably breathe deep sighs of relief and feel far better. If there's an especially tight spot in your body, even a few minutes of work on it can work wonders. Not only does massage help you feel better, but your body will thank you profusely for giving it some TLC. Johari claims that massage also brings an increased supply of oxygen to the brain, relaxes the nervous system, and raises the level of pranic energy to stimulate our activities.

To learn about the 107 *marmas,* or pressure points on the body, and how to offer a balanced massage, you can read Harish's fully illustrated book, *Ayurvedic Massage,* which describes traditional techniques to manipulate energy in the physical body to stimulate healing. It demonstrates how to best pat, rub, squeeze, knead, and gently press the entire body from head to foot.

Breath Control, or Pranayama

Purpose: Stimulating second-chakra energy flow.

Sit or lie in a comfortable position. Take three breaths in which you do no more than sense your breath moving in through your nose, down into and then back up out of your lungs, and out of your nose. With awareness, sense your breath as you slowly inhale and exhale.

Now close your eyes and find your inner center of balance. Sense your incoming breath making its way to this inner center, and steadily hold your breath for a short count of your choice (probably a count of at least 3 but not more than 6) before you slowly exhale.

With your next inhalation, as you breathe into your inner center and briefly hold your breath, put your attention on tightening the muscles in your pelvic area and surrounding area (extending to just below your belly button) while your lungs fill with air.

As you begin to exhale, slowly release these muscles. When these muscles are being isolated and tightened, it may feel like you are lifting your sacral area, and when you release these muscles, the opposite movement will occur.

As you practice, you will be strengthening your connections and stimulating the nerves in this area. Consistent practice is beneficial. If you are a beginner at breath training, start slowly with no more than five repetitions. Continue with as many complete repetitions of this exercise as you wish and feel comfortable with.

Concentration

> **Purpose:** Focus and insight.

Water is so important that we can't live without it. We drink it, bathe in it, swim in it, sail boats on it, and use it in sacred ceremonies. It helps us enter the world through the birthing canal. Symbolically, water is the fluidic pathway from worldly sensations to the infinite ocean of transcendent consciousness. As the ruling element of the second chakra, it represents the fluctuating nature of feelings and the flow of emotions and the creative imagination.

The following exercise helps to develop mental focus and acuity.

First find a glass and fill it with water. Set the glass in front of you so that you can see the water.

Sit comfortably and relax into the moment by breathing deeply and slowly. Look at (or down into) the glass. Examine it closely. Take in every little detail, as if you were about to turn around and draw a picture of it from memory.

Now close your eyes and visualize the glass of water (or mentally describe it in words if you have a hard time visualizing). Every time your mind drifts from your inner picture (or words) of your glass of water, open your eyes and look at your glass. Once you have focused on it and have it clearly in view, again close your eyes and look inwardly at your glass of water. In your mind's eye, how do you see the water? Learning to watch your emotions just as you are watching your glass of water may help you better understand which choices you want to make.

Polarity-Balancing Meditation

> **Purpose:** To benefit inner clarity.

Start by selecting a line from the "Second-Chakra Possibilities" table on page 79 to 80 that fits one of your own challenges or wishes for growth. Once you've chosen your concern (such as contentment or jealousy), use it as your focal point for this contemplative mediation. For detailed instructions, see the "Polarity-Balancing Meditation" on page 70. Take at least ten minutes for balancing, breathing, releasing tension, and at least a little Tratak before you begin the contemplative meditation itself.

As you meditate, if you feel disturbed by some kind of mental or emotional distraction, don't be critical of yourself. With your witness consciousness (or mindfulness, if you prefer), "step behind yourself," and when you can, mentally release any discomfort. Just let it go. When you start judging what happens in your meditation as right or wrong, notice that too. What you're doing in your mind is not good or bad—it's just what you're doing. Both easy and difficult meditation sessions develop your inward concentration and can help polarity balancing. No two meditations are alike, and almost every meditation can be beneficial.

Affirming Positive Emotional and Creative Qualities

Purpose: Emotional centering.

Take several deep breaths. With each breath allow yourself to relax more deeply and drink in the bliss of your inner essence. Think about what emotional or creative attributes you were born with or you have developed, their special importance, and how you can best use them. Can you expand your perspectives by opening your mind to new possibilities that exist in the freshness of the present moment?

Next, imagine yourself wielding your scepter of self-control, discipline, and authority over yourself. Are you tempted to clamp down and give in to limiting or negative feelings about yourself or others, or are you willing to open up to constructive new possibilities? How can you use your will to make desired changes in your emotional or physical life, to improve your family connections, or your relationships to your community or wider world? What qualities and actions do you see as you look within? What have you contemplated that leads toward greater enjoyment and more positive potentials for your future?

Then listen to the spirited song of your soul and confirm your inspiration to live with abundant joy.

Sound Healing

Purpose: Raising positive energy and strengthening beneficial emotions.

 ### Mantra Chanting

As well as chanting this chakra's seed sound, VANG, mantras or words of power related to this chakra (given below) can be spoken out loud or silently from within your inner space. They can be a chanted or even be a chorus of a song. Your mantra will become stronger if you communicate it with heartfelt energy and if you can feel its vibrational energy within.

SECOND-CHAKRA MANTRAS

MANTRA	PRONUNCIATION	MEANING
bhoga	BOWgah	enjoyment of the now, pleasure, delight
hridayam	HRIHdiihahm	the heart's light
shakti	SHAHktee	dynamic, cosmic, or strong feminine energy
sumati	sooMAHtee	kindness, benevolence, good disposition

Taking Action

Purpose: Using awareness to affect your words and actions.

As you meditate on your chosen polarity it might dawn on you that you want to become a more sensitive and skillful lover. Or you might wish to become more open-hearted and listen more closely to how another person thinks and feels. Maybe you want deeper emotional contact, and hope to perceive others as they truly are. Or perhaps you want to stop having the kind of pseudocontact in which you pretend to be what you think the other person wants you to be, while putting on masks that stop you from being truly seen, heard, or touched. What, if anything, do you do or avoid in order to keep a "safe" emotional distance?

How do you or don't you reach out? Are your arms glued to your sides as if you're afraid to touch, or do you move only your hands and forearms, as if a rope holds your upper arms against your sides and chest? By contrast, do your hands and arms reach outward in welcome or in invitation? Throughout the day, notice how you express or don't express your feelings in your posture and movements with others. You can also notice your physical posture as you meet or interact with others.

Alternatively, you might seek to follow the tantric path that leads toward doing austerities or *tapas* (acts of purification) of the right-handed path. Such action requires discipline, but also generates beneficial upward-flowing energy that can open higher chakras. Perhaps you may give up food for a time by fasting, or like the naga babas, renounce all worldly possessions.

"Austerity develops endurance," explains Gurumayi Chidvilasananda, "which is the backbone of yoga. In yoga, you need that power of endurance. Constantly enduring whatever happens, never falling apart. . . . You have many obstacles to overcome, so you must gain strength. . . . For a meditator, tapasya also includes accepting whatever happens as the best thing for your sadhana, and not being disturbed by any discomforts, inner or outer, that you may experience."[6]

When working with this or any chakra, it's important to reflect on your own experiences and make your own choices about it. What's right for someone else may not be right for you. How can you use whatever new awareness you are developing to benefit yourself and others?

The time you spend working with second-chakra energy can open the way to learning more about your emotional truths and sexual desires. The possibilities are legion and your insights will guide you in how you can best strengthen your soul commitments. Now as you move to the next chapter, get ready to step into the world of the third chakra, where we can play big games.

6

THIRD OR MANIPURA CHAKRA

The Power Chakra

In the third chakra you find your strength, power, and self-control. You can use these qualities to cooperate or to dominate, to help others find their strength, or to try to weaken them.

Respect for each other is a common principle. . . . If you want your rights then you also have to be conscious of the rights of others. . . . Balancing this chakra can be achieved by selfless service, serving others without desire for reward.

HARISH JOHARI AND WILL GERAETS,
*THE WISDOM TEACHINGS OF HARISH JOHARI
ON THE MAHABHARATA*

Third or Manipura Chakra Correspondences

Key Phrases: Ego, power, assertiveness, control, sense of identity, possession, wealth

Physical location: Solar plexus, the navel region

Endocrine gland: Pancreas

Astrological link: Sun

Day of the week: Sunday

Element: Fire

Sense: Sight

Sanskrit Derivation: mani (gems); *pura* (city)

Massage: Shoulders, arms, stomach

Leela Game of Self-Knowledge: Third row: Plane of Karma, Charity, Atonement, Plane of Dharma, Celestial Plane, Bad Company, Good Company, Sorrow, Selfless Service

THE ESSENCE OF THE THIRD CHAKRA: EGO, POWER, AND INITIATIVE

The third or Manipura Chakra is linked with the gravitational center of the body, having self-command, and being balanced within your *chi,* or personal energy. It is also connected with willpower, drive, ambition, and the desire for achievement and enjoyment of good times and good company.

On one hand, this chakra's qualities can contribute to developing the strength of our ideas, intentions, and personal sense of power. We mature in awareness and unlock our potential to move revitalizing and uplifting energy throughout the body.

On the other hand, third-chakra potentials can develop in egocentric directions that can involve treachery or controlling others to serve our own interests. This may include lying to ourselves about our motives and the effects of our actions, and manipulating others for our own benefit. We often justify this with self-centered insensitivity and egotism. At the third-chakra level, says Johari, "the ego is addicted to power. 'I want to be top dog.' 'This is MY decision.' 'This is MY organization.'"[1] He writes, "Kingdom and territorial complex are attributes of third-chakra energy, which creates many problems. The kingdom may be big or small, but the feeling is the same: 'I won't allow anybody to intrude in my kingdom.'"[2]

When self-glorification accompanies an egocentric attitude, then both worldly and personal problems may become severe. Self-righteousness often results, such as when people claim that they're "on the right side, or doing what's good for everyone" or "just doing God's work," while they look down on others and deceive themselves about their motives. Blind ego-driven pride and attempts to dominate and subdue can be their prime motives, even when that means harming others or causing needless suffering from financial loss or even death, whether in uniform or a gang. With luck and work on oneself, at a certain point in evolution, such challenging tactics may change into planting the seeds of the third-chakra qualities of atonement and performing acts of kindness, charity, or selfless service.

Most of us have the potential to move beyond self-consumed perspectives. Speaking to others in ways that help them feel better, refusing to support harmful agendas, and acting boldly for the good of the larger community or ecosystem are potent third-chakra attributes. But there's a catch. We have to have the willingness as well as the potential. And since almost everybody likes to "show that I'm somebody," it takes more than a little spiritual discipline to be humble about our accomplishments, acknowledge that we received help and luck from known and unknown sources, and hold back from bragging about what we've done.

The third chakra is also about inspiration and initiative. It includes the determination, drive, and focused perseverance that is often needed to realize our goals. Without such resolve and persistence we may have a wealth of good ideas that somehow seldom lead to success. A danger here is that we may identify so strongly with our craving to realize our goals that we fall into rage or depression when we don't. In the Bhagavad Gita, which is part of the Indian epic the Mahabharata, Sri Krishna tells Arjuna:

> *The seers say truly*
> *That he is wise*
> *Who acts without lust or scheming*
> *For the fruit of the act:*
> *His act falls from him,*
> *Its chain is broken,*
> *Melted in the flame of my knowledge.*
> *Turning his face from the fruit,*
> *He needs nothing:*

The Atman is enough.
He acts, and is beyond action . . .
What God's will gives
He takes, and is contented.
Pain follows pleasure,
He is not troubled:
Gain follows loss,
He is indifferent:
Of whom should he be jealous?
He acts, and is not bound by his actions.[3]

These words convey the positive spirit of the third chakra. We may choose to do what we can, for ourselves or even for our community, our nation, and the Earth itself. If our efforts succeed, wonderful! If not, well—we did what we could. The light we share has the power to brighten someone's path, even if it's a flickering candle flame. We don't have to browbeat ourselves if we can't do more. Using our strength, passion, and will, we can watch for the next chance to act in a constructive way that resonates with the higher purpose of our heart and soul.

Finally, writes Johari,

It is in third chakra that the player becomes conscious of the social and political influences which have influenced the development of his personality. Thus the player becomes self-conscious. Egoism becomes the impetus of action as the ego seeks to extend its influence in ever-broadening circles. . . . It is a moment of sobriety. At this point one becomes aware of the Law of Karma.[4]

We then truly realize that virtues are actions that help others and other beings, while vices are actions that harm them (or ourselves).

Opposite is a chart that lists some possibilities of this chakra. As with the first two chakras, these are not either-or dualisms. Rather, each is a continuum of qualities. One aspect of chakra balancing is moving from the less personally and socially helpful side toward the more helpful side. Sometimes even a small movement can make a big difference.

THE MENTAL PATHWAY FOR WORKING WITH THIRD CHAKRA ENERGIES

The Bright Side of the Third Chakra

Gifts and Strengths: The potential to engage one's highest intellect, confident and energetic action; willingness to help all sentient beings; relating to others from a stance of equality and cooperation.

"Manipura," writes Swami Satyananda Saraswati, "is the center of dynamism, energy, willpower, and achievement. Often it is compared to the dazzling heat and power of the sun."[5] Here you can develop balance between an urge to react impulsively and an inclination to delay action until you've thought through a situation fully. (For instance, you decide to sleep on it before making a big decision.) You strengthen abilities needed to follow through on your intentions. And you learn to avoid or step out of attitudes and actions that lead to unnecessary antagonism or conflict. Among the most common of these are power struggles where the matter at stake is trivial and the real issue is "Who wins?" or "Who's right?"

THIRD-CHAKRA POSSIBILITIES

OPPORTUNITIES	OBSTACLES
Confident, capable	Dominating, aggressive
Knowledgeable	Arrogant
Shares power	Power hungry
Respectful and democratic	Authoritarian
Helpful, engaged in service to others	Uncaring, out for oneself
Dynamic	Restless or lethargic
Centered	Off-center
Empowering	Demeaning, condescending
Clear sense of self-other boundaries	Fuzzy self-other boundaries
Stands up for oneself and others	Timid or weak-mannered, gives in easily
Genuine humility	Feels conceited or worthless
Attitude of equality	Egotistical, egocentric

Learning to sidestep such power struggles and save your energy for things that truly matter is a major accomplishment. The combination of conscious awareness, personal understanding, and willingness to step out of power struggles may save a job or a relationship.

Having balanced energy in your third chakra helps you be yourself, attract soul-nourishing experiences and friends, and give respect and consideration to others. You may even decide to carry out random acts of kindness and perform *seva* or selfless service and charitable deeds. Those who willfully work on staying centered within their own world of personal power and also work on self-improvement will gain greater self-understanding, more easily fix mistakes, and maintain healthy balance of their chi or flow of life energy. Behaving in such life-enhancing ways and cultivating the attitudes that go with them leads toward enduring peace of mind. As Paramahansa Yogananda put it, "Making others happy, through kindness of speech and sincerity of right advice, is a sign of true greatness."[6]

The Dark Side of the Third Chakra

Issues and Challenges: Abandoning one-upmanship and other habits of demeaning or insulting others; letting go of complexes at both extremes, such as "alpha" (superiority) or "doormat" (inferiority); replacing dominance with respect.

The third chakra is linked with your torso's physical center and feeling either balanced or out of balance in relation to the ways you use your strength. Power struggles that involve respect versus domination can be seen in career or romantic relationships, family, politics, and many organizations. Someone ensnared in the drive to dominate, with little or no respect for others or consideration of their needs, tends to cause damage and suffering that could otherwise be avoided. Some call this the alpha complex.

On the other hand, someone who has not accepted and owned his or her own strength is likely to have trouble getting important needs met. Think about feeling a knot in your stomach. Such a knot often points to feeling powerless in a situation, unable to affect events that deeply concern you. Chronically knuckling under to others, also known as the doormat complex, causes the inner fire associated with the third chakra to turn to smoldering ashes. If you're caught in this pattern, you let others walk all over you. Clinging to what's left of your deflated ego, you do what they want you to rather than what you want to. You work hard at placating everybody so they won't get mad. In a sense, you let the other person intrude into your territory and define who you are. Decisions made or actions carried out when someone else is telling you how to be are likely to lead in ineffective or mistaken directions.

Someone whose energy revolves around needing to feel superior or to control others may feel a sense of success from manipulating or forcing them to obey his or her wishes (even if another person's ideas or procedures are better). But such a person stays stuck in a state of consciousness that is self-defeating in crucial ways, and tends to blame others for their own misfortunes: "It's all your fault!" Gurumayi says, "It is so convenient in life to blame others for your misfortunes. It is such a habit to be critical of people."[7]

The sense connected with the third chakra is sight. "It's not what you see that gets you into trouble," adds Gurumayi. "It's what you *think* you see that gets you into trouble."[8] What we *perceive* is what we see, hear, and feel in our bodies *after outside events have passed though the transformations performed by our neural circuits*. Swami Muktananda says, "When you find faults in others, where do those faults really reside? Do they reside in that person . . . in that place? . . . Or in your own eyes?"[9]

Jungian psychiatrist Jean Shinoda Bolen suggests that people who lock themselves into responding from a self-centered third-chakra perspective often suffer from an atrophied or never fully developed ability to truly love unselfishly. This easily leads to ending up emotionally crippled, so that they miss out on half of what they could be and half of the enjoyment that life can hold.[10]

Spiritual ignorance, an inappropriately fiery temperament, attraction to bad company, ego trips, hedonism attached to insatiable desires, being deaf and blind to others' needs or feelings, excessive lust for power, and a sense of isolation or alienation from others are all third-chakra opportunities for personal growth. Using your power in considerate ways rather than bludgeoning others through the force of your demands brings better results and usually better responses.

Past Roots of Third-Chakra Problems

A parent's definition of a parent-child relationship may be a power struggle in which the parent must dominate and "win." "You'll do what I tell you to, or I'll show you what's what!" The parent gets to be Big Boss, perhaps with the aid of a beating, and the child learns to passively shut up and do as commanded while crying or pouting and feeling disregarded and demeaned.

Sometime between the first and third birthday a child learns the magical word *No!* What a discovery! This is a normal and necessary stage in the child's development of his or her ability to act effectively in the world. Tragically, some parents fail to realize that they are mutilating their child when they almost always demand compliance and seldom allow the child to find his or her own way, or to express opposition. Some fathers (and occasionally mothers) are extreme authoritarians, imitating the behavior of a drill sergeant, such as a giant of a man who barks harsh demands at his very small, very sad-looking five-year old son. On one hand a good parent can set sensible, reasonable limits that are expressed and enforced in a kind, loving, compassionate way. On the other hand, a parent's commands can be articulated with such an overbearing and inflexible attitude that a child isn't allowed to feel even a little personal power.

While many children respond to their parents' insistence on always being top dog by becoming timidly obedient, others become chronically rebellious. Too many stories are told about the child who is beaten and then goes to school and beats up and bullies others. Often such children end up mired in negative third-chakra fiery or angry reactions to almost all authority, even when it's benevolent. Although this chronic opposition may seem justified in the child's mind, it can become a pattern that leads to a spectrum of future problems.

Domination and submission issues can play a role in developing conscious awareness. In speaking of the classic example of dominance, hitting a child to make him or her obey, Baba Hari Dass says, "Discipline yourself first and the child will come around. The child is your mirror. Spanking a child is like training an animal to do as you say without understanding why. The best thing is to help children understand what is right and what is wrong. But you have to understand your own emotions first."[11]

THE BODY AND EMOTIONS PATHWAY: FEELING TONES IN THE THIRD CHAKRA

Personal Transformation in the Third Chakra

Power is widely interpreted to mean power to control what other people (or organizations) do. Instead, to open a doorway to personal transformation, think about the life-giving, regenerative power of being centered and aligned with the core of your true center—the most brightly lit point of your inner self. Focus your total mind, body, emotions, and spirit in health-conscious, thoughtful ways, such as actions that generate inner alignment with your strengths, talents, aptitudes, and sense of higher purpose. Increasing your willingness to fulfill your responsibilities with a sense of trust in the ultimate outcome helps you connect with and nourish yourself.

As you become more aware and accepting of your own identity and deep inner truths, while ignoring or sidestepping others' attempts at manipulation or intimidation, your power to be true to yourself grows. If you have a strong urge to compete, whether or not a situation is inherently competitive, practicing an attitude of unconditional self-acceptance will help you witness the one-up and one-down syndrome that plays out when you compare yourself with others. Of course there will always be some natural alphas in various areas of life, like a gifted athlete who can outdo all competitors, or a business executive who rises quickly to become CEO or chairman of the board. Such a person may have an urge to compete, but no desire to dominate others or make them feel small.

Inevitably you'll also meet some who strive for name and fame, or to otherwise increase their status, at others' expense. Such people are lost in the alpha complex described previously, in which they feel okay only when they express the attitude "I'm number one!" or at least, "I'm better than you." (Some Native American peoples, like the Navajo, went to great lengths to teach their children to avoid this attitude.)

Fortunately neither the alpha complex nor the doormat complex is an incurable condition. One-upmanship is a one-down game. Many who are caught up in it eventually learn to respect others as they are. Some school bullies become decent, kind adults. Such learning comes faster to some than to others.

Letting go of the doormat complex begins by developing a clear sense of boundaries—of where you end and the other begins. Then you know what you feel and think and do, and how and when it differs from what someone else wants you to feel and think and do. A next step is to develop the ability to be appropriately assertive in asking for what you want and saying no to requests that you don't want to agree to. You stand your ground and say what you think and feel. You do as you wish rather than what others want you to do. This does not have to be an aggressive action. You can be appropriately assertive in a graceful way—even to the point of refusing a request in a way that helps the other person feel good about themselves despite not getting what they want. Your style of staying balanced within yourself, and your personal power can be kind, considerate, and firm. If you are solidly rooted in your own sense of who you are, then you will remember that in no way are you willing to be someone else's doormat. Your resolve can be unshakable.

Also, there are several paths out of the alpha complex. One is to realize that many people who are trying to put others down or be on top actually have pervasive unconscious feelings that they themselves are inferior, or no good or worth nothing. By humiliating someone else or making them feel small, they can feel "better than." So bullying others is a way to feel personally empowered. If soulfully attentive, if you discover this pattern within yourself, you can let go of it.

Historically, sociologist Herbert Spencer's gross misunderstanding and spreading of a wild distortion of Charles Darwin's ideas contributed to people feeling like they have to step on others' heads to be "top dog" in their office or company or industry. Spencer badly misunderstood Darwin's idea that every plant and animal and person seeks to find an "econiche" where it can survive. The cultures that have endured longest on our planet are those where people learned to cooperate—not those where people constantly tried to get the best of each other.

In sum, power is not inherently good or bad. How you use it makes it so. Learning to use the positive potentials of power for the good of others as well as yourself (without lying to yourself about what's good) is a step in the direction of true personal empowerment. Becoming centered in this chakra keeps the eternal fire of striving for higher consciousness burning brightly, and enables you to take a step up the ladder of conscious personal evolution by opening the fourth-chakra faculty of genuine unselfish love.

Relational Transformation in the Third Chakra

Anybody can become angry—that is easy. But to be angry with the right person, and to the right degree, and at the right time, and for the right purpose, and in the right way, that is not within everybody's power and it is not easy.

ARISTOTLE

All too often, in most relationships, many so-called arguments are actually power struggles in disguise. In these, "Who wins?" is the hidden agenda that drives the apparent question of "What are we going to do?" Fortunately, such struggles are relatively easy to recognize once you become alert for them. You can feel them in your body, or you may recognize another person's particular power-driven emotional tone and demanding stance, which may be hot and explosive, or hard and cold, or brittle and rigid, or . . . there are many variations.

Getting into power struggles with people, whether near and dear to you or not, makes it hard to relax and enjoy your present situation. When experienced over time, it may also contribute to long-term health problems like chronic high blood pressure.

Once you start to sense yourself getting into a "Who wins?" power struggle, you can choose to step out of it. You might even find it useful to say the words, "Wait a minute—I think we've gotten into a pointless power struggle. Let's take a break from this intense energy and then talk about what we want in a different way." With greater awareness, you can explicitly look for ways to share power. Perhaps you need to consider letting your partner or other counterpart make more decisions. Conversely, you might insist that you have an equal voice if your partner/counterpart has been too domineering. Or you might agree to take turns in decision-making. When sharing of power between people becomes mutual, it lays a strong foundation for more caring, effective, and empowering relationships—whether in the family, at work, or elsewhere.

Another way of looking at third-chakra relationships is explicit in the title of one of the books by Ram Dass and Paul Gorman, *How Can I Help: Stories and Reflections on Service.* The orientation is, "What can I do for you?" or "What can I give you?" rather than "What can I get from you?" They also ask, "How does who we think we are affect what we have to give?"[12]

THE PATHWAY OF SPIRIT:
IMAGERY IN THE THIRD CHAKRA

The Triangle, the Lotus Petals, and the Seed Sounds

Everything in the picture surrounds the red downward-pointing triangle, a symbol for the element fire, this chakra's element. Fire is linked to the solar plexus and the stomach, which is the "furnace" that burns the food we need to survive. Here we find the sun. Since the sun is said to be related to intellect, in this chakra we experience our intellectual abilities to organize and manage. The nature of fire is one of purification, and also destruction. What goes into the fire may get purified. But when the fire gets out of control, it will destroy or be destroyed.

The sense organs here are the eyes. We see forms and colors. The work organs are the legs and feet. With them we can explore the new world that opens up in front of us. Here society gets its shape through the faculties of organization and management.

After the point and the circle, the triangle is the simplest form. Since the red triangle faces downward, it indicates that movement in this chakra is downward toward the first two chakras. From here those chakras are organized and exploited.

The three lines in the triangle represent three forces that are called *gunas*: *tamas*, or inactivity and laziness; *rajas,* or energy and activity; and *sattva,* or illumination. Or the lines can refer to our mental tools (ego, mind, and intellect), or to India's three main deities: Brahma the Creator, Vishnu the Preserver, and Shiva the Destroyer and the lord of yogis.

A central problem of the third chakra is attachment to our interpretations of the phenomenal world of names and forms. When energy and power are added in, the world becomes more complex and so also do our emotional and mental worlds. Brahma created the world, but inside ourselves we create our own—and that's the one we see and hear.

The ten lotus petals represent ten more inner phenomena that we have to learn to handle. They can all contribute to keeping the illusion of our own created world alive. Johari identifies them as spiritual ignorance, thirst, jealousy, treachery, shame, fear, disgust, delusion, foolishness, and sadness. We can think of these as side effects of getting too entangled in the power games of this chakra.

Figure 6.1. This drawing depicts the deities—Braddha Rudra and Lakini Shakti Devi—and core imagery shown in the painting of this chakra (plate 6: Third or Manipura Chakra).

The seed sound of the element fire is RANG. The *RA* sound originates in the navel and the *NG* sound brings the energy to the brain. Articulating this seed sound is said to increase the digestive fire and may help to live a long life.

A Short Visualization

1. Visualize the ten lotus petals, starting with the one to the right of the one on top. As you visualize each petal, moving clockwise, utter its seed

sound: DANG (palatal), DHANG, RLANG, TANG, THANG, DANG (dental), DHANG, NANG, PANG, PHANG.

2. Then visualize the downward-pointing triangle.
3. End with the seed sound of the element fire: RANG.

The Ram

This animal symbolizes the nature of the third chakra. Here it is shown facing left. As the vehicle of the deity of fire (Agni), it stands for the power of inner as well as outer illumination.

The ram is physically powerful, muscled, and a strong fighter. He will not give up easily! Once he makes up his mind to attack, he does not look up to consider the consequences. If needed he will go to war. That makes the ram a symbol for our ego, which gets its full shape in the third chakra. In the first, ego was connected to our boss, who satisfies our need for food and shelter. We serve him with our muscles. In the second, ego was very busy with the other (usually the opposite sex), and fixated on looking beautiful and young. Now ego expands and becomes more self-centered. When we are strongly ego-centric, we feel special and better than others in some way, and want everybody to know and see it at any cost. We may even be willing to sacrifice family and friends.

Whether the people we associate with are influenced by us in positive or negative ways becomes very important, because we can expand our effects in either direction. To gain more power and self-centered glory, people organize themselves and create institutions that can help, exploit, or dominate others. We have to learn to recognize and understand this ram inside us. But we also need to understand that without this chakra the world cannot run! Without its power to organize and manage, complex societies cannot develop.

Braddha Rudra

Braddha Rudra is shown here with his white hair and beard as the Old Shiva who reminds us that our ego can become very rigid and not open to change. He is sitting on a tiger skin that represents our mind running in the jungle of desires, indicating that he has the mind under control. Johari writes, "Braddha Rudra (Old Shiva), the wrathful form of Shiva, rules the Southern direction and represents the power of destruction. Destruction of one cycle of creation is also the beginning of the next cycle. . . . Rudra also implies weeping and lamentation because *rudra* comes from the Sanskrit root *rud* which means 'crying.'"[13]

Young Shiva is commonly viewed as Lord of Destruction and the deity of yogis, but that Shiva is not Rudra. That Shiva is the peaceful, transcendent aspect of this chakra, of the kind that alone remains when creation and preservation stop. Rudra, on the other hand represents the fearful, destructive power of destruction, death, or sleep.

We fear death. We fear catastrophic change. But a self-centered ego thinks it is very special and the ruler in its own world. It is Rudra or the process of destruction in the manifest world that destroys this false identification of the ego. Rudra releases the misconceptions in our mind that make us feel bound to worldly life.

Whenever we perform destructive acts, we still are part of Rudra, where destruction is manifest, bringing change and new life, but often also great suffering. When we stay in the third chakra, the world is still governed by fear, much as in the first chakra. Braddha Rudra is firm in his acts of destruction, sometimes for our own well-being and sometimes not. But if we meditate on him, he can remove our fear and anger. We have to understand the role of karma. Our actions can have useful or harmful consequences. As we face Braddha Rudra within us and realize our karmic responsibilities toward our own inner Self, we also begin to comprehend our karmic responsibilities toward the world.

Lakini Shakti Devi

Shakti is the cosmic energy that pervades the world and the universe. Always female in the yogic literature, in this powerful chakra she is a compassionate deity. The first thing we see are her three heads, which show that our world has become larger. At the everyday level, after the physical plane of food and shelter, and the astral or mental plane of fantasies, the celestial plane or plane of thoughts is introduced. Now we acquire the ability to organize our food and shelter and to convert the fantasies of the second chakra in practical ways.

Johari tells us that Lakini Devi can lead us toward "meditation on

Braddha Rudra in his calm and pure form, the guru of all spiritual knowledge, [in which he] absorbs all the cosmic principles by which the aspirant is bound to worldliness, [and] enables the aspirant to attain success in yoga."[14]

Lakini Devi shows us how to create our own heaven, where following dharma gives us joy and blessings. No longer restricted as we were, now we learn to relate to others and our world in harmonious ways. Many religions talk about heaven as a place without pain and suffering, using the concept of heaven to try to raise the spiritual level of the masses. The desire to create a heaven on Earth can unite people in a cooperative spiritual flow.

How does Lakini guide us? The thunderbolt in her upper left hand reminds us of the energy that this chakra is always giving off. Her upper right hand holds the pot that contains the fire that can purify or destroy. It symbolizes not only the fire in our stomach, but also the fire of austerities, called *tapasya*, a potentially powerful spiritual practice.

Lakini holds three arrows. The biggest arrow is dharma, or following the laws of nature. She and Braddha Rudra show us what needs to be done. "The arrow of the second chakra," writes Johari, was "shot from the bow of Kama, the lord of sexuality and sensuality. The arrow in the third chakra is shot by the desires for accomplishment, freedom, independence, and autonomy."[15] The first step here, says Johari, is to do everything consciously in the reality of the moment. To live according to dharma there are ten points of attention like the ten lotus petals of this chakra. We start with being firm in our intention. We forgive others and don't blame them for what happened. We realize that we are in command of our actions. We learn that we can't have everything we want. The "ten signposts of dharma," Johari writes, "are firmness, forgiveness, self-command, restraint, non-stealing, cleanliness [purity], control of the [senses and actions] truth, and absence of anger."[16]

The last two arrows are discussed in "The Bright Side" above and "Taking Action" below. One is an attitude and the other is concrete actions of charity, seva (selfless service). "Never hurt, always help,"[17] said Harish. What is good for others is usually also good for us.

With her last hand Lakini is giving boons and blessings. She shows us the immense spiritual possibilities of this chakra and will lead us to a meditation on a calm and pure Rudra, who in the fourth chakra will become the guru of spiritual knowledge. We understand the truth behind dharma and no longer feel separated from the spiritual realm. We are part of a whole that is larger than our own small world. Now we perform our duties without expecting rights or rewards. We can use this energy for the good and well-being of all people and all beings. Then this chakra shines like a precious gem.

Visualization of the Manipura Chakra

1. Start with visualizing the ten blue lotus petals, with or without the seed sounds.
2. Then put the downward-pointing red triangle inside the lotus petals.
3. Add the ram.
4. Then add the seed sound of the element fire, RANG.
5. Visualize Lakini at the left side of this chakra.
6. Visualize Braddha Rudra on the right side.

Reflections

In this chakra we face the destructive power of our ego. That brings fear and anger. As long as we remain selfish, Braddha Rudra will keep us from moving upward. With the help of our intellect we can start understanding our real nature and act accordingly. Instead of destroying, we can create a better world inside and outside ourselves. Helping and expressing kindness when we can, and avoiding doing harm or causing other suffering will help us to stay true to our dharma as we act out our different roles. Slowly we learn that the Manipura Chakra offers unexpected wonders.

PRACTICAL TOOLS FOR THIRD-CHAKRA WORK

Relaxation

Purpose: Becoming sensitive to and letting go of physical tension.

The following exercise is a relaxation method invented by Edmund Jacobson in 1929.[18]

You can do this relaxation technique in a meditation posture, or lying or sitting or even standing comfortably, such as if you're waiting in line.

If possible close your eyes, but you can also have them open. Then, inhale, focus your attention at the top of your head, and tighten all the muscles in your upper head and face, including your eye muscles. Continue to tighten these muscles until you can't tighten them any more.

Then exhale, and let go of any sense of tension that remains and relax as completely as you can.

Inhale, tense the muscles of your jaws and mouth area, then exhale and relax.

Repeat with your neck, and then your shoulders.

After that, continue tightening and relaxing your muscles in the same manner all the way down your entire body to the tippy-tip-tips of your toes. By the time you finish, you should feel at ease in your body and very relaxed.

In the future you can go through this relaxation sequence, or any part of it, any time you notice that some part of your body feels needlessly tense and tight. Once you've done it as described above, you might choose to relax without the preliminary tensing.

Breath Control or Pranayama

Purpose: Deepening your breathing and maintaining mental focus.

Here, you add one element to the breath-control practice given in the second chakra on page 93. Be comfortable, but keep your spine straight (if possible, be lying down). Imagine that your entire physical body is surrounded from head to toe by an infinity sign, or the number 8 lying horizontally on its side. Throughout the exercise, you will envision your breath tracing the line of the figure 8 or infinity sign.

Once you have a visual sense of your body with the figure 8 surrounding you, inhale and fill your belly with air while your chest is flat. Then notice the air flowing up into your expanding chest and imagine that the flow of air continues upward to go beyond your head to the very top of the figure 8.

When both stomach and lungs are filled completely with air, hold your breath for a count of 3 to 6 (your choice).

Then slowly exhale, retaining the air in your chest while your stomach empties. Imagine the air passing downward above your body, then crossing through your body at the navel to the back and exiting through the first chakra. As your stomach empties of air, begin to empty the air from your chest as well. Then imagine the air traveling downward beneath the back of your legs.

Full exhalation should coincide with the lowest point of the figure 8 beneath the soles of your feet. After fully exhaling, again count 3 (or whatever number you choose) before you let air begin to fill your belly again.

Then imagine the air moving upward from your feet, passing over and along the front of your legs, then going through your navel to start filling your stomach.

Start the cycle again in rhythm with your breathing.

After you are comfortable doing this breathing technique lying down, you can sit up and do it, and if you wish, even incorporate it into the Starting Sequence of your meditation. (In ancient Chinese texts this breathing pattern is called the circulation of the light.)

Concentration

Purpose: Focusing on the present moment and calming the mind.

In Hinduism and other Eastern religions, there are many different *mudras,* or seals made with the fingers and the hand to symbolically express various inner states of mind. Using a mudra can make it a little easier to focus your mind and be in the present moment.

To prepare for doing a mudra, you may want to briefly go through your preferred relaxation and breathing sequence, but if you do not practice meditation you can still do mudras. Before practicing a mudra, you may want to assume a meditation posture, but you can do mudras whenever you feel so inspired.

The mudra described here is often shown by statues of goddesses and meditators, with palms facing upward toward the sky and the thumb of each hand touching the index finger of the same hand to form a small circle. The three remaining fingers are extended and held close together, pointing forward or upward. This is called the Chin Mudra or mudra of wisdom. It can also be done with your palms and fingers facing downward toward the Earth instead of upward, which makes it easy to practice in a public place without anyone noticing.

To begin, notice and relax your breath and place your hands in a comfortable position on your legs with palms facing up toward the sky.

Next allow the top point of your thumb and index finger on each hand to come together to form a small circle.

For calming benefit, let your mind sit quietly with your hands resting in this position. Or you can do your mantra, your prayers, or affirmations. When your hands, the instruments of the mind, are in this position, energy moves upward to link with the wisdom of your higher Self.

To help keep your attention in your immediate present, if you like you can make your mudra into a moving mudra. As you inhale, let your thumbs and fingers separate by about an eighth of an inch. As you exhale, let them touch. Continue in this way.

Polarity-Balancing Meditation

Purpose: Greater awareness.

While first doing polarity balancing, you might not notice immediate results as you strive to fully develop or reduce deeply ingrained tendencies. Rather, such possibilities for change exist along on a continuum and you can take small steps. One step today, another tomorrow—or next week, or even next month—and before long you may find that you have made a major change. Your consistent meditation will build a momentum that encourages inner growth and balanced intellectual, emotional, and spiritual development.

This meditation helps you to get in touch with your center, where you are rooted in your confidence and, with a little luck, your truth. Move forward with your practice in a rhythm that is comfortable so that you are attracted to instead of discouraged about doing inner work. The only path to truth, awareness, and bliss is to listen wholeheartedly to your deepest inner soul truth.

> As with the first- and second-chakra meditations, when you're ready, choose a polarity from the "Third-Chakra Possibilities" table, and then follow the Polarity-Balancing Meditation instructions on page 46.
>
> If more than one polarity in the table feels relevant, select one for now. Later you can repeat the meditation with a different polarity. Since some of them tend to "hang out together," it can take some time to work through related and relevant polarities.

As an example of working with these polarities, you might think of statements or responses to questions that are related to personal power. You can imagine what you might say to an authority whose statements you normally shy away from questioning or answering. Or consider asserting your own power to make a demand, which you would normally only think in your mind, but never verbalize. For example, envision yourself acting with integrity and saying what you need to in a way that states your needs clearly, yet also communicates respect, and an interest in staying in well-balanced contact with the other person.

The other side of your polarity-balancing meditation might involve realizing that your words, voice tone, or posture are probably also sometimes intimidating or aggressive, and that you want to tone down all that. Through meditation you can become more alert to your gestures and posture that tell you when you're under the sway of a deflating or excessively forceful attitude, and how you might let go and feel more relaxed.

Affirming Strength

Purpose: Personal empowerment

Chills of anxiety, lack of confidence, and self-doubt can disappear—or at least shrink—when you connect with the source of your positive, egalitarian tendencies.

Close your eyes and look inward. With single-pointed attention of your mind's eye look inside your third chakra, the area of the solar plexus, and sense its location in your physical body. Now, imagine it as a whirling vortex of energy shining brightly. Let it quietly illuminate your sense of inner harmony and calmness. Chills of frustration, lack of confidence, or self-doubt can shrink or disappear when you inwardly focus on the strength of your inner core and its positive qualities.

With a deep breath, recover a warm memory from your past, when someone was very good to you, or you did a kind turn for another. Recall the feeling of strength you associate with it until it brings a smile to your face. Then continue to mentally connect with this place in your body where you feel physically centered. Inhale deeply and bring your breath into the matrix of this center. Again connect with your feeling of strength.

Exhale slowly with humble awareness of this potent energy flowing inside you.

Repeat these steps until you can do them easily, with a centered feeling of quiet confidence.

Sound Healing

Purpose: Listening with alertness.

 ### Outside Sounds

We are constantly bombarded by loud messages from media—e-magazines, TV, the Internet—that intentionally try to make us feel inadequate unless we buy the product they're trying to sell us. Even though such sounds sometimes drift out of our awareness to become background noise, it's important to hit the Mute button on your physical or mental remote.

Or try talking back: "Oh, shut up TV pitchman. I know you need a job, but I don't need that stuff you're trying to sell me. I'd rather be out of debt than buried beneath your not-so-great goodies."

Or walk to a tranquil outdoor environment and listen to soothing, healing sounds of the serenity of nature.

 *Mantra Chanting*

Many mantras are seed sounds that sprout shoots of transcendental realities when planted in the conscious mind. Some are sacred sounds passed by word of mouth from ancient times to the present, from master to initiate, to help the aspirant connect with truth beyond logic. Their repetition can spin the wheel of practical knowledge of the qualities linked with chakras. Some words linked with the third chakra that you can try are given below.

THIRD-CHAKRA MANTRAS

MANTRA	PRONUNCIATION	MEANING
ahimsa	ahHEEMsuh	nonviolence, harmlessness, noninjury
daana	DAYnah	giving, gift, charity, bestowing
sankalpa	sahnKAHLpah	determination, will
seva	SAYvah	charitable or helpful action
parmath	PAHRmath	seva as an ongoing way of being

Taking Action

Purpose: Finding your power.

Next time you or someone near you is feeling down, do your best to invoke the energy in your third chakra to remind you of the reserve of strength and power you possess. Whenever you're in a situation where you need to draw on your courage, go to your internal space where strength reigns, and let it inspire you to live with fiery passion, be centered in your courage, and know that you are strong (even if in a gentle way).

Be alert to notice when you find yourself slipping into anger or a challenging attitude that may evoke dubious responses. When you feel yourself falling into unproductive mental patterns, mentally and firmly tell yourself "STOP!" Take a moment to step away from heated emotion or negative feelings and be silent. Sense the ground with both feet and physically center yourself in relation to gravity. Breathe one full breath, release tension with the next breath, and for those two breaths, do nothing (unless you need to act immediately). Ask yourself, "What do I truly prefer to say or do in this situation? What's likely to be most useful?" (If the other person is uneasy waiting for your well-thought-through response, so be it.) Then say or do what feels best to you. If that seems too hard right now, start with smaller steps that are less emotionally loaded. Gradually work your way up to facing (and releasing) whatever feels disempowering.

Typically it takes at least two weeks for a person to start seeing changes in their behavior. The sequence is usually: (1) You notice what you just did; (2) you notice what you're doing while in the middle of doing it, and may even be able to stop right there and act differently; (3) you notice what you have an impulse to do and make a conscious choice whether to continue your old pattern or release and change it.

Another effective way to transform third-chakra energy is through seva, selfless service or works of charity for the benefit of others or nature. "Selfless service is the soap that purifies the mind," says Amma, the hugging saint.[19] (You can call on the energy of Hanuman, the monkey-faced god of selfless service if you want the feeling of an ally helping you.)

An important concept in most religions and many secular service organizations, seva is volunteer work offered without expectation of any rewards besides the good feeling you get from doing it. For example, each week a friend of ours picks up a supermarket's surplus food and delivers it to one of several local homeless shelters. The positive effects of such work can help you see more deeply into the nature of humanity, as well as the self, the mind, ego, and desires. The positive effects on you are stronger if you do it with humility rather than pride. Such service can be an effective path out of the obstacles side of third-chakra thinking. Also, it's a way to step up the ladder of conscious personal evolution by moving energy to the fourth-chakra faculty of genuine unselfish love.

At this moment, we each are who we are. A multimillionaire and a beggar can stand face-to-face, on the same ground, at the same time, looking into each other's eyes, recognizing their common humanity—or as some Native American peoples say, looking at "my other self." Once we discard the idea that one of us is better than another, we can cooperate toward common ends, and move toward sharing power more equally.

We can't leave this chakra without mentioning Mahatma Gandhi, who had inner strength beyond measure. The principle of nonviolence toward all living beings, *ahimsa,* is at the center of his philosophy. His best-known line may be, "An eye for an eye makes the whole world blind."[20]

Now on to the Anahata Chakra, where we hope to open the heart center—whether by the blissful touch of divine grace or by jumping over the blocks of our own ignorance. Are you ready?

7

FOURTH OR ANAHATA CHAKRA

The Heart Chakra

In the fourth chakra your heart opens to unselfish love and kindness.

The love and compassion of fourth-chakra persons makes them a source of inspiration to others who find peace and calm in their presence. Fourth-chakra persons . . . are harmless and everybody feels secure in their presence.

HARISH JOHARI,
CHAKRAS: ENERGY CENTERS OF TRANSFORMATION

Fourth or Anahata Chakra Correspondences

Key Phrases: Selfless love, compassion, kindness, transcendence of egocentric attitudes, clear awareness of feelings, openness, gratitude, living in harmony

Physical location: Heart, lungs, breasts

Endocrine gland: Thymus

Astrological link: Venus

Day of the week: Friday

Element: Air

Sense: Touch

Sanskrit Derivation: anahata (unstruck)

Massage: Back and chest

Leela Game of Self-Knowledge: Fourth row: Apt Religion, Irreligiosity, Good Tendencies, Plane of Sanctity, Plane of Balance, Plane of Fragrance, Plane of Taste, Purgatory, Clarity of Consciousness

THE ESSENCE OF THE FOURTH CHAKRA: EMBODYING UNSELFISH LOVE

"Let my soul smile through my heart and my heart smile through my eyes, that I may scatter rich smiles in sad hearts," says Paramahansa Yogananda, whose open-hearted nature demonstrated a love that totally transcends a "me first" attitude.[1] Overflowing the boundaries of personal concerns, such a love can light the spark of healing energies in others. It also points to love's potential to step across an invisible line of egotistical blocks into a more evolved consciousness. That realm is "higher," "expanded," "deeper," or "self-realized." It is the realm not only of "Big Mind," but also of "Big Heart" and deep compassion.

While the first three chakras are where most people's everyday lives take place (perhaps with an occasional glimpse into their greater potential), moving into fourth-chakra consciousness is a progression into a different state of being, such as when a blanket of fog lifts and we can see clearly what was previously invisible. As we tap into the treasures of this chakra we gain an expanded sense of self. We see and move beyond self-centered interests and concerns. "Forgetting your own self can sometimes be very helpful," comments Johari. Then he continues, "The fourth chakra is in the lap of God."[2]

Diverse spiritual traditions emphasize the importance of meditation on the heart chakra, considering it to be the temple of God. Living a compassionate life can awaken the fourth chakra. A person whose heart chakra is truly open:

Is generous in spirit and life

Has a balanced attitude in most situations, and is helpful when possible

Knows the meaning of patience and moderation

Inspires others and avoids harming animals, plants, and other beings

Gives others space to be themselves in their own ways rather than trying to remake them as he or she wishes

Has worked through and transcended many of the challenging qualities of the first three chakras

Gurumayi points out that at some point almost all of us have had just a flash, a moment of fourth chakra consciousness:

There have been times in your life when you have had a glimpse of unconditional love. Without any cause, you experienced love for someone. . . . Suddenly you loved the entire universe. For a few seconds this state lasted, and then it disappeared. You want to know what this is; you want to become anchored in this pure state of love.[3]

Few people, however, understand how to love unconditionally or do the work to awaken this chakra's energies. When you truly open your heart, you love life deeply, take care of your own real needs, and are willing to do the same for others without selfish interest. You have a clear sense of what others need, and of how to hear emotional truths. You readily move away from attitudes of fear, greed, and domination toward attitudes of respect, consideration, and loving qualities that are part of the teachings of the greatest saints and sages. "It is when the inner eye opens, when the eye of the heart . . . becomes active, that a person truly begins to see, truly begins to understand, truly begins to live in the light," says Gurumayi.[4]

When looking at the chakra's vertical placement along the spine, the fourth chakra sits with three chakras above it and three beneath it. It provides a centering point for sensing the concerns of the other chakras. Traditionally seen as a point of balance, it provides equilibrium between mind and emotions. It also bestows balance between being with others and being alone; balance between what you need for yourself and what you give to others. And it provides balance between the gentle and supportive aspects of your own being on one hand and the assertive and competitive on the other. This is especially important, since in our culture men easily get locked into thinking they have to be hard and aggressive and are "sissies" if they're soft, and women often get locked into being nurturing and giving without taking care of their own needs. To be a whole person, everyone needs some balance of heartfelt "masculine" and "feminine" qualities, integrated and expressed in our own ways.

Those who are centered in their fourth chakra are seldom preoccupied with the first-chakra concerns of fear, security, and survival, with the second-chakra concerns of sexuality, sensuality, and celebrity, or with the third-chakra concerns of power, authority, possessions, and status. Some are content to live in the light of love's passion to conjure a better world while others use their fourth-chakra awareness as a step on their path to developing the positive potentials of the fifth, sixth, and seventh chakras. Swami Rama Tirtha writes,

Since the eyes of my heart were opened,
I am able to see deep within.
Even when I look at the world around me,
I find my beloved wherever I turn.[5]

FOURTH-CHAKRA POSSIBILITIES

OPPORTUNITIES	OBSTACLES
Overflowing love	Anxious for love
Selfless love	Selfish love
Empathic, compassionate	Lacking empathy
Kind, altruistic	Unresponsive, uncaring
Nurturing to others and self	Careless of needs of others, self, or both
Conscious awareness in the present	Mental fog
Attentive to spirit	Neglectful of spirit
Open-hearted	Closed-hearted
Gives and receives easily	Has difficulty giving, receiving, or both
Emotionally forgiving	Hangs on to pain and troubles
Looks on the sunny side	Gets lost in the blues

THE MENTAL PATHWAY FOR WORKING WITH FOURTH-CHAKRA ENERGIES

The Bright Side of the Fourth Chakra

Gifts and Strengths: Loving others, and even other living beings, knowing that such love fills up one's own heart and enriches life regardless of how it is received or what is returned; the ability to keep a cheerful outlook.

In the fourth chakra we awaken in the high country of the human spirit. Dalai Lama Tyenzin Gyatso, a figure who radiates fourth-chakra energy onto the world stage, calls compassion, kindness, and unselfish love the most important qualities in life. He says,

> Many of our problems come from attitudes like putting ourselves first at all costs. . . . If something is missing in your heart—then despite the most luxurious surroundings, you cannot be happy. However, if you have peace of mind you can find happiness even under the most difficult circumstances. . . . The central method for achieving a happier life is to train your mind in a daily practice that weakens negative attitudes and strengthens positive ones.[6]

When your heart center opens, unexpected opportunities appear. The divine talent scout for enormous love sings inside your being, beckoning you to join its chorus of mesmerizing enchantment. You feel a greater sense of oneness and selflessness, sheltered from the fiery rages of the world by the cooling shade of the universal tree of life. Troubles lose much of their power to drag you down. More inclined to exist within your world of inward peace, you may access one or another of the attributes of an awakened fourth chakra that many sages call the "doorway to the Divine." Swami Satyananda Saraswati writes,

> The higher qualities of love, compassion, charity, mercy and so on are the expressions of a mind which is influenced by awakened chakras. This is precisely the reason why so much importance is given to the awakening of anahata chakra. . . . When anahata is awakened, we have a sublime relationship with God, with our family members, and with every being.

. . . Your values in life also change and the quality of your love and relationships improve immensely, enabling you to balance out the disappointments and frustrations in life. Therefore, you are able to live a little higher than you do now, and your attitude toward yourself and toward this life is much better.[7]

Fourth-chakra energy sustains a fountain of natural healing power. It can flow not only throughout your heart center, but can send beneficial effects through your entire body. Hopefully you know how much a warm embrace or healing touch can add to mere verbal reassurance. Jesus Christ, advocate for the power of love, healed through "the laying on of hands." Sri Mata Amritanandamayi, most often called simply Amma, or Mother, offers her miraculous open-hearted energy to the millions who come to see her as one by one they lay their heads on her chest and she cradles them in her arms. (And, in sites around the world where horrendous disasters have struck, she also offers her healing energy by providing such things as houses, hospitals, and schools to those in desperate need.)

The Dark Side of the Fourth Chakra

Issues and Challenges: Letting go of personal needs enough to hear those of others; feeling so inwardly wounded that one thinks "Loving just sets me up for disappointment when others go away."

Sadly, many people live out their entire lives with their fourth chakra almost completely closed. In some, the door that leads to it is not just slammed shut, but locked and bolted, because they're afraid that if the door to their heart is open someone might betray them. When that's the case, cautious attitudes and actions can provoke the kind of reactions from others that reinforce staying away from deeper emotional contact.

Since self-protectiveness also blocks us from being sensitive to another's needs, we may not develop the loving kindness that is essential to the fabric of a caring family or community in which all are nurtured and supported. That's widespread in a culture where separation through divorce, going away to war, or running away from home are common themes.

On the other hand, those who are so concerned with taking care of others that they neglect their own needs may ultimately lose the energy needed to take care of either themselves or another. When energy is overspent, a person can become drained of positive emotion and have a hard time accepting love from others. The conflicts and arguments that may crop up in such a relationship are akin to storms that blow across the surface of a lake or sea, whipping up waves and causing hurt or angry feelings.

Yet if we are lucky enough to possess positive fourth-chakra qualities, grumpy feelings quickly pass, leaving the deep abiding love that underlies them untouched, like a great ocean whose depths are untouched by storms that blow across its surface. Both (or all) who are involved in either trysts or lasting relationships usually know where each others' deeply sensitive and easily hurt spots are. Depending on the degree to which our heart is truly open, we may or may not avoid shooting hurtful emotional arrows at one another. Even though the fourth-chakra ideal is deep and unselfish love, each of us still decides about our feelings, words, and actions in the moment. We each make choices regarding how we feel about ourselves, our connections with others, and whether to direct the light of loving kindness toward those whose paths we cross. Yet another way of attaining balance is to be in tune with nature.

Swami Vivekananda articulates a fourth-chakra spiritual ideal in saying, "All love is expansion, all selfishness is contraction. . . . He who loves lives, he who is selfish is dying. Therefore love for love's sake . . . just as you breathe to live."[8] A related insight, widely attributed to Jallaludin Rumi, adds, "Your task is not to seek for love," he wrote, "but merely to seek and find all the barriers within yourself that you have built against it."

Past Roots of Fourth-Chakra Problems

When parents or other caregivers love a child, respect its autonomy, and set sensible limits that teach a sense of responsibility, they provide a solid foundation for realization of fourth-chakra potentials. By contrast, children who feel unloved often close the doors to their hearts, because it hurts too much to hope for love and have that craving ignored or spurned. Likewise, children who feel abandoned, such as when a parent dies or moves away due to a divorce, often become guarded in their ability to love. They may develop a tendency to pull away whenever someone gets too close, because in the past, loving led to heart-break. The "come close—stay away" blueprint is almost always a result of love lost in one or more painful past relationships. While such protective closing of the heart is not an inevitable response to painful relational experiences, it is common.

Being surrounded by takers who are mostly out for themselves and not sensitive to a child's needs is another past source of present problems. With few or no role models of giving and generosity, a small human being learns to close the doors to his or her heart but has little experience with opening them.

For these and other reasons, some people are just not skilled at handling the precarious balance between sensibly opening the heart and diving recklessly into heavy emotional reactions. When fiery passions mingle with fourth-chakra awakening, succumbing to the seductive nature of sensual gratification can be hard to resist. If well-established habits of hedonism reign, the soothing essence of pure love can be lost in the rallying cry for more pleasure. Tender green shoots of trust, kindness, and compassion may be replaced with deeply engraved first-, second-, or third-chakra responses of insecurity, possessiveness, anger, or "all of the above." When past memories and present cravings control our emotions, it's easy for an open-hearted experience of love to turn bitter instead of sweet. The Anahata Chakra involves outgrowing painful emotional relics of the past and replacing them with an attitude that acknowledges pain and suffering as part of life, along with love and joy. In it we develop the capacity to endure the former and replace them with the latter.

THE BODY AND EMOTIONS PATHWAY: FEELING TONES IN THE FOURTH CHAKRA

Personal Transformation in the Fourth Chakra

The words and the feeling "I love you," writes author Ken Keyes, "often mean, 'When I am with you, things you say and do help me experience parts of me that I regard as beautiful, capable, and loveable.'"[9]

The great sage Meher Baba added another dimension when he said, "Love is essentially self-communicative; those who do not have it catch it from those who have it. . . . It goes on gathering power and spreading itself until eventually it transforms everyone it touches."[10]

In conscious love, giving is as important as receiving. You are happiest when others are happiest. You accept each person fully as the unique individual he or she is. You neither try to make someone over to fit your agenda nor try to make yourself over to fit theirs.

In transcendent love, you enter the realm of the Divine where you radiate love regardless of circumstances. When you truly awaken your compassion you feel kindness for all, without self-righteousness, without looking down on anyone, without religious imperialism ("my religion is better than yours"), and without spiritual materialism ("my faith is greater than yours"). Anandamai Ma comments, "How can one impose limitations on the infinite by declaring 'This is the only path'?"[11] You just *are*, in your common humanity and your kinship of spirit with other people and living beings.

Transcendent love is unconditional. We love others not only for how special they are, but for how ordinary. The opportunity to feel such love is part of why people hang out with spiritual teachers who demonstrate or radiate true fourth-chakra values. We get a chance to feel their way of being in the world, and hope that some of that way of being emerges in us. Amma, the hugging saint, speaks of developing in ourselves "A love without beginning, without end."

But we don't have to be a saint or guru or spiritual aspirant to live and act with a "Big-Heart." Accepting each moment as it comes, without thinking that it should be different, or that the person before us should be different, helps us walk the heart center's path. If our heart has truly opened we can be friendly and loving in the present moment without feeling embarrassed, ashamed, or guilty about who we are or who we have been. Also, adds Johari, when the feeling of motherhood is awakened in a person, it can help open the heart to fourth chakra energy, "making the behavior of such a person very soothing to others."[12]

Relational Transformation in the Fourth Chakra

The conscious love and transcendent love that are fourth-chakra hallmarks are not so common, but by meditating on this center and making healthy emotional choices, we can feel and express the sweet scent of their essence. Since it lies beyond intellectual perceptions, the fourth chakra can be fully understood only through direct experience.

If we hope to move toward feeling and expressing conscious or transcendent love, part of what we need to do is pay attention, moment by moment, to the character of our words and acts of love. What do they suggest that we want or even demand without realizing it?

Others' styles of voicing or showing love may be different from our own. If we insist that others express themselves as we want them to rather than accepting their gifts of kindness and caring in the ways that come naturally to them, we may be closing the door to receiving what they are trying to give. We may also be sliding back into the third-chakra trap of trying to control who and how they are. One person may show transcendent love in words, another in generous deeds, another in hugs.

A major challenge of fourth-chakra consciousness or transcendent love is being willing to appreciate heart-opening experiences without placing demands on another, or making oneself miserable if another's gift of love is not offered. Sometimes that's easier said than done.

THE PATHWAY OF SPIRIT:
IMAGERY IN THE FOURTH CHAKRA

The Six-Pointed Star, the Lotus Petals, and the Seed Sounds

A person who vibrates in the fourth chakra, declares Johari, speaks from the heart. In this chakra we start looking for the divine spirit within ourselves and all beings. We enter the permanent invisible world, the plane of balance, which we cannot see but feel. Here we can touch the Cosmic Mind that is working behind everything. We can move beyond the gettings and doings of society and come to be in tune with nature.

The body itself speaks to us through sensations that we can interpret as either beneficial or disturbing. In the twentieth century, biofeedback taught us that we can learn to be far more sensitive to these signals and use them constructively. First among them is the heartbeat. The heart responds to every change in emotional tone, says Johari. That makes the heart our guru. After the heart comes our breathing, which we can also regulate. Biofeedback helps us control not only breathing, but also the workings of varied internal organs that we used to think we had no way to affect.

Anahata means "unhurt, unstruck, and unbeaten." In our heart, the dwelling place of our emotional self, our balance and energy can move upward. Our heartbeat and breathing pattern speak to us of the conditions inside us. When they are in balance, we are in balance.

Figure 7.1. This drawing depicts the deities—Ishana Rudra Shiva and Kakini Devi—and core imagery shown in the painting of this chakra (plate 7: Fourth or Anahata Chakra).

The hexagram or six-pointed star [at the center of the image] symbolizes the air element, which moves in all four directions as well as upward and downward. Air is the vital force (*prana*). The star is composed of two overlapping, intersecting triangles. One points upward, symbolizing Shiva, the male principle. The other triangle points downward and symbolizes Shakti, the female principle. The star represents the balance that is attained when these two prinicples are joined in harmony. The star also symbolizes the balancing of energy in the Heart Chakra between the three chakras above it and the three chakras below it.[13]

Around the green star is a circle with twelve deep red lotus petals. Energy, says Johari, flows to and from the petals in twelve directions as we inhale and exhale, activating twelve mental and emotional tendencies: hope, anxiety, endeavor, possessiveness, arrogance, incompetence, discrimination, egoism, lustfulness, fraudulence, indecision, and repentance. Through moment-by-moment awareness we can notice which petal is being activated and feed it our energy or withdraw it.

At the upper right of the picture is another lotus with eight petals that represents our spiritual heart. It is known as Ananda Kanda (Space of Bliss) or Hrit Pundarik (Heart Lotus). It can be felt right next to the physical heart. In the center of the Heart Lotus resides Narayan, or the human form of Vishnu. The most famous human incarnations are Ram and Krishna, the spiritual romantic heroes of the second chakra. They help in our quest to reach the fourth chakra. Narayan represents the character of our self in the waking and dream state.

The Seed Sound and a Short Visualization

The seed sound of this chakra is YANG and belongs to the deity of air, Vayu. When correctly pronounced it vibrates the spiritual heart and makes the energy move up.

1. Visualize the twelve lotus petals, starting with the one to the right of the one on top. As you visualize each petal, moving clockwise, utter its seed sound: KANG, KHANG, GANG, GHANG, YONG, CANG, CHANG, JANG, JHANG, UANG, TANG, THANG.
2. Then visualize the green six-pointed star at the center.
3. Then insert the seed sound of the element YANG in the center of the star.

The Black Antelope (or Musk Deer)

Like our heart, the black antelope at the bottom of the picture is sensitive, pure, and innocent. It runs restlessly around searching for the source of the smell of musk, without realizing that the musk is right in its own navel. We too can get caught by mirages and reflections that make us run to the corners of the Earth, seeking divine bliss. The supreme truth, however, is right inside us in our heart.

Shiva in Bana Lingam (A Highly-Polished Almost Egg-shaped Stone Found in the Narmada River)

The basic form of the self-born lingam in the first chakra, with its first spark of what some say is our immortal Self, now appears containing a shining image of Shiva at the top of both figure 7.1 and plate 7. Since we are entering the permanent invisible world, we see the form of Sada Shiva appearing. He is the eternal benefactor. He is always in a good mood! In this form we can experience the divine grace in the game of life.

He is also called Sabda Brahman or the eternal Logos, and created the causal world. As guru of spiritual knowledge, he gives reasoned discourse. To understand the causal world we need language. In yoga the first manifestation of articulate language is the monosyllable AUM (sometimes spelled OM), which is said to include all language and meaning. In the fourth chakra the love for inner sounds is born.

In the first chakra the lingam with the snake around it was in a sleeping state and the male and female energies were in their basic form. In the fourth this lingam becomes the same as conscience. It acts as the guru inside who seeks to guide us with every step we take. To be more in contact with this guru we should pay attention to our heartbeat. The intellectual understanding of the third chakra now has changed into the direct experience of inner light and feelings as an actual part of daily life.

Ishana Rudra Shiva

The deity of the fourth chakra is Ishana Rudra Shiva (shown on the left side of the drawing). When we were caught by the desires, emotions, and thoughts of the lower chakras, he appeared as the Destroyer, as Rudra. Here in the fourth chakra we can experience his true nature, which is continual happiness. This Shiva is no old man, but instead is ever young, peaceful, and beneficent. He has let go of worldly concerns and has only items from nature as clothes and garlands. He has tamed the snakes of passions. He is the ultimate yogi and sits on his tiger skin, which represents the ever-restless mind that runs around in the jungle of desires.

To control the mind he is teaching us the knowledge of pranayama, or breath control. In some forms of pranayama, controlled suspension of breath (*kumbhaka*) plays an important role. It is said to slow or even stop the movement of thoughts within the brain.

Shiva's trident represents the powers of creation, preservation, and destruction; or *tamas* (heaviness, laziness, darkness), *rajas* (active energy, passion), and *sattva* (tranquility, purity), as the occasion demands, as well as the ability to destroy evil. The *damaru,* or drum, in his left hand represents cosmic rhythm, to which we want to entrain the beat of our heart.

To understand the essence of Ishana Rudra Shiva is to realize that "I am Shiva." Although we can never become Shiva, we are a spark of him and he is present in all of us. Our challenge is to recognize it. A person who lives in fourth chakra awareness, says Johari, lives in harmony with himself or herself and with others.[14]

Kakini Devi

Kakini is the Shakti of this chakra and the one who opens its doors and shows us the way into it. Like air, she penetrates all, and pervades all, like Vishnu. Her four arms tell us that the emotional self is added to the physical, sensual, and rational self. And the heart is its dwelling place. Every change in emotion is registered by the heart, which is the psychic center, where we feel the effects caused by sense perception. When in balance we open ourselves for the emotional frequencies of devotional practice personified as Kundalini Shakti, who aids Kakini in bringing the energy up.

Kakini, who seeks the well-being of all, shows us our illusions (maya) of the first three chakras and shows us the divine play (leela) in this maya. Now we have to take a position in the game, so that we are able to follow our own spiritual path, *svadharma* (*sva* means "one's own," so this term means "one's own dharma," which suits our unique inclinations and our situation. Then we feel free to act. But in acting, we also have to bear the responsibilities and consequences of our actions.

Faith, devotion, or bhakti is the essence of this chakra. But when it is not in tune with cosmic principles or our inner nature, it can send us tumbling back down to the delusions of the first chakra. There we have blind faith without grounding in the laws of existence. Faith in tune with the laws of nature is *sudharma* (*su* means "good," so this term for good dharma is about following one's own true duty in a way), which is helpful to oneself and others. *Adharma* is that which is unhelpful, a breach of duty to oneself and others. Self-rejection and self-praise are both adharma. In this chakra we face the task of untying the knot of Vishnu (Vishnu Granthi), our identification with traditions and institutions, which lead us to believe in only one way and no other. (Guidance in untying these knots is given in chapter 11.) Then with an open mind we can act out our life.

Kakini Devi gives us tools that help us to elevate our minds to higher centers of consciousness. She is responsible for the creation of devotional art in all its different modes of expression: poetry, music, painting, sculpture, landscape, architecture, and the like. She transforms the worldly art of the second chakra into the devotional art of the fourth. Art now becomes a precise, compact expression of spiritual knowledge organized from within oneself. Art becomes inspired by Kakini. Here is no name, no signature. One hand makes all!

This kind of art calms the mind and brings peace, The absorption can be so intense that the sense of I-consciousness dissolves completely. In this way devotional art helps to find one's own dharma. For those to whom some form of art is calling, it can be a valuable way to express the fourth chakra.

Kundalini Shakti

The destructive snake of the first chakra has changed into a beautiful goddess sitting in a lotus posture above the central green star, Kundalini Shakti. The triangle in which she sits is facing upward, showing the tendency of this chakra to move energy upward. Now we see her in her beautiful and pure form, dressed in white, on her way to unite with her beloved. In this form she is the personification of bhakti, or selfless spiritual devotion. There is only love and the lover. It is no longer lust (kama), as in the second chakra. Now we find love everywhere in everything (*prema*). The heart gets filled with the devotional spirit of bhakti and brings a sense of cosmic unity.

With Kundalini Shakti we also find the embodiment of the cosmic sound that is present everywhere. It is known as *anahata nada,* or "white noise," and is the sound of the fourth chakra. In it we can hear AUM, the seed of all sounds. Here Kundalini Shakti appears in the form of *matrikas* (letters of the Sanskrit alphabet). With that she opens the world of mantras for us. They can be one syllable, but also full prayers. With the help of mantras we now can express our bhakti by continuously repeating them (*japa*). For some of those who follow the path of devotion, bhakti, the purification of the elements and the mind happens automatically. For them, everything is experienced as divine. A beginning step on this path is to mentally repeat the mantra AUM or *soham* in rhythm with our breathing.

Reflections

In the third chakra we started longing for balance and harmony in our lives. In the fourth we start living in tune with the laws of nature. This leads almost automatically to good tendencies. We pay attention to the quality of food and may choose to avoid meat. We practice *asana* (yoga posture) and pranayama, study spiritual writings, and discover our own path toward cosmic consciousness.

Following a traditional spiritual path may make it easier to realize the truths that are behind words. But dedicating oneself to a higher cause like removing suffering and ignorance also can make one a saintly person with no initiation into a particular path. People who don't believe in God in a traditional way can also have an unconditional presence in and enjoyment of each moment with an attitude of balance and harmony that can open the fourth chakra. One way or the other a person can find a guru, in whatever form he or she decides to appear. It may be your neighbor or a monk or a saddhu. Most important is to have an open mind. And to learn to truly hear the messages of our heart.

PRACTICAL TOOLS
FOR FOURTH-CHAKRA WORK

Relaxation

Purpose: To increase your sense of well-being.

Right now, connect with the deepest of your emotions and consider what you're feeling. Is what you feel connected with other people? Whatever you are feeling, your emotions and sensations live inside of you, not inside of others. Even if you don't have control over outside people and circumstances, you can exercise control over your thoughts about yourself and where you are in this stage of your life's passage. Whether you feel expansive and happy or constricted and anxious, whether you're accepting or non-accepting of life's events, the following simple exercise can help you enjoy your time and make better choices for your self.

Take a moment to think realistically about what you need to relax and enjoy life more. (Skip winning the lottery, dating a movie star, or other fairly unrealistic possibilities.) Consider what you'd like to do that is within the realm of potential realties, something that does not depend on someone else giving you permission.

Once you've thought of something that you'd really like to be doing, something that will enable you to enjoy your life more, make a commitment to do it. For example, you might make a commitment to enjoy each day and be the best person you can be to yourself.

In relation to your present commitment, let optimism rule your thoughts, believe in yourself, and trust that you can make time to do what is most important for your personal well-being and the fulfillment of your heart's desires.

Breath Control or Pranayama

Purpose: Releasing tension and building emotional strength.

If possible, open your windows to let fresh air into your room. Sit or lie in a comfortable position with your spine straight. Place your right hand over your heart and your left arm slightly away from your chest with your left palm pointed upward. Focus your awareness on the rising and falling motion of your right hand on your chest as you breathe. As you do, notice your thoughts.

Next imagine that universal healing energy is coming through your right hand to mix with the oxygen that is coming into your lungs and bloodstream while you inhale. The healing energy goes from your hand into your entire body, equal to the incoming prana that is feeding each of your cells, strengthening your health, and empowering your entire being.

Once you inhale, hold your breath and the accompanying healing energy to a count of five heartbeats before you slowly exhale.

With your exhalation, mentally envision your breath leaving your chest and going through your left arm down into your palm, where it exits your body. As the prana leaves through your palm, all anxiety, fear, or negative emotional concerns disappear.

Inhale peace and feel it expanding in your heart, exhale and release any strife.

Repeat this breathing cycle until you feel more peace within or have a better understanding of what you need to feel happier and healthier.

Concentration

Purpose: Maintaining focus and emotional clarity.

 ### Visual Splitting

This is especially useful for people who have a hard time keeping focus. You can more easily notice it when your attention drifts off. Such a focus is as useful in communicating a loving attitude as in any other area of life. If you're trying to send someone a message of love or caring but your attention keeps getting pulled away to other concerns, they're likely to think they're receiving a different message: "I must not be very important to him or her." This exercise will help you continue to develop your attentive focus.

After your meditative Starting Sequence (see the instructions for Tratak on page 29, look directly at a clearly distinct visual object some distance in front of you. Extend your arm and hand to point at the object. Focus your eyes on the tip of the finger you're pointing with.

Then slowly move your finger inward toward your nose, *while keeping a sharp visual focus on your fingertip*. As you do, you'll probably notice that the candle or other object you're pointing at divides into two objects. You'll see them move farther apart as your finger moves toward your nose. (If your object doesn't visually divide into two images that move apart, then you're keeping your visual focus on the object rather than on your fingertip. Keep practicing and within a few sessions you'll probably experience the phenomenon. If not, then this technique may not be for you.)

When your finger touches your nose, the two visual images will seem quite far apart. (What's going on? Each of your eyes is registering the object you're watching and you're seeing the two images separately, instead of fusing them into a single image as we usually do. An observer would see you getting cross-eyed as you do this.)

Now gradually move your finger from your nose back outward toward the object, still keeping your sharp visual focus on your fingertip. You'll probably see the two images approach each other and then merge back into a single object. (If you can manage, it's best to slowly inhale as you move your finger toward your nose and exhale as you move it away.)

Once you can do this, drop your arm and *imagine* your fingertip moving from the object toward your nose while you keep your visual focus on the imaginary fingertip, and notice the object divide in two just as before.

Then imagine your fingertip moving back from your nose to point at the object, all the while focusing on its location in space, as the two images move closer and merge back into one. Once you've mastered this method, you can try it with a complex visual field, like a patch of park or forest filled with leaves and sunlight and shadows, or a party or concert filled with many people and colors. As you move your focus toward your nose, you just might see your environment turn into an incredible kaleidoscope of forms and colors, and allow yourself heartfelt enjoyment of this new way of seeing.

Polarity-Balancing Meditation

Purpose: Deepening your connection with fourth-chakra energy.

Choose a polarity from the Fourth-Chakra Possibilities table on page 126. (Or ask your teacher or guru, based on his or her observations, to suggest a polarity that you would profit from working with.)

With that as your starting point, follow the Polarity-Balancing Meditation instructions that are described on page 46, and proceed to look within at whatever aspect of your situation needs most attention.

Evoke inner kindness while you listen to the feelings of your heart.

Affirming Love

Purpose: Attaining balance.

Find an unhurried moment and a quiet space. Move into a comfortable position, close your eyes, and relax your breathing. Now imagine connecting with the fourth-chakra forces of unconditional love and compassion.

As you inhale, embrace these positive qualities and feel them expanding within your being.

Then slowly exhale, and imagine that your outgoing breath is releasing any internal blocks or resistance you might have to opening your heart. In your mind tell yourself that you are connecting with the transformative healing power of divine love.

Next envision yourself being able to heal any of your own emotional pain or resistance to opening your heart. Remember that your heart has the miraculous power of forgiveness—toward others and yourself.

With each inhalation continue to breathe in love and compassion, letting it flow through your entire being, and then exhale and release any negative emotional associations you might have. Continue by inhaling love, exhaling fear; inhaling joy, exhaling stress, inhaling trust, exhaling antagonism. Keep breathing this way until you feel emotionally and mentally balanced and at greater peace.

Sound Healing

Purpose: Developing inner awareness using sound, as some people relate to the world best through hearing.

 The Music of Your Love

Dynamic feelings are like inner rhythms that can cause us to want to shout, cry, dance or sing.

Right now, move into a comfortable position. Take a minute to relax your mind and body, then find and feel inwardly your heart's center. Once you sense the area in your body linked with your fourth chakra, close your eyes, and with your inner ear listen to the sounds of your emotional spectrum. What melodies do you hear? Is there a rhythm to your feelings?

Let your mind envision imaginary musical instruments to help you create a melody to express the feelings you sense in this moment. (Or if you prefer, you can add words, or set your internal rhythm to a lyrical poem, or think of a song you know that fits those feelings.) You may even want to hum or chant your feelings or vocalize their sound in some other way.

Notice: What is your internal tempo? What is its mood? How might you like your melody to change? Are there any sounds of your emotions that you would like to repeat, repeal, or replace? Are there dimensions to your feelings that you've left out? Can you find a song or tune that encourages you to listen more closely to the symphony of your heart's rhythm and to love and live more fully?

 Mantra Chanting

Although you may work in different ways with mantras, or sacred words of power, you may also hear them in devotional singing or chanting. For instance, *shanti* (peace) is often repeated several times at the end of chants. One example is the mantra, *Om lokah samastah sukhino bhavatu, om shanti, shanti, shanti (AUM,* let the whole world be happy, peace, peace, peace). Chanting such mantras can connect you with the seeds of power that are echoed in their sound.

Select a word that works for you, either in Sanskrit or English.

FOURTH-CHAKRA MANTRAS

MANTRA	PRONUNCIATION	MEANING
ananda	ahNAAANda	delight, cheerfulness, happiness
anugraha	anooGRAH-hah	loving kindness, benefiting
karuna	kahROOnah	compassion, empathy
shanti	SHAWNtee	peace (of mind, in action, averting pain)

Taking Action

Purpose: Understanding the messages you speak with your heart.

To feel hard-hearted is to miss out on one of the greatest gifts the fourth chakra can offer you. Sri Anandamayi Ma remarks,

> *I find one vast garden spread out all over the universe.*
> *All plants, all human beings, all higher mind bodies*
> *are about in this garden in various ways,*
> *each has his own uniqueness and beauty.*
> *Their presence and variety give me great delight.*
> *Every one of you adds with his special feature*
> *to the glory of the garden.*[15]

Take a few moments and focus on the symbolic meaning of love in the garden of your own life. What does this mean to you? What seeds of self-nurturing are you presently planting to help your life evolve toward greater fulfillment? Are you willing to guide your inner spirit to turn up beneficial energy and turn down the negative, to engage more loving energy?

Which practical steps might you take to help awaken your willingness to love unconditionally? What can you do to feel more willing to give or ask for a hug (if that's appropriate in your culture in a public setting)? What message can you give to yourself to encourage healing and grow in your willingness to open your heart? The suggestions here don't mean you shouldn't ever be upset or angry. The question is how much of your consciousness you choose to give to each way of feeling and being.

Listen to your heart (but don't ignore your thoughtful mind or wise intuition when they add something valuable to your heart's message). Being in touch with the feelings of the heart chakra enhances possibilities to live with awareness and make meaningful choices. Now, with an open heart, we invite you to move toward the fifth chakra, where the power to communicate is central.

8

FIFTH OR VISHUDDHA CHAKRA

The Throat Chakra

Here you express yourself, listen within and without, and raise your potential to help others through communication.

[This] is the chakra of spiritual rebirth. It . . . includes prana, the vital life force throughout the body that brings balance of all the elements, and jnana, awareness that bestows bliss [and] understanding the laws of existence and [how] to synchronize with them. . . . The voice of a fifth-chakra person penetrates to the heart of the listener.

HARISH JOHARI,
CHAKRAS, ENERGY CENTERS OF TRANSFORMATION

Fifth or Vishuddha Chakra Correspondences

Key phrases: Communication, self-expression, listening, clarity, knowledge, integrity, truth, scholarship

Physical location: Throat and neck, mouth, ears

Endocrine gland: Thyroid

Astrological link: Jupiter

Day of the week: Thursday

Element: Akasha (space, the void)

Sense: Sound

Sanskrit Derivation: visuddhi (purification)

Massage: Neck, jaw

Leela Game of Self-Knowledge: Fifth row: Jnana, Prana-Loka, Apana-Loka, Vyaa-Loka, Human Plane, Plane of Agni (fire), Birth of Man, Ignorance, Right Knowledge

THE ESSENCE OF THE FIFTH CHAKRA: COMMUNICATION AND KNOWLEDGE

Fifth-chakra qualities help open inner vistas where the sacred can communicate with the mundane. In the fifth chakra they can form an alliance to meet or transcend earthly challenges. Fifth-chakra discrimination and awareness brings understanding of how to remove restrictive mental tethers that limit your potential. To fully realize the positive values of this chakra, you must seek knowledge that exceeds the ordinary, the familiar, and the previously accepted.

Such insight and energy allows worldly and spiritual values to come together seamlessly. This is a big step on a path of personal evolution in which normal communication has the potential to become magnificent. Receptive and conscious speaking and listening bring deeper understanding of the power of words and expression in the moment. It helps resolve communication problems.

When someone successfully taps into the warm, loving vibrations of the fourth chakra, their energy can naturally rise toward the fifth to promote clear, open-minded, effective speech and dialogue. People living ordinary lives can attain some beneficial fifth-chakra positive qualities, but it's easier if you first awaken the fourth chakra's energies. Among charismatic leaders who enjoy using their words to dominate others, however, you can sometimes hear fifth-chakra energies used in the service of third-chakra impulses. This is persuasiveness in the service of power, greed, and self-aggrandizement rather than caring and compassion. It often does more harm than good.

Spiritual masters tell us that the wise use of complementary qualities of sound and silence are what is important in the fifth chakra, but there is more. Swami Satyananda Saraswati explains:

> In this chakra the purifying and harmonizing of opposites takes place. . . . Vishuddhi represents a state of openness in which life is regarded as the provider of experiences that lead to greater understanding. One ceases to continually avoid the unpleasant aspects of life and seek the pleasant. Instead there is a flowing with life, allowing things to happen in the way that they must [as] parts of a greater cosmic whole. Proper understanding and true discrimination dawn out of this equal acceptance of the dualities and polarities of life.[1]

FIFTH-CHAKRA POSSIBILITIES

OPPORTUNITIES	OBSTACLES
Speaks clearly and accurately	Expresses self poorly, blocked
Speaks truth or not at all	Deceives or mystifies
Helps others feel better	Makes others feel worse
Communicates in depth	Communicates at surface level
Seeks to raise others' consciousness	Imposes own beliefs and agendas
Silent when nothing important to say	Talks much about trivia
Engages through dialogue and mutuality	Dominates conversations
Uses a pleasing tone	Speaks in a weak or harsh tone
Creative self-expression	Hindered in expression
Uses symbols and metaphors as such	Treats symbol and metaphor as reality
Listens well, hears others	Listens poorly, impervious to others

With fifth-chakra challenges, psychotherapists tend to focus on people who can't get their thoughts and words out in a way that is easily understood. They hope to help people find their lost voices. In contrast, spiritual teachers tend to focus on people who babble on and would profit from the discipline of periods of keeping silence. A reconciliation of these outlooks is seen in the principle that often a person's most useful line of personal work lies in developing abilities and qualities that do not come easily to him or her. So someone who has a hard time speaking can work on learning to speak effectively, while someone who never shuts up can profit from learning to be quiet and listen. Some people find value in developing both capacities. They learn to say less, while becoming more effective in what they do say.

THE MENTAL PATHWAY FOR WORKING WITH FIFTH-CHAKRA ENERGIES

The Bright Side of the Fifth Chakra

Gifts and Strengths: Speaks clearly with wisdom in ways that engage others; balanced between the mind and the heart.

Verses, songs, poems, and other messages that come from ageless depths of the soul's yearnings are transmitted in this chakra. When in touch with its magnetic currents, you can let your truth be heard without fear of reprisal. If you have developed a steady strength that can evenly balance logic and emotion, you may let your true self be more visible, and more readily spread good feelings and touchstones for constructive action.

A person whose fifth chakra is opening picks up on the "vibes" from others while retaining a clear sense of his or her own feelings and intentions. Such a person detects both the explicit words and the emotional messages another is sending. This provides a better sense of how to respond from a centered place—at least much of the time. With fifth-chakra energy, a person not only hears another's voice, but often also what lies beneath the words. Gestalt therapist Fritz Perls aptly describes this:

> *Do you sing, or do you saw?*
> *Is your voice dead, or soaked in tears?*
> *Are you machine-gunning me with the rapidity and*
> *   explosiveness of each of your words?*
> *Do you take my breath away with the and-and-and of your*
> *   anxiety? . . .*
> *Do you punish me with daggers of your Sunday-school*
> *   teacher's finger-pointing screech? . . .*

Or are you engulfing me in loving sound vibrations?...
The sound is true—poison or nourishment.
And I dance to your music or I run away.[2]

Self-mastery at the fifth-chakra level also includes the ability to hear your own diverse inner voices. Which aspects of yourself feel well-integrated and which do not? Confusion in the mind often arises, says Baba Hari Dass, because we are so busy chattering (either silently to ourselves or out loud to others) that we don't bother to listen to what truly matters, either internally or externally.[3]

It has been said that anyone who truly masters the positive potential of fifth-chakra energies can become a spiritual teacher. Such a person may follow any religion or none. For instance, one of the great psychologists of the twentieth century, Carl Rogers, was a secular figure, yet he raised the quality of consciousness of many around him whenever he spoke.[4]

Perhaps it seems contradictory for a chakra devoted to something as substantial as speech to be associated with the fifth element—akasha, or space or emptiness. But as we reflect further, we note that speaking is a subtle rather than material energy. It takes no space (except in the mind). And it involves silence as well as speech. The emptiness associated with akasha is emphasized in Taoism and Zen Buddhism. In emptiness many things are possible. It is the root of a flexible mind that clearly perceives concepts and symbols for what they truly are, rather than confusing them with what they represent. It also refers to an absence or decrease in egocentrism, a "shrinking of ego," which is a kind of emptiness of self-concern—especially an emptying of obsessions about how we're coming across. Such emptiness reminds us of André Gide's comment, "Believe those who are seeking the truth; doubt those who find it."[5]

Fifth-chakra energy can lead to making or breaking ties with worldly existence. It allows you to clearly perceive the stories you have accepted and believed since childhood, or since becoming influenced by some party or group. It also allows you to choose whether to keep telling your or others' old stories or to create your own new ones. This can help you sweep away prejudices that you've borrowed from others (we all have at least a few) and perceive the inner and outer realities that they obscure.

The Dark Side of the Fifth Chakra

> **Issues and Challenges:** Not seeking power or boosting your ego through your words or their absence. Not gossiping or spending so much time on the computer or texting or TV, focused on topics that take you away from obtaining deeper states of inner awareness.

The negative side of the fifth chakra may be mild, as in someone who simply has not developed the ability to communicate well, or deadly, as in a leader convincing people that they should commit acts against humanity.

At the everyday level, you may think, "What if I say things poorly, or I can't get my point across, or if people won't like what I say?" In your body, this can take the form of an anxious tight jaw or throat, or even holding your breath. Or if you're retelling a story you've told many times before as if you were playing a recording, you might be talking *at* your listeners rather than connecting with them.

Habits that hinder self-expression include telling others what you think they want to hear, talking "facts" when you're not certain about something, or expecting others to hear, understand, and appreciate your message. If you're not trying to meet others' expectations, you're free to speak from the truth of your inner journey or to remain silent. Willingness to be uncertain is an excellent way to escape the lurking ego's trap of feeling like you have to be right. "Of course, I may be mistaken" is often a useful line to add to the end of a statement. It can avoid useless arguments and defuse potentially antagonistic situations.

Psychotherapist Anodea Judith writes,

Being told we have no right to feel a certain way when in fact that is how we feel makes a lie of our basic experience. Hearing the words "I love you" while having the experience of being abused, neglected, or shamed makes a lie of love. Being asked to apologize for something we do not feel sorry about, to be nice to someone we clearly dislike, or to be thankful for something we didn't want are all experiences that teach us to lie.[6]

Double messages are another way we lie. Our words say one thing while our body language or voice tone says something else. When someone sends a double message, the nonverbal statement is usually the true one.

At a transcendent level, fifth-chakra concerns include, "I won't be able to hear others' emotional plights or help them feel better about themselves." If raw emotions involve pain or blame, it's a bottomless well without a flow to quench the pain of shame. What to do? One of our friends finds someone else to blame for anything that goes wrong in his life, instead of taking responsibility for his own actions that contributed to it. In his mind, he's always the victim of someone else's bad deeds. Ironically, he fancies himself a wise man.

Blame shoots arrows of negative emotion at the person blamed. The good news is this: As you learn to hear and see that pattern in others, when they blame you for something, you can *recognize it as attached to the blaming person—not to you.* Or if blaming is part of your own pattern, as you begin to hear it, you can let go of it. Even if you've already started to speak a blaming comment, you can interrupt yourself: "Oh, don't mind me. I'm just sorting things out." Then move to awareness of the power of your words, and call in wisdom from a different direction.

Blame often includes a put-down: "What you [or I] did is wrong and you [or I] are at least somewhat defective for having done it." Self-blame is usually an introjection of others' blame—often others in your past or even your childhood. They said you were no good and you bought their story. Now, even when someone makes a nonblaming constructive suggestion, you may turn it into self-blame. Once you start to notice such a pattern, as you begin to tell yourself how bad or ineffective you are, you can interrupt yourself by noting, "Oh, there's that old habit again. I can let it go. I'm basically just fine."

At its best, positive fifth-chakra energy is an enchantress of the soul, but negative fifth-chakra energy can appear in the form of the con artist and hustler who might be charming, but cares little or nothing about others as long as he gets what he wants. Such a person tends not to view that attitude as a problem and is seldom motivated to change it. Usually the best you can do is to protect yourself against getting hustled, by developing a sensor that warns you when someone seems too glib and charming as he or she makes a request that you feel uneasy about agreeing to. Unusual tension in your body, having a sense that something just doesn't feel quite right, and willingness to be convinced without solid evidence are all useful signals.

Someone who has developed fifth-chakra abilities without the tempering of fourth-chakra lightness of spirit might become successful in business, politics, or even religion—a person who speaks powerful words but can also mask the realities beneath them. Such a person often does a con job on him or herself as well, buying into the belief that the lies or half-truths hold merit. "Half the truth is often a great Lie," declared Benjamin Franklin.

Then comes the next layer of self-deception—"I am an honest person who speaks truth." Sometimes this includes the "high priest complex" of imagining that you are wiser than your heart knows you to be. The higher the position that a religious official holds, the easier it is to hide beneath the seductive mantle of power. The same phenomenon often occurs with executives, officeholders, and bureaucrats who drape their message in flags of pseudorighteousness to keep it from cracking open in the fiery kiln of truth, revealing the reality that it conceals.

Past Roots of Fifth-Chakra Problems

"Repeatedly telling a person he is wrong even if he tries his best is the easiest way to stop him from growing and make him feel he is not right," declares Johari.[7] This is especially true of repeated criticism and put-downs during childhood, whether from parents, teachers, or peers. It can also happen later in life, with people who are told they are worthless again and again, until they accept the message as true.

Those who hold back even when they have something worthwhile to say usually have an inner critic who warns, "Whatever you suggest is going to come out wrong, so you'd better be quiet," or "Better not write it."

The block may be situational, such as young children who are told to be seen and not heard. When someone is silent in a class but talkative in other contexts, often there was a past teacher who ridiculed that person and robbed him or her of feeling safe when expressing ideas in groups. Even a single such instance of ridicule, if it was traumatic enough, can make someone clam up through the rest of their school career. Or the block might arise when talking to authority figures like one's boss.

A different response to such early criticism may be anger and rebellion: basically, "Get off my back!" As an adult, such a person may be overbearing, belligerent, obnoxious, nasty to others in diverse situations, or even violent.

The negative side of another fifth-chakra polarity results from uncritically accepting erroneous stories about the world. When a statement is made over and over, whether by parents, a policeman, a pope, a politician, or even a scientist, a person may come to accept even a Big Lie as fact. We often receive approval from family, friends, employers, or members of our political party when we parrot the same beliefs they hold. Their approval can be a big incentive to think as they do, even when it means buying into ideologies that are actively harmful. (An interesting side note: George Washington refused join a political party. He regarded parties as inimical to the spirit of democracy.)

Having a history of physical, sexual, verbal, or emotional abuse is especially detrimental to opening the fifth chakra. Such abuse may be coupled with threats of "If you tell anyone, I'll kill you," or ". . . kill your parents." The abuser often also tells the abused that, "It's your fault—you brought this on," which piles guilt onto the shame and misery. No wonder the person becomes afraid to speak!

THE BODY AND EMOTIONS PATHWAY: FEELING TONES IN THE FIFTH CHAKRA

Personal Transformation in the Fifth Chakra

The Vishuddha Chakra is ruled by the planet Jupiter, which makes fifth-chakra persons interested in scriptures of ancient knowledge. Jupiter is called "guru" in Sanskrit, which means "dispeller of darkness." The writings of fifth-chakra persons are like scriptures, revealing and illuminating. Their very presence removes ignorance by opening up channels of knowledge within their listeners, enabling them to receive illumination and be freed from darkness.[8]

Real dialogue is an alternation of sound and silence. If we talk without pausing to make space for both the external and internal silence that lets us truly hear the other, we're carrying on a monologue masquerading as a dialogue even when we seem to be having a conversation. On the other hand, if we pretend to agree with what the other person says even when we don't, then that other person is carrying on the monologue.

Most of us enjoy talking. For most people, silence requires practice. To maintain a discipline of silence, whether for an hour, a day, or longer, is an austerity. Baba Hari Dass, who never speaks and communicates only by writing on his chalkboard, says, "Tapas (austerity) is a mental training to develop will power. . . . According to the mental level of an aspirant, one is given a particular kind of tapas to help train the mind. . . . Austerity means effort to control desire. It is chosen, not forced. . . . To watch yourself is the hardest tapas."[9] Gurumayi tells this story:

> Here in Shree Muktananda Ashram, we have a silent group and a talking group . . . in the dining hall. One group wants the signs that call for silence on every table. . . . The other group keeps taking the silence signs off the table. . . . It is difficult to say which group has a stronger case—the group that demands silence . . . or the group that has never felt the need for silence. . . . So it's a dilemma. If you ask for silence, you are the one who is making the noise. And if you don't ask for silence, no one seems to take any notice of it.[10]

For those in the silent group, one response to the dilemma would be to go into their own witness consciousness and listen to their mental grumbling about the noisy group. They would probably find that the inner voice of their minds is not so silent after all! Those in the chatterbox group lose out on the benefits of developing the discipline of silence. But most in both groups were completely missing the larger point, which was their egocentric attachment to the idea that their way was the right way and the other group was wrong. It was still "Me! Me! *My* way." And there they all go, sliding down the snake of ignorance back to the first chakra, whether talkative or silent.

Besides strengthening willpower, one benefit of practicing a discipline of silence for a specified period is the ability to be silent in any situation where it is useful. Life has many such situations.

Relational Transformation in the Fifth Chakra

When positive fifth-chakra qualities shine through your spirit, your relationships improve. Your attitudes, behavior, and motives help make the world a friendlier and more supportive, sustaining place, for you and for others.

Close attention to everyday attitudes and behavior can bring positive change. Psychologist Fritz Perls pointed out the importance of distinguishing between your preferences and your "shoulds." The former come from inside you. The latter are the programming you have acquired from others. For example, even if a child wants attention, he or she "should" sit quietly when his or her parents talk. Perls used the metaphor of swallowing whole without going through the process of chewing through and "spitting out what you don't want."[11]

With moment-by-moment awareness, you can start to notice your responses and whether you have an easier time saying yes or no. If your stomach tightens up as you find yourself agreeing to do something when you don't want to, then practice saying no (or a functional equivalent that is acceptable in your culture). Then look for occasions when you can refuse a request, in a way that feels comfortable for you (or at least almost so). Your style doesn't have to be confrontational—you can learn to do this with tact and graciousness.

On the other hand, you may tend to reflexively say "No, I'd better not," to protect yourself from giving in to unwelcome requests. If that's your pattern, then pay attention to those times when you'd prefer to say "Yes, yes, oh yes!" to a request or opportunity, and do so.

In addition, pay focused attention to other aspects of the contact you make. When you swallow what you want to say but don't have to, notice that. What kinds of statements do you bite back most often? Notice, too, if you uncritically agree with what others say. You almost always have the option to be silent, or to say something like, "How about that?" or "That's worth thinking about."

Your choice of words, the nonverbal messages that go with them, and your attitudes that underlie them can make a radical difference in the character and quality of your life. Listen carefully to what you say and how you say it and you just might find yourself becoming an enchantingly different person.

THE PATHWAY OF SPIRIT:
IMAGERY IN THE FIFTH CHAKRA

The Circle, the Crescent, the Lotus Petals, and the Seed Sound

In the fifth chakra we reach the last element, which is more difficult to understand. It is called akasha and can be translated as "void" or "space." For earth, water, fire, and air to exist, we need space. First we need a container; then we can put something inside. The nature of akasha is that of antimatter. When we see the atoms, we see there is space in between them, which is not made of matter. It has no other quality than void or space. The central circle represents this space, in which the whole of existence takes place.

The principle of sound creates akasha. Sound works with waves and needs space to move. The crescent within the circle represents the pure cosmic sound (*nada*). This indicates that the fifth chakra is the place of inner sounds. In the fifth chakra the increase of number of petals stops, as do the elements. The sixteen lotus petals around the central circle are almost all connected to musical sounds, frequencies in a harmonic scale and mantras to evoke divine energies in the body. Here the mental modifications become more peaceful and enjoyable.

After we have experienced the Divine in everything around us in the fourth chakra, now we have to realize this Divine in us. By going inside we will hear the sounds created by heartbeat, breathing, and blood flowing through our system. Before we could not hear them, because we were preoccupied by the impressions from the phenomenal world. Now when we become aware of these inner sounds, nerves will open, which also produce their sounds. A whole new world of musical sounds and mantras opens and with it new dimensions of experiencing. Now we start understanding more about the true nature of human existence, and knowledge comes. In the fifth chakra we reach the human plane where all the great religious teachings come from.

The seed sound here is HANG. When pronounced correctly, it will start vibrating in the throat, making the voice more sweet and melodious. It makes it easy for a voice to penetrate the heart of the listener, changing the space in the listener's mind. Prayers and stories come from the fourth chakra and are expressed by the throat. They can create a trancelike spiritual state. Mantras,

Figure 8.1. This drawing depicts the deities—Panchavaktra Shiva and Shakini Shakti Devi—and core imagery shown in the painting of this chakra (plate 8: Fifth or Vishuddha Chakra).

however, are created in the fifth and bring out divine energies. They give form to the formless.

A Short Visualization

1. Start with visualizing the sixteen lotus petals beginning with the one to the right of the topmost. Proceed clockwise.

2. Then visualize the silver crescent in the white circle.
3. Place the seed sound of the element, HANG, in the middle.

The Elephant

The elephant is considered to be the lord of the herbivorous animals. With great knowledge of earth, herbs, and plants, it moves through the jungle and the plains, creating space for other animals to move and plants to grow. Elephants create roads and water pools for everybody to enjoy. From them we can learn patience, memory, self-confidence, and the enjoyment of being one with nature. We can experience these qualities when we open ourselves to the inner sounds of the fifth chakra. The trunk of the elephant represents this pure sound. By adding NG to the letters of the Sanskrit alphabet, we create a nasal sound like the elephant. Doing so, we vibrate the outermost brain cortex, which we can feel when we put our hand on the top of the skull. Impressions that are stored there may be released and we are able to express them in a language full of wisdom and knowledge.

Panchavaktra Shiva

The deity of this chakra is Panchavaktra Shiva, or the Shiva with the five faces. Each represents an element and the principle by which it was generated. It is not possible to access the Supreme with the senses, speech, or mind. That makes it difficult to worship. We need a percept and a form. In many shrines in India one can find Shivalingams with five faces on them representing Panchavaktra Shiva. In this form he is considered to be the great teacher or master guru who shows us the limitations of each chakra. He makes us understand the human plane in its totality.

This Shiva is a combination of all the Shiva energies that manifested themselves in the lower chakras:

In the first chakra he shows himself as Brahma and is responsible for the creation of physical plane that we can experience through our senses.

In the second chakra we see him as Vishnu, who is responsible for the preservation of creation. In the astral plane we experience our mental and psychic energies.

In the third he becomes Rudra and is responsible for destruction. In the celestial plane we experience our mental body.

In the fourth chakra he appears as Ishana. In the plane of balance we can experience him, but cannot find him.

In the fifth chakra we see him as Panchavaktra Shiva. Here in the human plane he frees us from the illusion that we are separated from him. The self in us is the nondual cosmic consciousness. It is omnipresent, omnipotent, and omniscient. Here we discover our true identity.

In the fifth chakra a person is born as a human being. You do not belong to your parents anymore or a country or a caste or a religion. You are the child of God and relate only to the truth, untouched by desires. You can become synchronized with the divine laws.

As an instrument to communicate with the Divine, all religious rituals use fire (agni), which created our universe, including us. Sitting at a sacred firepit or fireplace is a very old ritual. Fire is a link between human and the Divine. Agni is the eternal witness that was and is always there. The divine essence of fire gives color and form to the phenomenal world. Fire is the gross manifestation or vehicle of energy. Now we can perceive our body also as a vehicle. Fire is called our grandpa and in front of him we perform our rituals, reminding us of the role we have to play.

Looking at Panchavaktra Shiva we see that he has four arms. One of his hands is in the *abhai mudra,* with which he conveys fearlessness. In the fourth chakra we experienced the grace of the eternal benefactor (Sada Shiva). In the fifth he reveals himself and leaves no more reason for fear. In the second hand he holds a mala or rosary, which is used to guide japa, the continuous repetition of a mantra or holy name. In the third hand he holds the drum that produces the fourteen sounds from which the Sanskrit alphabet comes. One can hear AUM in the overtones. In the fourth hand he has the trident showing the oneness in and behind creation.

Shakini Shakti Devi

Shakini invites you into the fifth chakra. She is the embodiment of purity. Her five heads refer to the five senses. Shakini gives us higher knowledge (jnana), a divine energy behind education and fine arts. Now we understand what is real and unreal. And maybe more important, we can live this discrimination in daily life. To be able to do this we have to free ourselves from value judgments. Our inner Self goes above the physical body and is beyond good or bad.

Shakini will instruct us through the spoken word of the guru. Speech is the essence of human beings for expressing our innermost feelings. But the spoken word also has its limitations. In the fifth chakra it is not only ordinary speech. Nonverbal messages also become important. Poetry and dreams are a way to express the truth. This is the center of dreams, and in dreams Shakini is teaching. When expressed they can become poetry.

Here knowledge is not yet realization, but awareness. Concepts are still the same, but we understand them. We become aware of how maya binds us to the world of desires. Whatever we have been trying to do only made us tired and was painful, because we were still perceiving ourselves as independent, individual beings. And the result was that we created only more karma.

When we gain more knowledge, ignorance can also pop up. When our so-called knowledge is incorrect and we don't realize it, we forget the illusory nature of existence. Ignorance is not in nature, it is inside us in our mind. As a result, the same place can be a heaven for one person and a hell for another. We should not only become aware of the truth; we also need awareness in our behavior. And that requires experience of reality. Otherwise it remains only information. After knowing through a direct experience of reality in the state of samadhi or conscious deep sleep, we return to the world with our own knowledge of what is right to do in the game of life. Once a wise teacher was asked where he got his knowledge. He answered: "By watching fools and not doing what they are doing!"

In one of her hands, Shakini is holding a skull to remind us to become detached from the illusory world of sense perception. The senses, however, are used by the mind. The real technique is then to withdraw the mind into the Self. To achieve that there are two steps. The first step is breath suspension (kumbhaka). When we stop breathing, Ida Nadi and Pingala Nadi (the male and female spiritual nerves) stop functioning and the spiritual channel (Sushumna) opens. The second step is to still the mind in the Self, which means taking the mind to a place where it normally cannot reach, where there are no senses. One way is to do mantra repetition (japa) or just listen to the breath as it makes the sound *soham, so* when breathing in and *ham* when breathing out.

In her second hand Shakini holds the *ankush* or staff to control the elephant of intellect. Here we are warned of the limitations of the spoken word, which can overintoxicate us with information or misinformation. In the end we talk about things that cannot be put into words or thoughts.

With the scriptures in her third hand, Shakini is giving us knowledge about the right way to live. But experience is also needed. In the fourth chakra, through purification we achieved an electrochemical balance, in which we experienced a feeling of intense happiness. To maintain this balance we have to understand the influence of chemicals, hormones, and subtle energies on and within our body and mind. It is said that when we are in disharmony with natural laws, we disturb the "airs" in our body, and that disturbs the mind. The quality of food is important. We have to understand what is right for us.

In her last hand Shakini Devi holds a rosary or mala used for mantra repetition. Mantras can help us communicate and make friends with all the deities, male and female. They can also help calm our mind and make our inner dialogue more peaceful.

Reflections

"Simple living and high thinking." It sounds simple, but it is not easy at all!

Contentment is our goal. In *satsang* (being in the company of a spiritual teacher or guru or others on our path) we find guidance and inspiration. Through self-study we gain knowledge. And this discipline can make us happy.

In the first four chakras we suffered all kind of mental modifications that created the melodramas and psychodramas in our life. Here in the fifth chakra we meet spiritual teachers and gain knowledge about the divine Self within us. By listening to the inner sounds we get more experienced with it. It is easier now to move toward feeling a state of bliss, the arrow of the fifth chakra. But sometimes for better and sometimes for worse, we are still under the influence of the three qualities (gunas), through which we experience life: the feeling of balance (sattva), the feeling of activity (rajas), and the feeling of laziness or inertia (tamas).

Plate 1. Seven Cosmic Energy Centers

Plate 2. Spiritual Alignment = Natural Harmony

Plate 3. Ardhanarishvara: Perfect Balance

Plate 4. First or Muladhara Chakra

Plate 5. Second or Svadhisthana Chakra

Plate 6. Third or Manipura Chakra

Plate 7. Fourth or Anahata Chakra

Plate 8. Fifth or Vishuddha Chakra

Plate 9. Sixth or Ajna Chakra

Plate 10. Seventh or Sahasrara Chakra

Plate 11. Soma and Kameshvara Chakras

Plate 12. Yantra Form of the Seventh Chakra

Plate 13. Narasimha, Man-Lion

Plate 14. Union of Male and Female Consciousness in the Tree of Life

Plate 15. Animal Representations of the Chakras

Plate 16. Pantanjali and the Chakras

PRACTICAL TOOLS
FOR FIFTH CHAKRA WORK

Relaxation

Purpose: Finding rhythms that soothe your soul.

In modern times, feeling stress is often more common than taking time to relax. If you commit to making a little time to unwind, your body will repay you by feeling better and your mind will be recharged and energized. You can relax by making your way to some peaceful river or lake or seashore where you can listen to the rhythmic waves of Mother Nature, or listen to the wind blowing through the trees, or experience inner calmness by playing your favorite soul-soothing music.

When thinking about what music is best for creating a relaxing mood, look for inspirational music with unique tones that reminds you to step out of your norm and tune inward to uncharted depths of your being. Search for music that communicates healing melodies and helps you feel happy.

Breath Control or Pranayama

Purpose: Improving your connection with your fifth chakra.

Swami Satyananda Saraswati claims that when we mediate on this chakra we can develop our psychic hearing.[12]

To connect more deeply with this chakra, sit straight, align your spine, and relax. Close your eyes and breathe slowly and deeply. Bring your awareness to the air passing through your throat at the front of the neck.

While keeping your focus on your invisible breath, let it make a gentle sound like a musical note. It can be the natural sound of your breathing (*soham*), or the cosmic sound of OM/AUM, or the seed sound of this chakra, HANG. Extend and exaggerate the sound of *mmmm* or *nnngggg* and feel this tone vibrating over your vocal cords along with your breath. You may feel it going downward and vibrating into your heart chakra or going upward past your ears toward your sixth chakra.

Inwardly watch the air entering and exiting your throat passage and notice the scope of the feeling tone your breath is making. Continue this practice for at least twelve breaths or until your mind tells you that it is time to stop.

Concentration

Purpose: Enhancing effective hearing and speaking.

Move your body into a meditative position and take some relaxing breaths to quiet your mind.

Then inwardly sense the area of your body associated with the fifth chakra and think about how that feeling is connected with the inner spirit of your communicative nature.

Next, with eyes closed, look inward and try to see your thoughts in pictures as if you were watching a video on a large screen. If you can't see imagery on your mental screen, let silent words in your mind create your visions. Notice the feelings and the inclinations toward action that your mind-movie evokes.

Now, from your inward journey vantage point, contemplate the form your communicative qualities take when you relate to others. Can you see thoughts that determine your attitude? Or can you feel an underlying attitude that gives rise to your thoughts? In either case, what do the thoughts or the attitude feel like?

Notice any positive or negative associations you have in this present moment. Now release any negative associations that you might have by envisioning your inner spirit opening a door to let them fall out of your body and mind through the power of your exhalations. If any don't want to leave and insist on continuing to sit in your mind and emotions, notice that. Then mentally move them to one side and open the rest of your mind-body-sensations-actions self to the next step below.

Then free-associate and link your thoughts with the words *self-mastery, letting go, love, hope,* and *wisdom.* Use these words in a way that allows you to see possible choices you can make about your communication skills that will instantly allow you to feel better?

Finally, check back with your jaws, hands, stomach, and sphincter again to see if there is any more unnecessary physical tension you can let go of. Or notice any residual tension that your body is using to tell you something you need to hear. Then visualize the area around your throat and ears having an expanding light, which brightens, healing and enlightening your comments, thoughts, and feelings.

Polarity-Balancing Meditation

Purpose: Achieving inner balance.

As with previous chakras, select a polarity from the Fifth-Chakra Possibilities table. If you are so inclined you can follow the Polarity-Balancing Meditation instructions in chapter 3. If you follow them daily or almost daily for an extended length of time the results can be impressive.

You might even find that when working with this chakra, meditation may seem to be only the beginning of your inner process. Although meditative states are valued as important for having a direct experience of fifth-chakra energy, not all meditation involves looking within. Sometimes we need to quiet our mind and look and listen outside ourselves.

One example is Veronica, who had moved frequently as a child, and had too much experience always being the new kid in town, and a target for the put-downs of bullies of both sexes on the playground and in the hallway. As a result she had developed a habit of an avoidance of and escape from harsh communications. So she frequently missed opportunities to voice her opinions. In college she decided to work on overcoming her attachment to the negative end of the polarities, included holding back what she wanted to say and talking with a weak voice. In her meditation she was able to witness her attitude and behavior that stopped her from taking a more active or even assertive role in conversations, as appropriate.

Then one evening at a gathering of about a dozen students around a long table in a local cafe, an older student at the other end of the table made a belittling and insulting remark to her for all to hear. She was burning inside but did not respond. Some twenty minutes later, he made another similar comment. That was too much. She replied in an equally sharp and cutting voice, "You're pretty damned hostile tonight, aren't you?" Instantly everyone at the table fell silent. No one said a word. The bully, unmasked, looked away. Very slowly conversation at the table resumed. The bully never spoke to Veronica again, which was fine with her. The incident was a turning point. She began a process of learning to confront people when necessary, often responding to someone who made a negative remark *by identifying what they were doing*—and no longer taking the blame or feeling too weak to stand up for herself in relation to mean-spirited comments.

Her meditation practice, combined with a willingness to dialogue, transformed her sense of powerlessness into fifth-chakra strength and sway. Effective speaking and hearing became friendly companions in helping her resolve conflicts effectively.

Perhaps as you meditate on your fifth chakra, you will realize that you want to make some kind of change in the way you communicate. If you do discover some alteration you wish to make, you have to actually *do* it, whether it be asserting the power of your words with more confidence, caring, or grace, falling silent, or letting others have the communication spotlight.

Affirming Your Ability to Listen on Deeper Levels

Purpose: Learning to hear feeling tones.

To enhance your ability to hear the nuances of feelings and messages in other people's voices, you might try the following.

As you go through a day, each time someone talks to you, imagine music playing in the background. What kind of music goes with their voice? Is it a mournful teardrops-in-my-whiskey-glass country song, or measured chamber music? Is there emotional or mental stress in a message that reminds you of a romantic dance, heavy metal, or rapid rap? Listen with awareness to specific voice qualities that suggest the kind of music you seem to hear.

After doing this for an extended time, let your mind relax. What did you learn by listening in that way? Notice your ability to hear people on deeper levels improving as you become sensitive to listening with your inner ear as well as your outer attention.

Sound Healing

 Inner Listening

The shabd yoga path taught by the Sikh Great Masters is useful in helping us become more aware of our fifth chakra. Most of the time people listen to sounds that exist in the outer world. In this method however, we listen to the sounds that are occurring within our inner self.

Find a very quiet place. Some people use earplugs to soften external sounds. If every place else in your house is noisy, you might find a friendly environment for this practice in a clothes closet. The clothing as well as the door will help block out sound.

Once you've found your quiet place, assume a comfortable sitting posture and go through the Starting Sequence of breaths in which you pay attention to your physical balance, breathing, and releasing unneeded body tension. Then as you continue to notice your breathing, turn your attention inward and listen.

Within your own body, not produced by anything outside, you will probably hear a sound. Listen carefully. Is the sound high-pitched or low-pitched? What are its qualities? As you continue to sit, it will probably fade into and out of the background.

Keep listening until you notice a different sound, with a different tone and quality. Continue to listen and you may discover several different sounds in your own inner symphony, produced by processes occurring within your body. As you notice them, some sounds may be high-pitched, some may be low, and some will be subtler than others.

As you do this meditation, take note of any images or thoughts that bubble up into your mind and note them down if there is something you need to remember. After you feel finished and begin to listen to the outer world again, you may find that the quality of your listening, your speech, or both is different than it was before.[13]

Fifth or
Vishuddha
Chakra

Altering Consciousness through Sound

Earlier chapters have already mentioned repeatedly chanting a mantra, an ancient technique that you can use to sharpen fifth chakra sensitivity. The following words, considered to have transcendent power, can help you calm and focus your mind.

FIFTH-CHAKRA MANTRAS

MANTRA	PRONUNCIATION	MEANING
satya	SAHTyah	truth, reality, that which actually exists
sumati	sooMAHtee	kindness, benevolence, good disposition
saprathas	sahPRAthahs	sounding or shining far and wide
zara	ZHYAAHrah	essence, real meaning, main point

Taking Action

Purpose: Effective communication.

The next time you are in a conversation, when appropriate, take time to listen to the quality and character of your voice as you respond to others.

> As you hear yourself speak, use a nonjudgmental inner focus to notice what music seems to go with the tones of the sounds your voice makes.
>
> Or if your mind prefers to look with the power of images, does your voice offer the other flowers or thorns? What do you feel in your tone: harmony or conflict, attraction or repulsion, duality or unity?

This simple practice can help you realize fifth-chakra potentials at both everyday and spiritual levels. Taking this practice to another level, you can ask, "is it necessary to talk, or will silence offer more in this situation?"

Anandamayi Ma encourages us not only to listen to what we say, but also to question whether we need to talk so much: "So long as speech has to be employed, use your words sparingly. . . . What is the hidden motive behind talkativeness? Is it not to display superiority or erudition or else to defeat someone by argument? The force of action is much greater than mere words. Superficial conversation and discussion will not take you far."[14]

While studying the fifth chakra, our focus has been on inner and outward communications, our worldly self and our higher Self. Now, as we become aware of the nondual nature of the essence of existence, there is more work we must do to climb the ladder of chakras and view the promise of the sixth. Do you dare?

 **9**

Sixth or Ajna Chakra

The Third Eye

In the sixth chakra you transcend normal abilities and can see into others, life situations, and yourself.

In the Ajna Chakra [there is] a balance between the solar and lunar energy within the body. . . . The yogi [embodies] all of the elements in their purest form. . . . The person . . . reveals the divine within and reflects divinity within others.

HARISH JOHARI,
CHAKRAS, ENERGY CENTERS OF TRANSFORMATION

Sixth or Ajna Chakra Correspondences

Key phrases: Intuition, meditative and self-awareness, mental and emotional clarity, truth; combines knowing, acting, and feeling; balances and integrates "masculine" and "feminine" qualities

Physical location: The point between the eyebrows, center of forehead

Endocrine gland: Pituitary or pineal (light-sensitive; regulates sleeping and waking)

Astrological link: Saturn

Day of the week: Saturday

Element: mahat, the essence of all other elements

Sense: Intuition

Sanskrit Derivation: ajna (order, command)

Massage: Forehead, ears, sides of head between eyes and ears

Leela Game of Self-Knowledge: Sixth row: Conscience, Plane of Neutrality, Solar Plane, Lunar Plane, Plane of Austerity, Earth, Plane of Violence, Liquid Plane, Spiritual Devotion

THE ESSENCE OF THE SIXTH CHAKRA: CLARITY, TRUTH, AND UNITY

Often referred to as the abode of the "third eye," the sixth chakra is where intuition and transcendent consciousness take priority over ordinary logic. When this center is open, you can see clearly into another's heart and soul—or into your own—with a knowingness that transcends the need to speak of truth or wisdom. It also helps you sense the vibrational currents and underlying substratum of situational forces. When this capacity is stimulated, you have the ability to see how past directions influence present choices and the future potentials toward which they are pointing. Reasoning, wit, spontaneity, and mental flexibility all become highly developed at this superconscious level where you can distinguish between what realities seem to be and what they truly are.

Right livelihood and truth steer the soul's rudder of a person living from the evolved awareness of the sixth chakra. For those who walk this path, universal messages of higher truths are the lens through which they view life and clarify their perceptions. Part of this state of conscious awakening is being able to discern what is beneficial and helpful to humanity and other beings and what is harmful—to whom or what, when, and in what specific ways. Using this awareness constructively is the gem of right livelihood that is often viewed as a major component of a spiritual path.

Also, the sixth chakra is often called the dwelling place of the meditative faculty. It embodies the mantra *hamsa*, which is Sanskrit for "swan," a revered bird that is said to be able to distinguish truth from untruth as it flies to places that ordinary people cannot reach. Just as no one can see electricity or microwaves, or just as a dog or deer can hear many sounds that no human ear can hear, the subtle internal hum of this mantra goes unheard by the many who live mostly in their lower chakras. But a master of this energy center who practices right livelihood can go beyond the limits of logical thought. By meditating on the sixth chakra and opening the mind to the universal qualities of the web of life that links all beings, a person stands on the threshold of the portal of divine oneness where he or she can become a *paramahamsa*—one who dwells in supreme consciousness.

For most people, development of sixth-chakra capacities typically occurs along a continuum of growth. Such development takes different forms depending on each person's chosen path. A few people are naturally disposed to the development of sixth-chakra powers, but most of us have to practice meditative techniques to free the mind from worldly tethers and work earnestly to awaken our dormant potential to experience the gift of using more than our five senses.

SIXTH-CHAKRA POSSIBILITIES

OPPORTUNITIES	OBSTACLES
Uses intuition, third eye opens	Resists intuition, rigidly rational
Feels oneness with others	Views others as completely different
Hears others	Hears others through own concerns
Perceives totality of life	Distracted by details
Sees, hears, and senses own inner truths	Has rigid internal walls, self-deceiving
Alert and aware	Dreamy, not quite here
Hears messages from own body	Ignores messages from own body
Taps into deep inner wisdom	Engages in sloppy thinking, foolish action
Uses insights about others for their benefit	Uses insights about others for personal gain
Deep or meaningful communications	Surface or trivial communications
Detached from pride associated with ego	Ego-attachment to powers (*siddhis*)
Evolving consciousness	Descending consciousness, conceited

It is said that Ajna Chakra qualities may also include the development of *siddhis* (powers) such as clairvoyance (the ability to see what is happening somewhere else), the ability to leave your body while remaining conscious and then return (astral travel), and the power to communicate with the departed who are on the other side. While such aspects of sixth-chakra consciousness can seem beyond normal life, and may be or not be attractive to you, what is important is to harness the energy of this higher center. With consistent effort you can learn to use it to experience states of consciousness in which you enhance your ability to awaken direct perception of the sacred or act in ways that are helpful and healing to you and to others.

THE MENTAL PATHWAY FOR
WORKING WITH THE SIXTH CHAKRA

The Bright Side of the Sixth Chakra

Gifts and Strengths: Penetrating intuition; finds beauty in each moment; senses the infinite and responds with a vibrational sense of boundaries between self and other.

Ajna Chakra consciousness can perceive and effectively use first- through fifth-chakra energies and sharpen awareness of vibrational energy. It asks, "How can I make better use of energy from a certain chakra?" Known as the commander, it can fine-tune energy from the other chakras: if energy from one chakra is so strong that it overpowers energy from another, the sixth chakra can provide balance between them. In that way it is like an airport control tower that keeps the other chakras working in harmony with one another.

Sometimes an open Ajna Chakra can empower a person to look directly into another's reality, using clairsentience or clairvoyance, inner voices, and dreams. Although this ability is rare, weak, or absent in most of us, through practice we may be able to strengthen it.

Your third eye can give you a bountiful harvest of gifts, including the ability to see through deception or see or hear in your mind's eye an image of an event that includes details that have not been mentioned. Or you might just have a nagging sense that something more important lies below the surface of what someone says, and tease it out verbally. Since this chakra makes it possible to perceive people and experiences directly, without an intervening curtain of illusions and delusions, it helps avoid problems that result from mistaken perceptions. You might hear concerns that someone is trying to conceal from you, or even that they themselves are unaware of. They may have just a vague sense of internal events that they have not learned to describe, such as certain kinds of painful feelings or physiological or muscular responses.

When functioning at a sixth-chakra level, people tend to be imaginative and creative. Living at the Ajna Chakra level makes it easy to find beauty and wonder in each moment, and personal meanings in cosmic knowledge.

In this state "one does not *know* Truth, but *becomes* truth" writes Kedernath Swami, a disciple of the twentieth-century saint Sri Anandamayi Ma. "It is an experience 'in silence' of Being. . . . In philosophy the death of the ego is the life of the soul. In psychology the falling of the 'persona' (mask) is the revelation of the real person. In both, the pseudo-self must disappear for the real Self to appear."[1]

At points of awakening in the first through the fifth chakras, you can shrink your self-centered ego so that it takes up less of your mind and feelings and exerts less power over your actions. This transformation begins in earnest in the fourth chakra. But only in the sixth and seventh chakras can you fully transcend egocentrism. Not always; not everywhere; no guarantees—but at least sometimes. Others can often feel the energy field of someone in whom this has taken place, and offer their respect without a word being spoken. Communication tends to become easier and more to the point.

Here R. Sanjiva Rao tells of such a silent transmission and reception of energies:

A conflict of a particularly difficult nature arose in my mind. . . . No amount of wrestling with it or attempts to quiet the mind in order to dissolve it was of any avail. . . . I asked for an interview with [Anandamayi] Ma. . . . I could only tell Ma that I had a problem. I was not in the position to explain [it]. So I sat quietly in front of her. She spoke no word. . . . Within a couple of minutes, the mind was in a state of deep stillness and the problem was effortlessly dissolved; I was in a state of an ineffable peace.[2]

She "was so untainted by prejudice, so present to all," adds Richard Lannoy in his collection of her talks, "that each felt that she met their innermost needs with unerring precision. . . . [She had a remarkable] capacity to provide totally opposite advice or instruction at the right time with extreme precision."[3]

As you develop an ability to open your third eye, whether you label it intuition, psychic awareness, or something else, you usually become better able to see and hear another's inner truths.

The Dark Side of the Sixth Chakra

Issues and Challenges: Clinging to mental wandering and daydreaming; attachment to "powers"; imagining and telling others that one is more enlightened than one really is.

The negative side of the Ajna Chakra can take the form of either deficiency or overexpression of its qualities. Deficiency includes being insensitive to others, blocking our awareness of their feelings and inclinations. "In most people this inner eye remains closed," says Swami Satyananda Saraswati, "and though they see the events of the outside world, knowledge and understanding of truth cannot be gained. In this sense, we are blind to the real possibilities of the world, unable to view the deeper levels of human existence."[4]

It is easy to fall into misinterpretation or projection. Your biases, preferences, and prejudices (we all have some) may cause your intuition to be wrong, or cause you to draw mistaken conclusions about others' meanings and motives. Sri Aurobindo Ghose reminds us that "I am . . . inwardly real to myself but the invisible life of others has only an indirect reality to me except in so far as it impinges on my own mind, life and senses."[5]

To counter these tendencies, consider this: When you think you perceive something, check it out. You can tell others what you think you're seeing, hearing, or feeling in relation to them and ask whether your perceptions are right or not. If they say you're not, accept their statement, at least on the surface. *Nothing useful will be gained by insisting that you are right and they are wrong.* At the least, if someone says you're wrong but you're fairly sure you're right, hold it in your mind as a guess, a hypothesis. It might prove useful or even vital. However, it might not, or it might be useless or cause you to act badly.

Challenges of the sixth chakra include the development of siddhis or supernatural powers and the danger of getting lost in egotism when using them. This is common among aspiring gurus and can be a major obstacle on the path of psychospiritual development and soul liberation. The greatest saints and gurus have said that such powers, dazzling as they may be, are digressions or blocks on the spiritual path.

It would be convenient if the problem of egotism were blown away by the winds of aspiring efforts to penetrate the veil of maya and were absent in someone trying to become self-actualized. The reality is, no such luck. The Sanskrit word *sankalpa* means something like "will, intention, resolve, directed energy." Willpower or sankalpa can help you move in either a helpful or harmful direction. The intention to realize the positive qualities of a given chakra, desires, ambitions, the wish for fame or fortune, the certainty that you know what is best—each of these can be a sankalpa. Someone with the sankalpa to realize sixth-chakra qualities can nonetheless get caught up in egocentrism: "Look at me. See how spiritual I am." The ego game goes on, and suddenly you've slipped back down to your lower chakras.

The sankalpa of certainty that our political or religious path is the right one, along with the aspiration to make everyone else agree with us, is the greatest danger of the sixth chakra—especially, notes Johari, for dictators or the founders or high officials of religions who are so sure their ideology is right that they are willing to torture or kill anyone who stands in the way of expansion of their power. History offers many examples. "In sixth chakra," writes Johari, "establishment of a creed, cult or religion inevitably provides the motivation for excessive force.... The [person] believes he has all the Truth—that he is, in effect, God or his agent. Those who fail to agree are wrong. Therefore any means is justifiable to convert them to one's own truth."[6] This is one of the major causes of wars and brutality in the world. Charismatic figures go about earnestly spreading useless or even toxic values that promise instant entry into what they conceive of as higher consciousness without doing the work in the lower chakras needed to actually get there. The result is that such dangerous leaders become lost in a haze of delusions, self-righteousness, and rigid finite thinking of the logical mind. Typically they are clueless as to their true motives.

Past Roots of Sixth-Chakra Problems

Everyone has at least a little intuitive capacity—even those who seem locked into their intellectual consciousness. Failing to use our intuition is dumbing ourselves down by shutting off a source of information that our mind-body organism may be able to receive and perceive.

Children and young adults are often actively discouraged from developing their intuition. "Think logically," they are often told. "Don't be a daydreamer." Also, children who have imaginary friends are often discouraged. People who want to use the right hemisphere of the brain (imaginative and creative) are often persuaded to overemphasize use of the left side of their brain (logical and solution-oriented) and neglect the right side. Some are advised not to develop their artistic abilities because they need to make a good living and money will be scarce if they're not logical about career choices. When they say they have intuitive experiences, others may suggest that they're crazy.

Johari explains the difference between fantasy and intuition. He claims that you can use intuition after you have studied a subject thoroughly, just as an astrologer can use all his knowledge intuitively. Without study, sometimes it is intuition and sometimes it is fantasy.

For example, Sylvia, a graphic artist, had all kinds of intuitive experiences in her business but she didn't get validation for them. When she talked about them, others sent her explicit or implicit messages that it was not okay. As a result, she put them out of her mind. Now, however, even business magazines are running articles suggesting that the leading edge of managerial thinking includes intuitive development.

THE BODY AND EMOTIONS PATHWAY: FEELING TONES IN THE SIXTH CHAKRA

Personal Transformation in the Sixth Chakra

Awakening the Ajna Chakra opens unexpected realms of possibility and beauty. We discover that we are more than we knew, or even more than we ever imagined we could be. We see our experiences from fresh vistas and find ourselves in an improved state of consciousness in which we can clearly perceive how we are affecting and being affected by the people, places, and patterns around us. This is an inner rather than an outer transformation. (An observer watching us might notice no difference.) Instead of being stuck in a quagmire of words and worries, we have an opportunity to bring more grace and joy into our lives.

In the dance of duality ever present in our daily lives, there is always a chance of getting lost in a maze of potential obstacles to attaining peace of mind. Keeping our psyche focused on the sunny side of the Ajna Chakra path is easier when we can fully embrace an inwardly balanced expression of witness consciousness. "Ajna is the witnessing center where one becomes the detached observer of all events, including those within the body and the mind," writes Swami Sivananda Saraswati. "When Ajna is awakened, the meaning and significance of symbols flashes into one's conscious perception, and intuitive knowledge arises effortlessly and one becomes a seer."[7]

"Witness consciousness implies watching without being affected, without making any judgment," adds Swami Muktananda. "Say, for example, there are two people quarreling and one person is watching. The one watching, who does not get involved, is the witness. Similarly, the indwelling Witness is the One who observes all the activities of the waking state without getting involved in them."[8] Some teachers compare witness consciousness to watching a movie. You sit in the theater and are completely focused on what is happening on the screen in front of you, but do not act in the movie. It's a nice ideal, but it too can occur on a polarity scale from little to much. (Check out the tension in your toes during a scary scene. If they're curling or twitching, you're still in the realm of desires and emotions.) In total witness consciousness, self is untouched, just watching. Short of that, you can notice your toes curling.

Gurumayi Chidvilasananda suggests,

As you watch another person, give your blessings. . . . Extend your support, your help. . . . Be the Witness. . . . In order to do that, keep your heart in the Witness state as well. . . . If you practice this discipline in seeing, it will purify the way you see the world. . . . When you look at people in this new way, you will act and speak to them differently. . . . From this inwardly balanced state, you will be like a divining rod that intuitively knows how to . . . touch both the minds and hearts, and most likely, your own heart will be happy.[9]

Also, the Ajna Chakra can bring a harmonious integration (yoga, or union) of masculine and feminine qualities within your inner self. You begin to have available almost all the capacities and sensitivities of both genders while feeling totally free to be true to yourself. This includes union between your gentler, nurturing side and your more forceful, assertive side. It embraces union between logic and intuition, and union among the qualities of all the chakras, as you draw on the kind of energy that fits your present situation.

Intuition, one avenue of sixth-chakra perception, requires openness and trust (which paradoxically includes trust for signals and information that tell you when not to trust). It is basically a right-brain mode of responding, more akin to meditation and creative illumination than to the left-brain mode of reasoning and calculating. Balancing the energy of both hemispheres helps you get more in touch with your higher Self. Sixth-chakra reality is part of a mystic realm that is logically understood only in glimpses by those of us who are more worldly by nature—that is, most of us—since it functions beyond the realm of the five senses.

Sri Aurobindo notes that:

> The illumined Mind does not work primarily by thought, but by vision; thought is here only a subordinate movement expressive of sight.... Our first decisive step out of our ... normal mentality is an ascent into a ... mind no longer of mingled light and obscurity or half-light, but a large clarity of the spirit.... It ... is a unitarian sense of being ... capable of the formation of a multitude of aspects of knowledge, ways of action, forms and significances of becoming.[10]

Such depth of insight can guide us to act in ways that honor our own inner spirit, to benefit others and all living beings, and to cherish the living spirit of others as one with our own. Our mind becomes a private temple with a simple, firm foundation and living scenes of remarkable beauty, wonder, and unfathomable mystery.

Relational Transformation in the Sixth Chakra

In the Ajna Chakra you go beyond names and forms, seeing through the name to reality itself. Rather than applauding or cringing at a name or label, you might grant it little importance, or even none. You don't go for the outside form or name; you see the inside spirit. You see the person behind the clothes, the job, the car, the house.

In the fifth chakra, you learned to clearly distinguish between words and concepts on one hand, and the underlying realities they represent on the other. Here you take another step. You fully discern that what is, is. That which exists, exists. You perceive realities that no one has named, as they are beyond words. At times you might identify with what you perceive, as if you and it are one and the same. As you do, you may even sense the essence of your identity being one with other persons and living beings. "To get into the universal Self—one in all—is to be liberated from ego," says Aurobindo. "Ego either becomes a small instrumental circumstance in the consciousness or even disappears from our consciousness altogether."[11] When your third eye is open, you can look outward at the world at the same moment you are looking inward at yourself and perceive a higher consciousness in yourself, others, and other living beings.

THE PATHWAY OF SPIRIT: IMAGERY IN THE SIXTH CHAKRA

The Square, the Lotus Petals, and Seed Sound

A luminescent white circle shown in the center is the basic form of this chakra. The circle is an expansion of the point, an individual unit in cosmic consciousness. The circle represents infinity.

The element here is called *mahat* or *mahatattva,* which can be translated as "the supreme element that embraces all other elements." It is said by some that creation all starts in cosmic consciousness or with pure thought. This is still unmanifest. To become manifest we need an individual independent perceiver. The point (*bindu*) represents this moment and is considered as the origin of all forms of manifest existence. It is also called universal intellect (*buddhi tattva*). With the point or the self (microcosmos) comes the principle of individuality. In the sixth chakra we have to untie the last knot, the knot of individuality or Rudra Granthi. (Guidance in untying the knots is given in chapter 11).

Figure 9.1. This drawing depicts the deities—Ardhanarishvara and Hakini Devi—and core imagery shown in the painting of this chakra (plate 9: Sixth or Ajna Chakra).

The two lotus petals represent the male and the female, the sun and the moon. According to yoga they work in our body as the two spiritual nerves, Pingala and Ida. These nerves or nadis are physically present in our nose, where they end (Pingala in the right nostril; Ida in the left). When we watch our nostrils we can notice that most of the time only one is working or is dominant. The one that is working brings air up, which cools the brain on that side. This makes the other side warmer and more active. So if the right nostril (male) is dominant, the right hemisphere of the brain will be cooled and the left hemisphere will be active, and vice versa.

If both nostrils are open, the Sushumna (the invisible spiritual nerve with no direct physical location) will activate, which is the path to awakening. This happens automatically at the moments of sunrise and sunset, which are widely recommended as the best moments for meditation.

In the image of the sixth chakra we also see the last lingam, called Itara Lingam. It belongs to Itara Shiva, who keeps the desires coming from the lower chakras under control.

With the help of the knowledge acquired in the fifth chakra, we now hear inner sounds and our own voice of inner wisdom. This is called conscience (*vivek*) and can be seen as the third eye. All that humanity has learned through the ages in different cultures is in us in the form of the collective unconscious (although we may choose to block out our awareness of some of it). In yoga this is seen as the teacher or guru sitting on our head (the seventh chakra). We can avoid the material world with all its political and social games, but we cannot stop the inner voice. In the sixth we hear this inner voice as our teacher talking. It is a great moment to meet a teacher physically. But it is even more so when we realize that the teacher is within, always present.

The seed sound of this chakra is AUM. We have seen it appear many times in the lower chakras. We accepted AUM as the sound of sounds. Now we start recognizing it as the presence of the Divine. To have a real experience of this we have to surrender to austerity or hard work on our self (tapas). Like a yogi we have to sit for a long time in our cave, which is within us. To do yoga we have to be able to be alone. Then we can hear the mantra AUM in everything.

A Short Visualization

1. Visualize the luminescent white circle.
2. Then add then two lotus petals, while silently producing their seed sounds: HANG and KSHANG.
3. Then add the lingam (shown as the arch that surrounds the Shiva/Shakti figure Ardhanarishvara).
4. In the middle place the symbol for the seed sound of this chakra: AUM.

Ardhanarishvara

The half-male, half-female Shiva-Shakti depicted at the center is the deity of this chakra, considered by many as one of the most beautiful forms of the Divine. Shiva occupies the left side of the figure and Shakti the right side.

When we look at our bodies, declares Johari, we see three basic types of energy: electric, magnetic, and neutral. Electric energy is sun energy and related to the male. Magnetic energy is moon energy and related to the female. Male and female have been meeting each other throughout the lower chakras. However, they were not balanced, as the masculine energy had problems accepting its opposite nature. But like the sun when it shines too much, when the masculine electrical energy is unbalanced, it will burn and destroy. Although it is a source of many creative actions, it alone is not conducive to meditation. For that we need the magnetic female energy.

When the sun and moon are balanced in our bodies, the neutral or psychic energy can flow through the Sushumna. In the sixth chakra negative and positive fade or disappear and only neutrality remains. And we are able to maintain this state for longer times.

Now we become a witness of the game of life. Just closing the two eyes may make the third eye open. Its nature is fire, in which we can burn the source of harmful desires. For this we have to sit and practice concentration until we find peace in the silence. It is said that then only the desire to be one remains. The mantra *soham,* "I am that," becomes reality. Here it becomes *hamsa,* the mythological swan that can separate milk from water, the real from the unreal. Truth becomes very simple.

Shiva holds in one of his hands the trident representing cognition, volition, and affection. It tells us that the Divine is omnipresent, omnipotent, and omniscient. The other hand tells us to be without fear.

Shakti holds a lotus flower symbolizing purity, beauty, and knowledge. Although the lotus, one of the most beautiful flowers, comes out of the mud, it is untouched by dirt. In her other hand Shakti holds the *ankush* (staff) to control the elephant of unhelpful desires coming from the lower chakras.

Now that we have more understanding of our female side, we are able to see Earth as Mother Earth. We experience her as a living organism, giving life to all that exists on and in her. Before we only saw her physical part, which we exploit as we pleased. Although we treat her badly, she keeps on giving gold, diamonds, and all the materials to create our modern world. Now we start seeing her spirit, her intelligence, and her love. Realizing this, we can discover new patterns, new ways of play. Freed from obscuring involvements with the lower chakras we can experience Earth in all its purity and beauty and it becomes a divine playground.

Hakini Devi

Hakini is the one who opens the way into the sixth chakra. She gives us what is needed for being and staying there. In each chakra Kundalini Shakti gets one more head. Now she has six and they represent the possible achievements here: enlightenment, thought control, undivided attention, perfect concentration, unobstructed meditation, and superconscious concentration.

Hakini's six heads remind us to continue to work on our ability to concentrate. When we are one-pointed, problems can be seen in their real proportions. We can come up with solutions that have a vision behind them. There are many ways to work on our concentration. One way is visualization of the chakras, starting with the first and gradually going to the seventh, where we can experience the peaceful silence of the Divine.

Whether you are doing a short or long visualization, usually it's best to do the one that fits the chakra and personal quality you are working on. If that means one meditation session, or a few, so be it. Or if you've decided to take a month or a year to focus on a given chakra, you may find it useful to draw and visualize the figures in that chakra for that time. Do what feels worthwhile for you. If you feel bored or distracted, *stop* until you're ready to focus on the drawing or painting (or one of its elements) again.

Keeping the mind focused on a mantra, yantra (an image), or just a point can be used everywhere. Whenever we have to wait, we can practice this. Fine arts also demand high concentration. Painting a yantra is spiritually one of the best exercises to focus both hemispheres on one subject. When we talk about meditation, we usually mean this deep concentration, where we practice fixing and holding the mind. Thoughts are still there, so it is not yet a total meditation that is uninterrupted and undisturbed. But it can take us toward a meditative mood in which the mind becomes one-pointed and there are no thoughts. Coming back from this state we perceive new possibilities.

In one of her hands Hakini is holding a lotus flower, showing us the purity, beauty, and knowledge behind her energy. In another hand she holds the damaru or hand drum, which is producing AUM in its overtones. All the concentration exercises take us to a place very close to deep meditation, where we hear the refined sound of AUM all the time. In Hakini's third hand we see the skull representing detachment.

In the sixth chakra we perceive ultimate reality as the unity of all existence. In the lower chakras we were pushed and pulled by unending desires, which gave us the idea of being separated. To see the Divine, we have to be fluid, with an open mind and few or no value judgments. This is part of a formless essence in which we find total peace with ourselves.

In this chakra we find great yogis and also great demons or dictators. In the conviction that all is one, each reached the highest position in their own realm. Ego is still present, with the power to develop visions and convince others. These can be small or big, on a personal level, an organizational level, or a political or spiritual level.

To show the spiritual possibilities, in her last hand Hakini shows us the mala or rosary as a device for centering. It becomes a symbol for spiritual devotion (bhakti). This not a path for everyone. It demands surrender. Intellectual teachings are no longer sufficient. After the realization of unity in all comes the task of living this practically in daily life. When we experience this, everything seems equally important and we see the immense diversity in which this unity is expressing itself.

Now we understand that everything that happened in the lower chakras was needed to bring us here. We understand more about what love means. A loving mother is not always nice. Sometimes she has to set limits or consequences to correct our behavior. When we experience this always-present care in our lives, we become curious about what more life has to offer. Please, Mother, keep on correcting us! Then we can become the drop that is going to the ocean, knowing that the ocean is already inside us.

 Full Visualization

1. Visualize the circle with the lotus petals and produce their seed sounds. HANG and KSHANG.

2. Then we add the lingam, which looks something like a tall arch that covers the Shiva-Shakti figure of Ardhanarishvara.
3. After that visualize Hakini with her six heads and four arms.
4. Then comes Ardhanarishvara, the Shiva-Shakti deity of this chakra, with four arms.
5. End with AUM in the middle.

Reflections

Shiva and Shakti now work as one, becoming silent. We became one-pointed and focused on our final destination: cosmic consciousness. If we can experience all as filled with divine love, there are no more obstacles and there is nothing else to do other than to enjoy wherever the divine play takes us.

PRACTICAL TOOLS
FOR SIXTH-CHAKRA WORK

Relaxation

Purpose: Communication with atman.

Meditation with your spine straight has its own value of calming the mind, and is also an activating force for moving energy upward to invoke higher, deeper, and broader consciousness as you select and carry out your daily actions.

Take a few moments to reflect: What one choice can you make right now that will help you cut the tethering cord of intense attachments that stop positive sixth-chakra energies from opening? What practical step can you take to free your spirit to become more relaxed, awake, and aware in the moment?

One practice is to follow the advice of Sri Mata Amritanandamayi. For a period of time, perhaps an hour or two a day, consciously remember that you are not just your mind, emotions, and attitude. Relax your mind and tell yourself, "I am the atman (that within you which is you and who is also your connection with all beings)." During that time, let this outlook be reflected in how you see your self, your choices, and actions.

Breath Control or Pranayama

> **Purpose:** Letting your breath tell you about your body.

By now you will usually immediately sense when you are holding your breath, if you are not doing so intentionally as part of a practice. You will probably also sense, almost automatically, when your breath, your heartbeat, or both speed up.

If not, you can spend a few minutes of every meditation or even when you have a few spare minutes in your daily life focusing your witness consciousness on your breath and its natural rhythm and any other events you notice in relation to it that are occurring in your body. These messages can be useful in telling you what your total self does or doesn't want to do, even if your intellect hasn't quite figured it out.

Concentration

> **Purpose:** Continued enhancement of concentrative focus.

"You cannot truly meditate until you have developed your ability to concentrate," Johari said again and again. By *concentration* he meant the ability to focus your attention where you want it to be at any given moment, keep it there for as long as you wish, and move it somewhere else when you are ready to do so. This capacity is basic to your ability to work with all seven chakras.

Some people misunderstand concentration. They think it means consciously pushing something out of your mind. Ah, the impossible dream! You might give it a try: Right now, for the next sixty seconds, don't think about lizards.

How did you do? If you're like most people, you thought more about lizards in that minute than you had all day. Concentration is not achieved by pushing away, but rather by placing your mental focus where you choose. A thought about lizards may creep in. That's okay. Just notice it with a sliver of your mind and move your attention back to where you want it.

This ability to direct your mental focus is also valuable in conversations. Suppose you have an agenda, something you want to accomplish. Others in the conversation have their own interests, and time and again start talking about them. Since most people are easily distracted, the conversation may meander here and there. But you, with your mind that can maintain its focus, are able to notice and hear all that is happening and you can say something like, "Yes, that's fascinating. I want to hear all about it. But what we need to do right now is . . ." and you bring the focus of the discussion back to the primary agenda, where you want it to be.

Another way to develop concentration is through art, as described on page 65. When you are truly focused on your art, all attention is on the subject. There is no time consciousness. There is little ego. Drawing and painting can serve as concentration exercises, and perhaps most important, we learn to play. The same goes for music.

Polarity-Balancing Meditation

Purpose: Becoming whole.

Sixth-chakra polarity meditation is done in the same manner as the first- through fifth-chakra polarity meditations, with the difference that you choose a polarity from the Sixth-Chakra Possibilities table as your starting point and metaphoric "candle flame."

In Ajna Chakra meditation, said Johari, you provide a place within yourself for your consciousness to become whole. You allow diverse fragments of perception, awareness, and knowing to come into contact with and inform each other. Most people's minds usually function as if they are divided into compartments that contain thoughts and feelings that are kept secret from those in other compartments. As positive sixth-chakra consciousness develops, this compartmentalization and separation disappears.

When something uncomfortable comes into your awareness, you no longer distract yourself by jumping to another place in your mind, or push it into your unconscious, but turn it over mentally, inspecting, feeling, sensing, and intuiting first one side of it and then another. When you think you have integrated something into yourself and can notice or contemplate it at will, then you can turn your attention to whatever occurs next with an open and unbiased mind.

Affirming Integrity:
"I Live the Wisdom of Self-Mastery"

Purpose: Balancing the masculine and feminine sides of your self.

The sixth chakra is the meeting place where the masculine and feminine qualities of our being, or two hemispheres of the brain, become integrated, as symbolized by Ardhanarishvara. We can relax into accepting both those sides of ourselves, the left masculine (solar) side and the right feminine (lunar) side instead of feeling compelled to maintain a strictly masculine or feminine façade and attitude. Johari suggested that the masculine, or left, hemisphere processes information in a more complex and abstract manner, with a more diverse vocabulary. Conversely, our ability to distinguish between sounds and general perceptions lessens in this hemisphere. He argued that our right, or female, hemisphere more easily recognizes nonverbal communication, increases imagination, and evaluates the physical forms of shapes and objects. In this next exercise you can check out your own thoughts and feelings about such matters. Everyone can develop both these sides of himself or herself.

 For Females

Stand comfortably and well balanced, with your feet about shoulder width apart.

If you are a woman or girl, let all the feelings, attitudes, and qualities of femininity run through you as they usually do, permeating your being.

Then imagine that the back half of your body is that of a man or boy. Drawing on all your life experiences with the other gender, allow yourself to feel what it's like for those masculine energies to flow through you.

Imagine these energies moving forward in your mind and body and becoming dominant. Then with these masculine qualities available and accessible to you, imagine what you can say and do, how you can act and be, which you may find unbecoming for your usual womanly self.

Speak, shout, or sing out a few words or phrases from this "manly" side of yourself. If you like, walk around from your more masculine stance, not necessarily exaggerating it, but rather feeling relaxed and comfortable as you do.

After you've finished, ask yourself, "Are there any of these qualities that I'd like to make part of my usual way of being?"

For Males

Stand comfortably and well balanced, with your feet about shoulder width apart.

If you're a man or boy, do just the opposite. Face the world as usual, expressing your maleness in the ways that come naturally to you.

Then imagine that the back half of your body is that of a woman or girl. Give yourself permission to experience fully how those feminine energies feel as they flow through you and move to the front of your body.

Are there ways you can hold and move your body—and your mind and feelings—that are more comfortable now than as your usual masculine or even hypermasculine self?

Then contemplate what kind of integration of "feminine" qualities into yourself might make your life feel better to you.

In this way, both genders can relax into allowing qualities that are typically attributed just to the other to become part of themselves. This opens the potential to become a fuller, more capable, more sensitive person.

Sound Healing

> **Purpose:** Mental focus, feeling better, altering your state of mind and feeling.

Mantra Chanting

Chanting a mantra while doing japa can help fine-tune inner listening and connect you with your ability to hear inwardly. For example, you might repeat the seed sound of this chakra, AUM (OM), over and over for as long as you can maintain your focus. You can also try to hear this sound as an inward primal hum that reputedly contains the energy of the sun, moon, and fire. Or you can try the following exercise.

Select from the following list a word that works for you, either in Sanskrit or English.

Then repeat it in rhythm with your breathing during your meditation, or continually chant or write it in japa fashion throughout your day.

Keep that mantra as long as you wish, letting it become part of your consciousness.

SIXTH CHAKRA MANTRAS

MANTRA	PRONUNCIATION	MEANING
soham	so(rhymes with toe)-HAHM	that I am, I am that
hamsa	HAHMsaw	truth beyond that which others can see
vijnana	veezhNYAnah	consciousness or intelligence
OM (AUM)	ohhhm or ahh-uuu-mmm	primal sound of the sixth chakra (in either pronunciation the sound is drawn out at length, which may mean until you have exhaled completely

Taking Action

Purpose: Visualizing your best course of action.

Close your eyes and look inward. Bring your awareness to the center of your forehead above the bridge of your nose. Imagine that you are looking into a panoramic video screen.

Visualize a picture of yourself as you were in your past when you were doing something that you took pride in doing fairly well.

Once you have this picture of yourself clearly in your mind, imagine yourself in present time performing this exact same action. (If you don't think in images, paint these pictures in words). How do you see yourself acting now compared to the way you carried out this same action in your past? Do you look or feel any different?

Next, project a mental picture of yourself into the future. Imagine yourself repeating the same course of action with less concern about the results and what you and others will think of you. What possibilities, if any, do you imagine or want that differ from your past and present experiences?

To move from the Ajna Chakra into waking up the energy in the crown or seventh chakra, we dive into a pool of deep inner silence that ultimately flows into "the garden of the thousand-petaled lotus." Even if our path is farther from the portal of self-realization than we might like, we can listen to what the masters have taught about its essence and ponder our life choices in regard to moving our energy toward our higher or lower centers.

 # 10

SEVENTH OR SAHASRARA CHAKRA

The Crown Chakra or Thousand-Petaled Lotus

Crown-chakra consciousness transcends most everyday concerns, and brings a divine spirit into feeling, thought, and action.

The yogi is . . . beyond bondage and liberation . . . and ceases to be a slave of habit. . . . His [or her] being becomes more finely attuned to reality [and] becomes light, illuminated. . . . Seers and saints who experienced this space . . . became lenses of the lamp of pure knowledge, holding on to nothing, understanding everything. [One] who reaches here attains harmony, a balance with the forces of the cosmos.

HARISH JOHARI, *LEELA: THE GAME OF SELF-KNOWLEDGE*

Seventh or Sahasrara Chakra Correspondences

Key phrases: Joy, bliss, and unity consciousness as an everyday mind state; awakening to the inner Self; nonattachment, truth, and beauty; universal brother and sisterhood; identification with all beings; "the guru within"

Physical location: Cerebral plexus

Endocrine gland: Pineal

Astrological link: Ketu

Day of the week: Monday

Element: Beyond elements

Sanskrit Derivation: sahasrara (thousand-petaled)

Massage: Scalp, crown of head

Leela Game of Self-Knowledge: Seventh row: Egotism, Plane of Primal Vibrations, Gaseous Plane, Plane of Radiation, Plane of Reality, Positive Intellect, Negative Intellect, Happiness, Tamas

THE ESSENCE OF THE CROWN CHAKRA: ILLUMINATION

"Think of a time when, all of a sudden, you were happy," suggests Gurumayi. "You didn't do anything to make yourself happy, but you were happy." To know how to attain that state and to remain in it for longer periods, however, is a great challenge.[1]

We came along too late to meet another yogi and mystic, Sri Ramakrishna, one of India's most beloved saints, who lived from 1836 to 1886. Ramakrishna spent much of his adult life in a small room on the Dakshineswar temple grounds on the outskirts of Kolkata. Typically he sat almost naked in a loincloth, caring nothing for material goods. Recognized by all as a spiritually realized being, Ramakrishna opposed all dogmatism, oppression, and rigid belief that one spiritual path is better than others. "Harmony of religions is not uniformity; it is unity in diversity," writes his disciple Swami Adiswarananda. "It is not a fusion of religions, but a fellowship of religions based on their common goal."[2]

Ramakrishna's transcendent outlook was carried to the West by his disciple Swami Vivekananda, who first came into the public eye in his turban and robes at the 1893 Parliament of Religions in Chicago. He said, "Condemn none: if you can stretch out a helping hand, do so. If you cannot, fold your hands, bless your brothers, and let them go their own way." He added:

We are what our thoughts have made us, so take care about what you think. . . . When an idea exclusively occupies the mind, it is transformed into an actual physical or mental state." He summed up his own and Ramakrishna's view by saying that the only place we can truly find God is "in our own hearts and in every living being. . . . You have to grow from the inside out. None can make you spiritual. There is no teacher but your own soul.[3]

"In every living being?" you might wonder. "How can that be?" Sri Anandamayi Ma replies,

A man who hears the word 'Himalaya,' without having actually set eyes on the mighty range will be under the impression that it is but a single mountain, whereas once face to face with the Himalayas he will realize that they consist of hundreds upon hundreds of peaks, stretching over hundreds of miles, with millions of trees, animals, birds, insects, with streams and waterfalls. Similarly, the farther one penetrates or the deeper one penetrates on the path of sadhana, the more clearly *will be perceived the One in the many and the many in the One.*[4]

Amma offers this metaphor:

If the sun shines down into a thousand different pots filled with water, the reflections are many, but they are each reflecting the same sun. Similarly, if we come to know who we truly are, we will see ourselves in all people. When this understanding arises, we learn to consider others, overlooking their weaknesses. From that, pure love will dawn from within.[5]

One like Ramakrishna who lives in the seventh chakra has everything even if they have nothing. Often others take care of their needs and wants, although they may not want much. People are attracted to such masters, just as they wanted to be around Ramakrishna and in our own time want to be near Sri Mata Amritanandamayi. They want to be bathed in the vibrational field of their guru's angelic consciousness. As such rare beings move through the world with their caring, loving, deeply perceptive, big-hearted attitudes, profound events occur just because they are there. Those who live at the level of the seventh chakra may have some special talents or none. They don't worry about having powers, since consciousness is all they need. They don't feel better than others, since without ego attachment they can speak with anyone, listen to anyone, or hug anyone on a plane of equality with love in their heart.

"Isn't that all just a fairy tale?" you might wonder. "Are there truly such people?"

Think of the great prophets and saints. Think Jesus. Think Buddha, Mohammad, St. Francis, Teresa of Avila, Hildegard of Bingen, Confucius, and Lao Tzu. Think Bodhidharma and Padmasambhava, and Dogen Zenji. Think Rumi, Gandhi, Martin Luther King, Babaji, Meher Baba, Ramana Maharishi, Neem Karoli Baba, Aurobindo, Vivekananda, Yogananda, Anandamayi Ma, Adi Shankara, and in our own time Dalai Lama Tenzing Gyatso.

Few people have ever heard of most other seventh-chakra figures except for the few devotees who live with them and serve them. Such a person may be a benevolent pastor of a small-town church or an obscure ashram, a village shaman, an indigenous medicine teacher, or even someone who lives just down the street whom you've never heard of.

The Soma and Kameshvara Chakras

Two little known "sub-chakras" are said to be located *within* the seventh chakra: the Soma Chakra and the Kameshvara Chakra (both depicted together in plate 11: Soma and Kameshvara Chakras, as well as in figure 10.1 shown opposite).

 ### The Soma Chakra

The Soma Chakra is located just above the sixth chakra. The yantra form is a silver crescent surrounded by twelve lotus petals. On top of this is standing Kamadhenu, the wish-fulfilling cow.

Soma can be best understood as the "nectar from the moon," which seeps out of the space between the two hemispheres of the brain (*brahma randra*). This space is also called the cave of the bumble bee. Soma is said to be directly connected to semen and is considered to be the origin of all desires.

In a normal person this nectar will go down to the third chakra, where it is burned in the stomach. Yogis, however, are able to drink this nectar of

Figure 10.1. Two sub-chakras within the seventh chakra:
Soma and Kameshvara.

immortality before it reaches the throat. For that they practice a special technique of "swallowing the tongue" (*khechari mudra*). It is done in such a way that breath cannot reach the lungs and is suspended. When prana becomes still, mind becomes still. Both are kept in the void between the two hemispheres. This can only be practiced under guidance of an experienced teacher.

With the help of pranayama and especially the suspension of breath, we prepare ourselves to be and stay in this chakra. This can only occur after passing through the sixth chakra, where our I-consciousness has dissolved. Johari writes, "Soma is connected with the moon and makes the yogi very peaceful, self-contented, calm, and cool. Bliss is cool."[6]

Kameshvara and Kameshvari

In the second sub-chakra Kundalini Shakti finally joins her lord Shiva. Our individual consciousness is no longer a separated unit. Now it is fully united and absorbed in the supreme consciousness.

Kameshvara is source and lord of the desire principle (kama) and represents Shiva himself. In the beginning there was a desire to create, from which all came. This desire manifests itself as the seed of thoughts. Kameshvari is the goddess of desire, who wants to unite with Shiva, the source of desire. Through the central canal in the Sushumna (Brahma Nadi) she rushes up to meet him. Here she becomes Tripura Sundari, the most beautiful of all and ever young. In the first chakra she became individual consciousness and was sleeping. Through a great deal of spiritual practice and devotion, the goddess was awakened and rose upward until she reached above the Soma Chakra. Now she unites with Shiva and ushers in an altered state of consciousness called *turiya*.

The state of turiya is somewhat similar to deep sleep, but the person is neither conscious nor unconscious. There we experience samadhi, in which mind, ego, intellect, and sense perceptions are all dissolved. In this superconscious state we are able to "see" the Supreme Spirit. In turiya we experience ultimate detachment. We can now return to the world of desires, but our perspective has changed. Everything seems different. The One who desires is now one with the One who fulfills desires.

The basic yantra form (in which Kameshvara and Kameshvari are centered in the drawings), is a downward-pointing triangle in a circle surrounded by eight lotus petals. The triangle represents the three aspects of consciousness: knowing, feeling, and doing. Now we realize them as truth (*satyam*), beauty (*sundaram*), and goodness (*shivam*). This is how someone who has reached seventh-chakra consciousness perceives the world and shows it in behavior.

Transcendental Consciousness

These two mini chakras tell us that we have reached the seventh chakra. The mind is still. Whatever we express or do now is for the good of all. There is no more ego. Except, that is, for those moments when the adept stumbles and falls into an egocentric thought such as "Look how advanced my consciousness has become." Then, with a little luck, the wish-fulfilling cow appears. "Earth appears as a cow before Vishnu," writes Johari in *Leela,* "and asks him to relieve her of the burden of egotism." Vishnu replies that she need only realize that she can do it for herself.

Research has revealed at least two distinctly different forms of transcendent consciousness. In one, nirvikalpa samadhi, a person may let go of mental contact with the surrounding everyday world. In the other (found in highly accomplished Zen meditators) a person develops such an intense awareness of and responsiveness to both internal and external events that he or she does not habituate to recurrent stimuli such as a gong being struck again and again, but rather responds as if every recurring sound is something new that is occurring for the first time.

In the Hindu literature many different descriptions of samadhi can be found. All are variations of the first of the two kinds of states described above, and few of them are based on Western-style research. We did not scour the Zen literature for descriptions of the second form of transcendent consciousness, since this book is based on the literature of India. We suspect that there are diverse forms of samadhi, since the consciousness of no two individuals is exactly alike. There are, however, distinct brain-wave patterns that can be influenced by meditation and are found in many different people. These can be seen using biofeedback and neural imaging instruments.

Philosopher and psychologist William James wrote,

Our normal waking consciousness . . . is but one special kind of consciousness, whilst all about it, parted from it by the filmiest of screens, there lie potential forms of consciousness entirely different. We may go through life without suspecting their existence, but apply the requisite stimulus, and at a touch they are there in all their completeness.[7]

Philosopher Ken Wilber adds,

The most fascinating aspect of such awesome and illuminating experiences ... is that the individual comes to feel, beyond any shadow of a doubt, that he is fundamentally one with the entire universe, with all worlds, high or low, sacred or profane, his *sense of identity* expands far beyond the narrow confines of his mind and body and embraces the entire cosmos. For just this reason R. M. Bucke referred to this state as "cosmic consciousness."[8]

Those who attain states of transcendental consciousness seldom discuss their experiences, since the audience of those who can comprehend them is small. Sri Aurobindo offers these words:

[Such] spiritual consciousness is all light, peace, power, bliss. If one can live ... partly in it or keep himself constantly open to it, he [or she] receives enough of this spiritual light and strength and happiness to carry him securely through all the shocks of life. What one gains by opening to this spiritual consciousness depends on what one seeks from it; if it is peace, one gets peace; if it is light or knowledge, one lives in a great light and receives a knowledge deeper and truer than any the normal mind can acquire; if it is strength or power, he gets a spiritual strength for the inner life or Yogic power to govern the outer work and action; if it is happiness, he enters into a beatitude far greater than any joy or happiness that the ordinary human life can give.[9]

No accepted vocabulary exists for most of the states and phenomena that can be experienced within transcendental consciousness. It is a realm beyond words. And even if we had such words, they would be like the shadows on the wall of Plato's cave compared to the realities they would represent.

SEVENTH-CHAKRA POSSIBILITIES
Draws on universal life force
Finds beauty in everyone and everything
Feels one with all people and beings
Has purified mind and senses
Feels cradled and guided by divine spirit

Filled with transcendent awareness

Honors diverse life paths

Incisive vision into what is occurring

Awareness of nonduality

Needs the minimum required to survive

Can meditate anywhere anytime

Humble, notices and releases egotism

Does not fear death

THE MENTAL PATHWAY FOR WORKING WITH SEVENTH-CHAKRA ENERGIES

The Bright Side of the Seventh Chakra

Gifts and Strengths: Bliss consciousness; feeling connected with all beings; living as a divine child of the universe; great wisdom.

Seventh-chakra consciousness is more than an expansion, widening, and deepening of our mind. It is a transformation in the quality and character of our way of being. Someone who dwells in the seventh chakra feels deeply connected with all creation. This may be manifested as God, the universe, all people, or all beings, including trees, plants, and animals. The finite, limited self feels connected with the infinite, both within and outside all boundaries of time and space. Pain or pleasure, humiliation or honor, wealth or poverty—none matter in seventh-chakra consciousness.

Anyone who can truly live at the level of the Sahasrara Chakra is a spiritual master, regardless of their place and path in life. In India such rare people are venerated and may have thousands or millions of followers. In the West they may be regarded as kooks who just don't get what life is really about (that is, getting and spending and gaining wealth and power).

A seventh-chakra person may identify with all reality, from the Earth's beginnings to its end as the sun becomes a red giant and spreads outward to engulf our world billions of years from now. He or she may have a direct sense of our place as one planet in a galaxy of millions of stars and planets amid a universe of uncounted galaxies.

Seventh-chakra awareness brings a rare ability to respond to every situation well, rather than blowing our gaskets because it is not different than it is. In the seventh chakra there is no spiritual materialism, or political, business, religious, or scientific imperialism.

Such consciousness also brings a wondrous ability to discard the trappings of our individual personalities and egocentric attitudes, and truly survey a situation from multiple perspectives. It includes an ability to communicate without speech. A glance, a touch, or even a mental and emotional transmission can change the character of a situation just through the energy that radiates from the opened "thousand-petaled lotus" of the crown chakra.

Life at the seventh chakra is radically different from what most of us can logically understand. In the presence of such a master of the mind, most will feel that something is different. But not everyone. There is the ancient saying "When a pickpocket meets a saint, he sees only his pockets." But even that is not always so.

One day when Santosh Puri returned to his ashram, he came upon robbers who had been filling their pockets with cash and valuables. Police who had been alerted were taking them into custody. He sized up the situation and the robbers, and told the police, "Let them go. I owed them money and they were taking what I told them they could have to repay the debt." Actually he owed them nothing. It was a straightforward robbery, and they would have gone straight to jail. After the police left, the thieves threw themselves at Santosh Puri's feet, begged for his forgiveness, and became his disciples, working in whatever ways were needed. They were transformed by his kindness and saintly influence.

The "integral self-knowledge. . . [that occurs in the seventh chakra]," says Sri Aurobindo, is gained "by a patient transit beyond the mind into the Truth-Consciousness where the Infinite can be known, felt, seen, experienced in all the fullness of its unending riches."[10]

The Dark Side of the Seventh Chakra

Issues and Challenges: Thinking you're more enlightened than you actually are; forgetting others' needs in your own quest for illumination.

When you stand in sunlight at noon on a cloudless day, there is no darkness. Even your shadow is temporarily invisible. Similarly, being awake in the seventh chakra is something like standing in the zenith of your own inner light. However, even the seventh chakra has a dark side. A person who is trying to awaken their seventh chakra can get lost in their psyche's shadows while falsely thinking he has attained greater illumination than he really has. Unfailingly, the ego blocks such people from reaching mastery of the self and holds them prisoner in their wandering mind and wayward emotions. Pilot Baba says, "Come with me to live in a cave in the Himalayas for six months and you *may* be able to attain transcendent consciousness." Even that is no guarantee. No instruction manual can get you there.

People may talk about living in their seventh chakra, but until they experience it, it's like lip-synching rather than actually singing. Part of the problem is being unable to recognize or acknowledge what we don't know. The reality of the seventh chakra is unknowable except through direct experience. How can someone who has never seen or felt something know the true meaning of a word that refers to it?

"What is known comes under the field of knowledge, thus a limitation to him who is beyond knowledge," says Anandamayi Ma.[11] R. Sanjiva Rao, late principal of Queen's College in Benares, adds:

> Ma . . . contacts the world around her, the world of people and of things, without the mediation or interpretation of the mind. The mind . . . is . . . like an extraordinarily sensitive photographic plate, capable of recording without distortion or exaggeration the physical and psychic influences in the world around. . . . To anyone who has not had experience of the super-mental condition, the idea of silencing the mind being a condition precedent to the manifestation of a higher state of consciousness is completely unintelligible. But Ma's life demonstrates that [when this occurs] the Real, the Eternal comes into being.[12]

If this sounds complicated to you, imagine the analogy of coming up to a high wall that you can't climb or see through, and when you meet people who have been on the other side of it (of whom there are only a few), they have no words for what they experienced there. All you know is that they send out remarkably good vibes.

We did not include an "Obstacles" side in the Seventh-Chakra Possibilities table as we did for the other chakras. Nonetheless, there are a few. To get to the seventh chakra you have to have worked hard to till the soil of cosmic consciousness so that the seeds of the atman in your being can sprout. You may need a guide to work your way through limiting habits and thought patterns of each of the lower chakras. Only a master who is awake in the crown chakra can see and hear some of your self-defeating patterns, model seventh-chakra consciousness for you, and offer suggestions that can help you on your path.

If you think you have attained cosmic consciousness when you are nowhere near it, you have a problem. We met one young man who set out to meditate for hours every day, with no guidance from any master. After a few weeks he started turning into a sort of zombie. He became dysfunctional in daily life, and grumpy and unpleasant when not meditating. (No, we don't know the end of that story.)

Here's another part of the seventh-chakra paradox. If you're trying to reach that state and feel upset that you're not there yet, you're still stuck in egocentric consciousness: "I must become enlightened." Sahasrara consciousness, it is said, creeps up on you only when you have given up the craving to attain it and simply accept yourself as you are and your life as it is. And even after you cross the threshold of crown chakra consciousness, there is the danger of feeling unhappy if you fall out of it. Drat!

And there's laziness. It's such a blast to hang out in feeling blissful that you might give up on doing anything useful for anybody else. Let them just soak up your great vibes. By contrast, the most enlightened spiritual teachers who are recognized by the public as being such devote much of their time to helping ease the suffering of others.

Past Roots of Seventh-Chakra Problems

By the time someone has evolved to the point of cosmic consciousness, most past roots of psychological problems have been worked through, transformed, dissolved, or transcended. But if you try to claw your way to seventh-chakra consciousness yourself, with no guide who has been there and knows the routes and stumbling blocks, you're unlikely to succeed. Another error is to select as a guru someone who thinks he or she has reached the Sahasrara Chakra but actually has not, and doesn't see or admit his or her limits. Trying to follow the path laid out by such a self-congratulatory flawed guru will lead you into circles and blind alleys. But if you perceive that guru's limitations as well as his or her greatness, you can learn what's valuable in his or her teachings without expecting more.

THE BODY AND EMOTIONS PATHWAY:
FEELING TONES IN THE SEVENTH CHAKRA

Personal Transformation in the Seventh Chakra

"[The] Spirit or Oversoul," says Sri Aurobindo, "is ultimately our own highest, deepest, vastest Self."[13]

But how can we get there? *Can* we get there?

Not from here. Except for the rare souls born into seventh-chakra consciousness (from time to time it does happen, but seldom), we have to prepare the way by realizing the positive potentials of the first through sixth chakras. Don't expect do it in a weekend workshop.

How do we make the leap from sixth- to seventh-chakra unity consciousness? It's as easy or as hard as sprouting wings and flying upward. Working your way through the obstacles and opportunities of the first six chakras is a way to sprout those wings. But once you truly find yourself living within sixth-chakra consciousness, you can remember Mataji Narmada Puri's observation that you can aspire to continue to tread your path of spiritual evolution while being fully present and content with where and how you are. Then hang out with one or more teachers who have found their way to the crown chakra and, with a little luck, you'll begin to feel like you're being surrounded by wisps of fog softly drifting in from the sea. Then to your great surprise, one day the misty gray of fog lights up with the spectacular hues of a golden sunrise or sunset; you and the fog and all else around you become a single inseparable reality, and all the powers of all the chakras are part of you. So it is told.

As it happens, not many of those who have developed the ability to enter crown-chakra consciousness spend most of their time there. Sri Ramakrishna, who did so, was an exception. Like Pilot Baba emerging from samadhi as the scientific instruments spring to life, most spend the majority of their time moving through the worlds of chakras one through six—but in a different way than most people. They bring the awareness and insight of Sahasrara consciousness into their travels through the worlds of the other chakras. Just as you can move upward through the chakras, you can move downward through them, moving energies from obstacles to opportunities. As you do, each chakra will glow with a brighter light than it did before. Mataji Narmada Puri said this very clearly:

Working on the highest chakra is also working on the lowest. When you awaken the [positive potentials of] the chakras at the top you also awaken those at the bottom because they are all connected. When I am doing chakra meditation, the same energy that is working in the upper chakras is working in the lower chakras. . . . Your upper chakra energies help you go in a purified way back to your body in your first and second chakras. What is a saint? He or she has a body like you. Whether you are a saint or a businessman or a farmer, in every chakra your understanding will draw upon what you have learned by opening [some of] the potentials of your upper chakras. It helps you overcome the limitations of each chakra.[14]

In every life situation it can be useful to ask yourself, or be intuitively sensitive to the question, "What kind of chakra energy, and which of its dimensions, is going on here now? Is it working well? Or is another kind called for? Are my thoughts going in a direction that will alleviate suffering, or am I caught in maya's grip?"

Relational Transformation in the Seventh Chakra

A dramatic effect of Sahasrara Chakra consciousness on our relationships lies in the remarkably openhearted quality of those who experience it. Sri Mata Amritanandamayi describes this:

As love becomes more subtle, it gains power. . . . Finally you will reach the state of total identification with the Beloved where you realize that you are not separate. This is when you become one. It is the ultimate step. . . . When your heart is full of innocent love, you are absent; the ego is absent. In that state, only love is present; individuality disappears, and you become one with the Divine . . . loving each and every aspect of creation, seeing the Divinity in everyone and everything.[15]

THE PATHWAY OF SPIRIT:
IMAGERY IN THE SEVENTH CHAKRA

The basic yantra form of the seventh chakra (seen in plate 12: Yantra Form of the Seventh Chakra) is the circle as a full moon with an umbrella of a thousand lotus petals in the colors of the rainbow. The deity is the guru within or our own inner voice of wisdom. The Shakti (form of energy) is Chaitanya, or the pure consciousness or cosmic intelligence.

Here the deities disappear and the formless Divine remains. This kind of meditation has its fruit in samadhi, the last step in the tantric path. Here the individual self becomes the supreme Self, the atman. Although the Divine is without form, it takes on a form in the person of the yogi or yogini, whose body radiates purity. In such meditation we feel bliss and are able to enter the fourth state of consciousness called turiya. In the seventh chakra we can experience uninterrupted meditation (*dhyana*). Such meditation is the fruit of deep concentration in the sixth.

There are two types of meditation: with form (*saguna*) and without form (*nirguna*). Up to the sixth chakra we needed the forms of the chakras and the deities to understand the spiritual essence of the different aspects of consciousness. After we have practiced meditation with form extensively and have internalized the form, in the seventh chakra we open ourselves to meditation without form. In this type of samadhi the I-consciousness dissolves in the supreme consciousness (*samprajnata samadhi*). There is nothing to concentrate on and even the consciousness of meditation does not exist. No words exist to describe this state. Mind is only blissful illumination. One is not only experiencing, but is also being in truth and bliss (*sat-chit-ananda*).

After experiencing this a yogi again usually returns to the world and stays in a state called *sahaja samadhi,* where one remains one's own self, yet a spark of the Divine is present. In the seventh chakra we reach the plane of reality (Satya Loka), where we achieve self-realization and know transcendent reality. Liberation is very near.

But even with liberation within our reach, our ego resists. It sticks to old patterns and does not surrender easily. When ego refuses to identify with the whole, we can become very egotistical. We might think we are the only one and feel entitled to get whatever we want. After a lot of effort and hard work we reached the peak, the seventh chakra. But the higher we go, the farther we can fall. When ego becomes too big and powerful, Vishnu himself, who has ego as his food, can come to slay this dragon of egotism.

PRACTICAL TOOLS
FOR SEVENTH-CHAKRA WORK

Relaxation

Purpose: Feeling oneness.

If you are in the blissful state of samadhi you won't need to do this. Congratulations! In any other time and place, if a twinge of tightness shoots through your body or just lightly tickles your awareness, it's a signal that you've slipped out of the attitude of total acceptance into a different state of mind. If the triggering event is dangerous, act! If it offers something that you find attractive, you may want to act. In other cases, notice the signal, then, if you can, slip back into the consciousness of feeling no need to evaluate. Let go of the tension that was triggered and continue to simply watch or participate in the great adventure of life. Enjoy the majestic sea of both storms and tranquillity taking place around you.

Breath Control or Pranayama

Purpose: Greater presence in the moment.

The "Walking and Breathing" pranayama method described here is useful for keeping your greater presence of consciousness when you return to action in your daily world. It involves synchronizing your walking steps with your breathing, which keeps your attention in the present with every step you take. If your mind goes wandering, you notice it almost instantly. It is useful for someone who has been to the seventh chakra for maintaining a meditative presence of mind in the lower realms, and useful for someone who is just learning to meditate because of the immediate feedback it provides. It brings balance to the mind and gives you a signal to bring your attention back from worries, daydreams, memories, and anticipations to what's occurring inside your body and in your immediate environment. It is only for use while walking, but variations allow using it whether your main focus is on enjoying the sights and sounds around you or on getting somewhere quickly.

 ### Walking and Breathing Pranayama

For clarity, we will call one step with one foot a half step. We will call a step with one foot and then a step with the other foot a full step. To take two full steps, move your feet left, right, left, right. If you are in a place where you can walk, try it now.

Take two full steps as you inhale and then two full steps as you exhale. Count each step, silently to yourself or out loud, breaking each number in half with each half step so that you take one full step for each number: "Wun-" for the first half step and "-nn" for the second half step, and "Too-" for the third half step and "-oo" for the fourth half step.

In this way, count to two as you inhale. Then use that same counting pattern as you exhale. Continue counting to two and taking two full steps as you inhale and counting to two and taking two full steps as you exhale.

As you continue to walk in this way, feel your breath move in and out of your lungs, as well as sensing your physical movements and sensations. *The main thing is to keep your breathing and walking synchronized.* Whenever you notice that they're not, stop moving completely for a moment. Be motionless. Sense your physical centeredness and balance. Then start counting and walking with your steps and breath synchronized again.

You can vary the number of steps per breath. Maybe you're in a hurry, needing to get somewhere quickly for an important meeting. If your lung capacity allows it, take *four* full steps with each inhalation and each exhalation. That's a fast walk, but it still keeps you present. Even while you're getting *there,* you can be *here.* And when you get *there,* you'll be *present.* If you can't maintain an inhalation or exhalation for four full steps, then three full steps will probably work for you and still give you a moderately fast walk. By contrast, if you want to meander and take in the scenery, take just one full step with each breath. And one kind of traditional Zen walk uses just a half step per breath. With that walk, you may be challenged just to keep your balance!

As you use any of the walks just described, notice how you feel different from in ordinary walking. Since from the outside all but the last one of these looks like an ordinary walk, no one will even know that you're in a moving meditation, but you'll probably see and hear things that you otherwise seldom or never notice.

Figure 10.2. This drawing depicts the deity Saraswati and the core imagery shown in the painting of this chakra (plate 10: Seventh or Sahasrara Chakra).

And whether your usual abode is the seventh chakra or the first, you're guaranteed an altered state of consciousness.

Concentration

Purpose: Focusing the mind.

Here you can apply the tracing or drawing and coloring methods you explored in previous chakras to the line drawing of Saraswati's embodiment of the crown chakra shown in figure 10.2 opposite. Concentrate on your drawing, or on coloring without going over the lines; make this the central aspect of your drawing or coloring. Each time you notice that your attention has wandered, bring it back to a visual focus on your artistic play or work (call it what you wish).

Polarity-Balancing Meditation

Purpose: Alertness and awareness.

"When the mind becomes still, it resembles the Universal Mind—the mysteries and wonders of the universe are reflected upon it," says Sri Mata Amritanandamayi.[16] Aurobindo adds, "The Illumined Mind [is] no longer of higher thought but of spiritual light. . . A play of lightening of spiritual truth and power breaks from above into the consciousness and adds to the calm and wide enlightenment and the vast descent of peace."[17]

Select a line from the Seventh-Chakra Possibilities table on pages 200–201. Follow the Tratak meditation instructions on page 29.

Then once your mind is quiet and you feel present and focused, let the phrase you chose take the place of the candle flame or flower. Each time you notice that your mind has drifted off, bring it back to that phrase and whatever imagery or words hover around it. As far as you can, imagine your heart opening up to transform whatever thoughts come through your mind.

Or, in your imagination, see seven candles or a vase with seven flowers and let that represent all the chakras. Mentally scan through the past day or week of your life and contemplate which chakra is most highly activated by each of your activities. Ask yourself, "Is this chakra's energy helpful and appropriate for this activity? If not, which chakra's energy is? How can I better bring it into play in such situations?"

If neither of the above exercises appeals to you, a third alternative is to allow all thoughts to take up less and less of your consciousness and pure receptive awareness to take up more and more of it. Just be in your witness consciousness and notice thoughts, feelings, and sensations as they move through your mind and body.

Sound Healing

Purpose: Vibrating to higher consciousness.

The seed sound for this chakra is *visarga*, which Johari describes as a particular breathing sound in the pronunciation of Sanskrit. (That's all we can tell you. Sanskrit has been said to include all fifty sounds in the Indo-European language family, which is more than exist in any present-day language.)

 ### From AUM (OM) to Humming

Some scriptures tell us that everything begins with sound, with the Word. In yoga that word is AUM. To keep it simple: AUM is humming. We all do it, whether we are aware of it or not. We use it, for example, to show that we understood a conversation. Many artists use humming to get inspiration. Doing it intentionally is a great tool to relieve tension. It vibrates the whole system and especially the top of the head (the seventh chakra). Just put a hand on top of the head while humming and you can feel the vibrations.

 ### Mantras

Choose one of these, or a related word or phrase that pleases you, to use in your meditation or turn over in your mind and contemplate for at least a day and as long as you wish.

SEVENTH CHAKRA MANTRAS

MANTRA	PRONUNCIATION	MEANING
amitabha	ahmeeTAHbah	divine light, unmeasured splendor
kevala	kayvahhLAH	unity of spirit
moksha	MOWKshah	release, liberation, salvation, deliverance
vajra	VAZHhrah	diamondlike, thunderbolt

Taking Action

Purpose: Turning our ego to dust.

In the seventh chakra we behave like air. Air creates movements inside and outside the body. Gas is formless and can go easily and freely in all directions. In this state the ego can dissolve. Now that we can move freely, we can reach the highest vibrations. Like the sun we start to radiate and we give light to those around us. Dharma expresses itself in actions helpful to all beings (good karma).

In Kolkata (formerly called Calcutta), Victor once stayed for a week in what had been the home of Rabindranath Tagore, the first non-Westerner to receive the Nobel Prize. Tagore offers a few useful words: "You can't cross the sea merely by standing and staring at the water." And on another occasion Tagore wrote, "I slept and dreamt that life was joy. I awoke and saw that life was service. I acted and behold, service was joy."[18]

Johari sums up the seventh chakra in these words: "According to the scriptures, Sahasrara is the seat of the self-luminous soul or *chitta*, the essence of being. In the person who has attained Sahasrara, chitta is like a screen upon which the reflection of the cosmic Self, the divine, is seen. In the presence of the cosmic Self, it is possible for anyone to feel the divine and, indeed to realize the divinity within oneself."[19]

Now that you have some sense of all the chakras, we pause to look at the *granthis*, which you are almost sure to meet while traveling on this inward journey.

11

REMOVING OBSTACLES TO COSMIC CONSCIOUSNESS

Untying the Three Granthis or Knots

> *There are three obstacles (granthis) in the evolution of consciousness [that] prevent energy (prana) from rising.*
>
> HARISH JOHARI AND WILL GERAETS,
> *THE WISDOM TEACHINGS OF HARISH JOHARI*
> *ON THE MAHABHARATA*

Granthi can be translated as a "knot" on the way to cosmic consciousness. The journey is long, with many obstacles where we can get stuck, tied to a cascading flow of seemingly unending desires in a certain chakra or chakras. In some cases it can seem almost impossible to pass these points. They can keep us from reaching the point where we can enjoy eternal bliss and contentment. These knots or granthis are connected to three main deities, Brahma, Vishnu, and Shiva, whom we met in earlier chapters. They symbolize different aspects of consciousness.

Once Harish Johari was asked, "Why do people have problems?"

"That is why we are all different!" he replied.

Those few words say a lot. We all have different problems. We all have the granthis in common, yet they take varied specific forms in different people. Just as the chakras become more subtle the higher we go, so too do the granthis.

From the viewpoint of psychology, two of these knots don't have to be a problem. A psychologist can help someone function well in the world of survival, entertainment, and status or in the world of thoughts and emotions. A person who is not on a spiritual path can live everyday life just fine, enjoying the moment and growing in useful ways in regard to each of the granthis without moving through them. But on a spiritual path, we can't just skirt past these knots. We have to experience and learn from them. To go beyond them requires going through them.

THE BRAHMA GRANTHI

The first knot has to do with the world of names and forms. Because Brahma is said to be responsible for the creation of form, it is called the Brahma Granthi. Some place this granthi in the first chakra; Johari and others place it in the third, but actually we can meet it in any of the first three chakras. Johari says "The world is created by Brahma, but the world known to the individual consciousness is created by the mind. . . . The world that we know well . . . is created in our mind. . . . Untying this knot frees one from the bondage caused by attachment."[1] This includes attachments to much of the stuff our culture erroneously tells us we need. It includes attachments to many of our fears, both those we learned early in life and those we pick up by listening to what the media in all its forms sends out from morning until night. We start believing that what other people, media, and mind have perceived, processed, and presented to us is the real world. Because it looks like that's all there is, we get attached to it. We think it's reality. But sages call it samsara.

Science has shown that actually we only receive frequencies of waves and particles. Our sense organs and cortical neurons change them into images, tastes, smells, sounds, touches, and feelings. We are watching our own body and the environment around it with the mental filters created by our sense organs and work organs. Quantum physicists are now looking for the essence of the universe in the material world. That essence just might turn out to be invisible strings and particles of energy. Yoga calls our visible, audible world *maya,* or illusion, because our perception of what is real can undergo dramatic transformations as it passes through our nervous system.

In this partly real and partly illusory world created by our minds, name and status play a major role. Name and status express themselves in things that we want to have or must have to belong to a certain group. That can be a car, house, job, clothing, hairstyle, parties and receptions, public appearances, art, music, TV, digital devices, and so on. We can get addicted to them and they can fill our whole life, leaving no time for anything else. It is our ego that wants all this and is using the mind to get it. Intellect sends us a warning, but ego ignores it. Desires and ambitions trap us. For many it looks like there is no way out.

To follow a yogic path that can help us come closer to knowing what's real and what's not requires a disciplined life. Obviously this is not for everyone. But if we're willing to give it a try, it is useful to begin with some purifications to get our body more in harmony with its environment. Changes in diet, fasting (such as of food, speech, or sleep), and also facing the hardships in life head-on can help.

The path of Patanjali (ashtanga yoga) can provide more discipline and structure in our life. The first verse of the Patanjali's classic *Yoga Sutras* leaves it very open. It just says: "Start!" It does not say which path to choose. Art is one. So too are the martial arts and all sports. Each can offer the ego the opportunity to surrender to something greater than itself. It may be an art piece or group spirit or total body control.

Hatha yoga also can help open this knot. With the guidance of a kind, loving, and experienced teacher, we learn how to be still as we perform our postures or asanas. With practice we can stay in an asana longer and longer. As the body becomes still, the mind becomes still. Slowly we can experience how it is not to feel compelled to satisfy our cravings. Gradually we become able to raise our sights and do things that we never thought we could.

For our spiritual path, opening this knot is important. When we see the world only as a material reality, we do not know what lies behind that reality. When we can see the unity in diversity, all objects become divine. They tend to appear when we need them if we are willing to "surrender to providence." To do so requires understanding the difference between need and desire. The easiest discipline to understand, if we are willing, is simple living. That leads to high thinking—or at least leaves space for it to occur. We're also likely to experience something else: a happiness and a joy that comes from within. We open ourselves to moving into the fourth chakra and experiencing the grace of being in balance.

THE VISHNU GRANTHI

This is located in the heart chakra, balanced between materialism and idealism. It reaches down into the third chakra at one end and up into the fifth at the other.

A strange phenomenon occurs as we begin to enjoy the loveliness of dwelling emotionally and mentally in the heart chakra: we come up against Vishnu's knot. What's going on? How can this occur when Vishnu has compassion for all beings? Even when we live with the beauty of devotion, faith, and compassion, we may discover in the heart chakra that beauty in living can become a knot. (It hardly seems fair!) As with the Brahma Granthi, this may happen when our compassion keeps us so fully in the world that we do not take time for introspection.

Compassion for all that lives is badly needed, and many religions have it as their message. Our intentions may be excellent. We want to serve the cosmic good, and we think we can do that by taking away the suffering and the pain in the world. We fight for the poor, oppressed women, badly treated animals, the endangered rainforest, ignorance, and the end of war. All these things we do not for ourselves, but for the greater good. Many people are doing a great deal of good work to reduce anguish and suffering, which has great value. A very valuable life can be lived on that plane. But even this, says Johari, can be an attachment:

> This attachment makes one a dreamer, a reformer, a savior, a preserver of ancient knowledge—a preserver of high spiritual qualities—but not a yogi. Instead of going back to the source through union, one adopts a bodhisattva vow to relieve the world from suffering. . . . The [yogic aspirant who aspires to reach the crown chakra] has to untie this knot, which creates emotional ties to traditions and idealism, thus trapping the energy at the heart chakra.[2]

A life lived out at this level can have profound value. Many people who reach this stage are content in it. This knot is not easy to understand, because for many people hardship, pain, and suffering are painfully real and not an illusion of any kind at all. Yet some suffering and pain force us to stand still and think about life. But when we spend all our time trying to relieve the world's troubles, we cannot reach a state where there are no thoughts, which for some yogis is their goal.

A very advanced yogi might realize that troubling events exist, yet no longer experience them as a source of suffering for himself or herself personally. Once Ramana Maharishi, one of the great twentieth-century saints, was asked if he was sick. He had cancer, but replied: "No, I am not sick! Body is sick and I am not body!" He was above worldly pleasure and pain, beyond liking and disliking. This is the path of those yogis who are not attached to the world and only interested in union with the source, which is within them.

To untie this knot we can work with prana, our vital life force. With prana we can control our mind and emotions. When we breathe slowly, our mind usually works more slowly. Kumbakha or holding the breath even stops the mind so that very few, or even no thoughts drift through it. As it happens, not many people, even among aspiring yogis, actually reach the state of consciousness where there are no thoughts. But that need not mean "Don't even try."

In meditation, we work toward being without thoughts, and keeping our witness consciousness alert to notice those thoughts that do come floating through our minds. Being without thoughts is like a holiday as long as it lasts. Then we can go forward with an empty mind that is open to what creation has to offer and untie this granthi.

THE RUDRA GRANTHI

Those few adepts who have gained great control over their senses, have left all restless thoughts behind, and emptied their mind of the outside world's distractions, can advance through the fifth chakra to relax in the silent peace of the sixth chakra. Since its obstacles and opportunities were discussed in detail in chapter 9, we need not repeat them here.

In this context Rudra is another name of Shiva (known by more names than any god or goddess besides the incredible feminine shape-shifting artist, Shakti). Here he is in the form of Shankara/Rudra, who lives in Kailash, and supposedly can destroy the universe back into black-energy form. With our experience of the peace of silence gained in the sixth chakra, we can now experience the immortal Shiva inside us.

It is said that doing many austerities for long periods, under the supervision of one who has attained seventh-chakra consciousness and knows the path well, can bring one to cosmic consciousness. So too, making devotional art in all its forms can become sadhana, when it is done alone. Artist Lawrence Weiner said: "When I paint, it makes no sense to worry about the problems of myself or the world. I concentrate on my job. All my thinking at that time is related to it."

The greatest of the masters who have attained diverse siddhis or powers have said that we can attain one of them fairly easily. What is that one most special power? *It is the ability to always speak the truth.* Most of us are so skilled at self-deception, even if subtly or unconsciously, that only by the time we reach the sixth chakra, if even then, do we always know the truth. It has also been said that if we always speak the truth, whatever we say will come true. Food for thought.

The attachment to ego creates our last problem. For an artist who has reached the sixth chakra, during the process of painting the ego is usually absent. All the mental focus is on the work. It makes him or her humble. But then ego pops up to put a signature on the painting. And with that the world of name and fame can start pulling the artist down into second chakra partying and enjoying the fame, and soon the artist may become lazy and not follow his or her dharma (making art) anymore.

Epics and other stories from ancient India are full of demons who gained enormous powers by performing difficult austerities. Tantra offers many possibilities for gaining siddhis, such as by repeating certain mantras in certain postures over a long period of time. A danger here is that one can learn to do japa not as a devotional discipline, but to achieve powers. Having done so, the demons in India's epics sometimes became convinced that they could not be killed. They started saying: "I am God!" or "I am God's messenger." And they would kill whoever was against them. Eventually things would get so bad that Vishnu himself would have to come to Earth and take a human or partially human form, such as the Man-Lion, Narasimha (depicted in plate 13: Narasimha), to finish off the demon. The aggressive nature of swollen egos in human beings has similarly resulted in many unholy wars. Rulers, executives, and generals who live in a world full of luxury and decadence can fall into the classic trap of demons and start thinking that suffering and pain are only illusion, and that death is just a transition, so: "Why let these people live in ignorance and unnecessary pain? It is better to free them from this miserable life and kill them." But very often, soon they too are dead.

Sometimes just meditating on the Infinite within us can open this knot. To stay out of the tempting world of siddhis or powers we can meditate on AUM or *soham*. They are neutral sounds. The siddhi they give is peace because of the absence of ego. Also a personal mantra, which we repeat for the rest of our life without any expectation and without any powers attached to it, can help to move past this knot. Then we just might be able to enjoy eternal bliss.

Is that the end of the story? Not quite. Our job is not done yet. More work is needed. We are still on Earth. Reaching here does not mean life has stopped.

We can now understand that dreams of saving the world, reforming religions, fighting for traditions, or ending war can be very useful, but they are not everything. "Under what circumstances should we act?" you might ask. The general answer is simple: when the means do not cause avoidable suffering and destruction, corrupt the end, or keep us from truly knowing our inner selves.

To have a job, family, and a social function in society can be very satisfying. The same is true when we work for spiritual organizations or for whatever virtuous cause these things inspire in us. People with vision who handle their powers wisely live in a world full of inspiration, advising on all levels and sometimes leading influential organizations and institutions. Knowing about the granthis can make it easier to avoid getting caught in them.

A key to untying the knots is to know to which chakra and which granthi your energy is most attached. If you don't, then return to chapter 2 and use Tratak meditation to develop your ability to focus, concentrate, and watch your mind. Then you'll be able to observe what your consciousness is doing now, where it's stuck, and where you need to work.

In daily life knowledge of the granthis can be useful in any chakra. Being aware of them can help you to stay focused and not get distracted by an overdose of incentives that might hold you in their grip forever. Then, according to yoga, if we stay disciplined, real happiness comes within reach.

ONE MORE OBSTACLE

Some observers consider another stumbling block just as important as those formally recognized in the granthis. Located in the third chakra, between the Brahma Granthi and the Vishnu Granthi, it involves clinging to power, greed, and self-glorification. On a spiritual path, getting past these obstacles is difficult because these achievements are often widely applauded in society, especially by those who enjoy their advantages and by the media. This barrier can deaden—or at least anesthetize—the inner spirit. Until, in Sri Chinmoy's words made famous by Jimi Hendrix, "the power of love overcomes the love of power!"

Then what? Or now what? Having seen the obstacles and opportunities linked with each chakra, and with the granthis, we have an enlarged sense of perspective on our inner world. All that we have gained will be useful in thinking about our next move as we turn to the last chapter and take a step toward merging with the sacred.

12

WHAT NEXT?

The pulse of the cosmos mirrors itself in the human body, with the beating of the heart reflecting the throbbing rhythm of the universe itself. The same elements which comprise the mantle of the earth are the very elements making up the human body, and the laws which govern their forms and actions are the same.

HARISH JOHARI,
DHANWANTARI

AS YOU WALK YOUR SACRED PATH

In these pages you've had an opportunity to travel into your inner world. If you have cleared and balanced your lower three chakras and live at least occasionally in Anahata or fourth-chakra consciousness, that's a *major* achievement. If you are integrating a few positive fifth-chakra qualities into your life, you are probably on a spirit pathway to realizations that will take you beyond the logic of words. And if the divine grace of sixth- and seventh-chakra qualities has become even a small part of your experience, we honor you. Cultivate the best qualities of all the chakras as fully as you can, and your life will serve as a model for others to do likewise. To fertilize and water the garden of your own personal consciousness is the work needed to sprout seeds that grow toward the light of cosmic awakening.

But if we are stuck in one of the blind alleys of the lower chakras (probably without realizing it), our attempts to guide others may be useless or worse. On the other hand, there is the phenomenon of a person who by his or her own nature and life history has a highly developed consciousness, and can help others tread that path too. To find such a guide is a blessing.

Once you've attained your own enlightenment, it is said that you can return to this earthly vale of tears, sorrow, and suffering to guide others through their troubles and into a more loving and caring way to feel and be.

It is also said that personal enlightenment cannot be achieved without helping others. One might even say that helping others is the best thing one can do for spiritual growth. Many great babas in India, like Swami Avdeshananda of the Djuna Acara, have as a general motto: "Help ever, hurt never!" In doing so we don't have to become front page news.

Learning about the seventh chakra allows a glimpse of the divine will that is behind the world of sensory perception. With this realization we start to merge into the source of it all, which is experienced as infinite space within the self. In that state of consciousness there is no more separation. Only the witness self is there, with full insight into everything. We surrender to the will of the Supreme. We now experience bliss (ananda) directly. It is the result of following the path of dharma. It is not possible to explain or express this bliss to others. It can only be experienced.

Once our individual consciousness has evolved to completion, a last purification is needed before it can disappear in cosmic consciousness. We know the truth (Vishnu). We feel beauty (Brahma). And we do good (Shiva). Now we simply do the job that the cosmic forces are asking from us. Throughout the whole journey through the chakras the search for truth was our guide. Now we realize this truth. If the Divine wants to make use of us, this is the moment where we are most useful. We are ready for it. We understand now the real problems of life. No more distractions, no more selfish motives—now only universal needs are the focal point. A little humor is all right, lest we be too grave and serious.

Among the most famous saints who demonstrate this way of being are Ramana Maharishi and Shirdi Sai Baba (not to be confused with Satya Sai

Baba). The first became famous during his lifetime, while the latter was almost unknown until after his lifetime. Jesus also belongs here. His messages expressed universal needs in a devotional, spiritual manner. He too became far better known after his death than while alive. All were humble and lived simply. They were one with their source.

Many saints, after realizing the truth, return to society and perform their duties with full passion. An example is Kathiababa, who was very high up in the Himalayas visiting the babas who live completely away from illusions of the world. He could have stayed there, but decided that his place was with the people. He sees himself as a servant of Vishnu, and decided that the best way for him to serve was by serving the creatures that Vishnu loves. He saw in Vishnu the essence of creation and the embodiment of cosmic consciousness giving life and penetrating everywhere in the universe. In such a vision Vishnu is the one who protects us, while we are climbing up in the chakras; all that we experience is his playful nature. Here he symbolizes all religions. That means he has many names. Or we can say that it is impossible to give him just one name.

There are many ways that lead to cosmic consciousness. Action is unavoidable. We can follow step by step the path of Patanjali, which is the path of yoga and of which Shiva is the lord. We can become spiritual devotees (bhaktas). We can search for true knowledge (jnana). And we can mix these and create our own path. Once we reach this point the nature of the game of life becomes simple. We just discover in what way we ourselves can reach home or cosmic consciousness. And there are many paths. We offer a few brief statements of varied views from those who have reached higher chakras. The following comments are borrowed from A. N. Sharma, who travelled widely to interview many little-known spiritual masters.[1]

Askari Darvesh "said that if we plant thorns we cannot expect to gather dates."

Swami Achutananda "wanted people to cast off disappointments like an old garment and to be confident that in the end things can and will come right however difficult and impossible they appear to be in the beginning. . . . He always said that great adventures, great creations and great discoveries have usually been nurtured in hardships, pondered over in sorrow, and established with difficulty."

Rajab Ali Patel remarked, "One should be very careful what one brings out of one's lips. As the wounds of tongue never heal—one must always think twice before uttering words which might hurt any one." He further said that "careless talk makes more enemies than friends."

Sri Anandswarup Sahebji Maharaj "[organized] small-scale industries of many types, so that the workers may benefit on co-operative basis. . . . He taught that the only way God can come to a hungry man is in the form of a morsel of bread."

Gangeshwaranandaji Maharaj "meets even the humblest of people with an open-hearted smile, full of love and affection. . . . Among his devotees there are people of all religions, communities, and countries. Rich or poor, learned or ignorant, young or old, men or women, all love and respect him and thus he has formed successfully one large family out of his disciples and followers."

Sri Dharm Devi "was fully intoxicated with divine love . . . a rare manifestation of the divine Spirit in one so young and innocent. . . . Her talks are so fresh . . . and elevating. . . . Her answers satisfied everyone . . . immensely when they heard a little girl getting up and making every thought crystal clear for their benefit. When asked, 'How to know a saint?' she replied, 'By the Light he radiates and the deep impression he makes on you by his words.'"

Some say that any transformation of consciousness on a widespread scale can occur only when people whose hearts are closed, who act with inhumanity and cruelty toward others, change their ways. Few have said this as clearly as Mahatma Gandhi who offers these words:

Man as animal is violent, but as Spirit is nonviolent. . . . There is always in me conscious struggle for following the law of non-violence deliberately, and ceaselessly. Such a struggle leaves one stronger for it. . . . Our anger controlled can be transmuted into a power which can move the world. . . . I do not believe that a man may gain spiritually and those that surround him suffer. . . . Therefore I believe that if one man gains spiritually, the whole world gains with him and that if one man falls, the whole world falls to that extent. . . . The principle of non-violence necessitates complete abstention from exploitation in any form. . . . He is no follower of ahimsa who does not care a straw if he kills a man by inches by deceiving him in a trade or who . . . in order to do a supposed good to his country does not mind killing a few officials. All these are actuated by hatred, cowardice, and fear. . . . It is the acid test of non-violence that in a non-violent conflict there is no rancor left behind, and in the end the enemies are converted into friends.[2]

WE ARE ALL PART OF NATURE'S LIVING FABRIC

Present-day spiritually oriented reformers who seek to end conditions of suffering and exploitation include Vandana Shiva and Sri Mata Amritanandamayi. They trace the roots of their outlook and work far back to the ancient times when the cultures of India were entwined in an intimate relationship with nature, recognizing that they needed to give back as much to our living Earth as they took from it.

Our own age is radically different from that of the rishis who knew that the forests in which they lived were a living presence of the Divine. Johari writes,

Earth is not only a planet. She is a living organism, the great Mother principle which has given birth to all that exists on Her breast. . . . She is the essence of tolerance and forbearance. Though Her children blast Her body and ignite Her soul, she gives them in return diamonds, gold, and platinum. . . . We see her body, the Physical Plane of first chakra. What we cannot see is Her spirit, Her intelligence. . . . To first chakra man [Earth] is but a coffer to pillage and loot as he chooses, without regard to consequences. Sixth chakra man recognizes the peril of this attitude as he sees the planet he loves facing imminent and possibly irremediable danger.[3]

We are part of nature, not apart from it. To be able to work on our inner selves effectively we also need to preserve the good health of the biosphere, and maintain the ability of every ecosystem to support life as fully tomorrow and in the distant future as it does today.

TANTRA, SHAKTI, AND THE INNER GODDESS

A background thread throughout this work is the union of male and female consciousness and energies as described in the Ajna Chakra (and depicted in plate 14: Union of Male and Female Consciousness in the Tree of Life). Men and women are part of the same tree of life. Exploiting or suppressing either gender, as many patriarchal traditions do, deadens something precious in the soul of the exploiter or suppressor as well as the exploited and oppressed. For the past several thousand years, since the decline of the ancient goddess cultures, men have dominated women's behavior and decisions, even though women's abilities and outlook are needed in every sphere of life.

It is strange to realize that our economy claims to categorize all our labor, but does not include the work of our mothers—as if raising children and maintaining family life and social interaction are not needed, not important. After listening to countless stories from women all around the world about oppression of the feminine, Sri Mata Amritanandamayi says that innumerable women have accepted the masculine story that they are inferior to men, when in fact they are not only equal in almost every regard but superior in some.[4] Surely there would be far more cooperation and far less conflict in the world if women held half the positions of power. The tantric tradition, of which the chakras are a part, notes Swami Prabhavananda,

> teaches the Motherhood of God—God as Shakti, or the power which creates and preserves the universe and dissolves it into herself. The concept [of] Mother, indeed, takes many forms, has many aspects. . . . The tender Mother shows her benign aspect to those who are her votaries, in whatever form or aspect they may worship her. And she is to be seen and realized everywhere in the universe. A beautiful prayer occurs in the Candi, a prayer book of the Sakta Tantras: "O Mother, thou art the embodiment of all knowledge. Wherever there are intelligence and learning, there art thou manifest. All women are thy forms. Thou hast thy being in the universe, filling and permeating all things." Thus spiritual aspirants are taught to look upon all women as the embodiment of Shakti, or Mother.[5]

Differences in people, places, and ways of life are like facets of a single gem. The light in your chakras shines out through whichever facet of the jewel is called for by a given time and place and circumstance.

We are blessed by Sri Harish Johari's precious gems showered throughout the world through his teachings that can come to dwell in every mind and heart that opens to them. This is a doorway to the cosmic light of the potential higher state of the world's collective consciousness, if one is willing to walk through it. Are you?

GLOSSARY

Airavata: elephant with seven trunks

Ajna Chakra: the sixth chakra, between the two eyebrows on the forehead

akasha: fifth element, related to space

Anahata Chakra: the fourth chakra, located in the heart center

ananda: bliss

Arjuna: loyal devotee of Krishna

artha: wealth, earthly security

asana: yoga posture

ashram: a spiritual gathering place, analogous to a church, often with monks, nuns, or other seekers living there

atman: Self, referring to the psychic state in which a person feels at one with all people and beings

AUM: sacred Sanskrit syllable

ayurveda: Vedic science healing methods that go back to more than 4000 years BCE

Brahma: lord of creation in the Hindu trinity with Shiva and Vishnu

brahmachari: one who abstains from sex

brahman: the Absolute

chakras: spinning wheels (centers) of light

dakini: female deity

devas: gods

devi: divine goddess

dharma: following the laws of nature

dhyana: practice of meditation and concentration to attain enlightenment

Durga: warrior-woman incarnation of Shakti

fakir: saint or seeker on a spiritual path; advanced yogi

Ganesha: the elephant-faced, human-bodied god

Ganga: the river Ganges

gestalt: pattern, whole, configuration

granthi: in tantric tradition, a knot in relation to chakras that slows progress on path to enlightenment

gunas: quality of thought (there are three gunas: rajas, tamas, and sattva)

guru: spiritual teacher who dispels darkness

hamsa: white swan

Hanuman: the Indian monkey-god devote of Rama

hatha yoga: one branch of yoga that practices physical postures

individuation: realizing your unique potential that is differentiated from others

Indra: lord of the gods

introjection: accepting some attitude or alleged fact uncritically ("swallowing it whole") without thinking or "chewing it through" for yourself

japa: repetition of mantra

jnana: knowledge

Kama/kama: Hindu god of love/enjoyment; desire

Kameshvara Chakra: enlightenment chakra above the Soma Chakra

karma: action

Krishna: divine incarnation of lord Vishnu; central in the Mahabharata epic

kumbh mela: holy festival in India

Kundalini: cosmic energy (said to be sleeping in the first chakra but able to be aroused by spiritual practices that lift consciousness to higher chakras; often visually depicted as a snake

leela (lila): game of self-knowledge; play; our lives conceived as cosmic games

lingam: symbol for Shiva and male energy

loka: plane of existence

mahat: great

Mahavidyas: great wisdom or knowledge

mala: prayer beads

Manipura: third chakra, located near the navel

mantra: sacred syllable or word

maya: the world of illusion in which we mistake our ideas for the realities they represent

moksha: final liberation

mudras: finger and hand positions that bring physical, mental, and spiritual benefit

Muladhara: first chakra, located near bottom of spine

nadi: nerve ending; Ida Nadi, the lunar psychic channel; Pingala Nadi, the solar psychic channel

naga (or nag) babas: sadhus who are naked except for ash

Narayana: a name for Vishnu

nirvikalpa samadhi: a state of dissolution of the self-conscious self

niyamas: ethical duties

Parvati: incarnation of Shakti who meditated while yearning for Shiva to come to her

prana: energy of the primal life force

pranayama: breath control

projection: thinking you see or hear in another something that's going on inside you (that you may not want to admit)

rajas: one of the three gunas related to passion and activity (adjective form *rajasic*)

Rakini: two-headed goddess of second chakra

Rama: a particular incarnation of Vishnu; central in the Ramayana epic

rishis: saints or sages with great wisdom

Rudra: Shiva

sadhana: spiritual practice

sadhu: pious man; wandering seeker

Sahasrara: seventh chakra, located at the crown of the head

samadhi: spiritual union between body, mind, and soul; absorption in God

samsara: repeating cycles of life and death

samskara or sanskara: impressions left on mind and body from past experiences

sankalpa: will, resolve, directed energy, intention

santosh: contentment; self-sufficiency

sat-cit-ananda: existence-knowledge-bliss

satsang: a spiritual gathering, or meeting of guru and disciple

sattva: one of the three gunas linked with pure energy (adjectve form is sattvic)

seed sound: sound that embodies the pure essence of a given chakra, often chanted as a mantra to resonate or connect with its cosmic origin (for example, OM or AUM is the seed sound of the sixth chakra)

seva: giving service to others without thinking of personal return

Shakti: female spiritual energy that pervades the universe

Shiva: male spiritual energy; God as the destroyer in the Hindu trinity with Brahma and Vishnu

siddhis: psychic powers

Soma Chakra: considered nectar of the moon, it is located above sixth and within the seventh chakra

Sushumna: central psychic nerve where Kundalini rises

Svadhisthana: second chakra located in pelvic region

tamas: one of the three gunas that represents inactivity or dullness (adjective form tamasic)

Tantra: tantric religion that seeks pathways to linking with divine energy

tapas: austerities

Tratak: a yogic method of meditation that includes staring at a single object such as a candle flame to develop powers of concentration and focus

tree of life: symbolic concept of the sacred interrelatedness of nature, humanity, and god

truth: perfect correspondence between an idea or statement and the reality it represents; unhindered direct perception or realization of the reality itself

Vedas: four ancient scriptures that teach the art of living

Venn diagram: a diagram representing logical pictorial, precise sets; also called mathematical set theory

Vishnu: God, the Preserver, balance between gods of creation and destruction in the Hindu trinity with Shiva and Vishnu

Vishuddha: fifth chakra, located in the area of the throat

yama: discipline to get mind and body in control

yantra: mystical geometric diagram with spiritual or tantric benefit

NOTES

INTRODUCTION

1. Aiyar, trans. *Thirty Minor Upanishads.*
2. Johari, *Chakras: Energy Centers of Transformation.*
3. Pilot Baba, personal communication 2013.
4. Maslow, *Motivation and Personality,* 15–45, 111–67. Also see *Toward a Psychology of Being,* 21–43.
5. Korzybski, *Science and Sanity.*
6. Narmada Puri, personal communication 2013.

1. AN INWARD EYE

1. Narmada Puri, *Tears of Bliss: A Guru-Disciple Mystery.*
2. Chidvilasananda, *The Yoga of Discipline,* 32.
3. Narmada Puri, *Tears of Bliss,* 250–51.
4. Ibid.
5. Narmada Puri, personal communication 2013.
6. Wilber, Ken. *No Boundary,* 261.
7. Pilot Baba, personal communication 2013.
8. Narmada Puri, personal communication 2013.
9. Pilot Baba, personal communication 2013.
10. Milk Baba, personal communication 2012.
11. Narmada Puri, personal communication 2013.

12. Pilot Baba, personal communication 2013.

13. Ibid.

14. Hari Dass, *Silence Speaks,* 31.

15. Johari, personal communication, 1993.

16. Jung, *Man and His Symbols.*

2. SOLVING YOUR PERSONAL MYSTERIES

1. Sivanand, "A Flood of Artistry."

2. Roger Bannister is widely quoted online, origin of quote is unknown.

3. Ram Dass with Rameshwar Das. *Polishing the Mirror,* 56, 82, 83.

4. Ibid., 55, 126.

5. Narmada Puri, personal communication 2013.

6. Pilot Baba, personal communication 2013.

7. Wynne, "Some Indications and Contraindications for Exploratory Family Therapy," 289–322.

8. Bettelheim, Bruno. *Freud and Man's Soul.*

9. Ram Dass, with Rameshwar Das. *Polishing the Mirror,* 146–47.

3. THE POLARITY PRINCIPLE

1. Kempton, *Awakening Shakti,* 26–27.

2. Johari and Geraets, *Wisdom Teachings,* 9.

3. Johari, *Breath, Mind and Consciousness,* 391.

4. Muktananda. *Play of Consciousness.*

5. Prajnapad, *Encyclopedia of Hinduism.*

6. Wertheimer, "Gestalt Theory."

7. Assagioli, "Balancing and Synthesis of the Opposites," 7–9.

8. Ibid.

9. Ibid.

10. Tulku, *Gesture of Balance,* 9.

11. Assagioli, "Balancing and Synthesis of the Opposites," 7–9.

4. FIRST OR MULADHARA CHAKRA

1. Saraswati, *Kundalini Tantra.*

2. Pilot Baba, personal communication 2013.

3. Chidvilasananda, *The Yoga of Discipline,* 2.

4. Ansbacher and Ansbacher, *The Individual Psychology of Alfred,* 241–42.

5. Pilot Baba, personal communication 2013.

6. Saraswati, *Kundalini Tantra.*

7. Yogananda, *The Essence of Self Realization,* 166.

5. SECOND OR SVADHISTHANA CHAKRA

1. Rama, *Living with the Himalayan Masters,* 248–49.

2. Odier, *Tantric Quest,* 72.

3. Johari, *Leela.*

4. Ansbacher and Ansbacher, *The Individual Psychology of Alfred Adler.*

5. Saraswati, *Kundalini Tantra,* 153.

6. Chidvilasananda, *The Yoga of Discipline.*

6. THIRD OR MANIPURA CHAKRA

1. Johari, personal communication.

2. Johari and Garaets, *The Wisdom Teachings.*

3. Prabhavananda, ed. *Bhagavad Gita,* 52.

4. Johari: *Leela,* 59.

5. Saraswati, *Kundalini Tantra,* 156.

6. Yogananda, *The Essence of Self Realization,* 166.

7. Chidvilasananda, *The Yoga of Discipline,* 3.

8. Ibid.

9. Ibid., 64–65.

10. Bolen, *The Ring of Power.*

11. Hari Dass, *Silence Speaks,* 180.

12. Ram Dass and Gorman, *How Can I Help?,* 21.

13. Johari, *Chakras,* 108.

14. Ibid., 109.

15. Ibid., 109.

16. Johari, *Leela,* 63.

17. Johari, personal communication.

18. Jacobson, *Progressive Relaxation,* 1929.

19. Canan, *Messages from Amma.*

20. Gandhi, *Gandhi,* ed. Kripalani.

7. FOURTH OR ANAHATA CHAKRA

1. Attributed to Paramahansa Yogananda, www.brainyquote.com/quotes/quotes/p/paramahans163486.html.
2. Johari, talks in Europe, 1990s.
3. Chidvilasananda, *The Yoga of Discipline*, 80.
4. Ibid., 75.
5. Ibid., 75.
6. Dalai Lama, *How to Practice*, 1, 3, 4, 5, 132.
7. Saraswati, *Kundalini Tantra*, 125.
8. Vivekananda. *Letters of Swami Vivekananda*. Passage can be found online at www.thehinduforum.com/threads/swami-vivekananda-on-love.342.
9. Keyes, *A Conscious Person's Guide*, 36.
10. Meher Baba. *Discourses*, vol. 1, 24.
11. Anandamayi Ma. *Sad Vani*.
12. Johari, *Chakras*, 122.
13. Ibid., 113–14.
14. Ibid., personal communication.
15. Fitzgerald, *Life and Works of Anandamayi Ma*.

8. FIFTH OR VISHUDDHA CHAKRA

1. Saraswati, *Kundalini Tantra*, 173–74.
2. Perls, *In and Out of the Garbage Pail*.
3. Hari Dass, *Fire Without Fuel*, 104.
4. Rogers, *On Becoming a Person*.
5. Quote found online at http://quoteinvestigator.com/2013/11/14/seekers. Original source, André Gide, *Ainsi Soit-Il, Ou Les Jeux Sont Faits [So Be It: Or the Chips Are Down]*, 1952.
6. Judith, *Eastern Body, Western Mind*, 310.
7. Johari and Geraets, 146.
8. Johari, *Chakras*, 132.
9. Hari Dass, *Silence Speaks*, 102–103.
10. Chidvilasananda, *The Yoga of Discipline*, 170.
11. Perls, *Ego, Hunger, and Aggression*.
12. Saraswati, *Kundalini Tantra*, 178.

13. Hall, personal communication 1971.

14. Anandamayi Ma, *Sad Vani,* 51.

9. SIXTH OR AJNA CHAKRA

1. Kedarnath, *An Introduction to Sri Anandamayi Ma,* 34–5.

2. R. Sanjiva Rao, quoted in Ibid., 57.

3. Richard Lannoy quoted in Ibid., xv.

4. Saraswati, *Kundalini Tantra,* 105.

5. Aurobindo, *The Life Divine,* 648–54.

6. Johari, *Leela,* 14–15.

7. Saraswati, *Kundalini Tantra,* 134.

8. Quoted in Chidvilasananda, *The Yoga of Discipline,* 71.

9. Ibid., 77.

10. Aurobindo, *The Life Divine,* 939, 945–46.

11. Ibid., 120.

10. SEVENTH OR SAHASRARA CHAKRA

1. Chidvilasananda, *The Yoga of Discipline,* 80.

2. Adiswarananda, *Sri Ramakrishna Biography.*

3. Vivekananda. *Words of Wisdom.*

4. Anandamayi Ma, *Sad Vani,* 28.

5. Amritanandamayi, *108 Quotes on Love,* 36.

6. Johari, *Chakras,* 145.

7. James, *The Varieties of Religious Experience,* n. 231.

8. Wilber, *No Boundary,* 261.

9. Aurobindo, *A Greater Psychology,* 209–10.

10. Aurobindo, *The Synthesis of Yoga,* 280–82.

11. Kedarnath, *An Introduction to Sri Anandamayi Ma,* 36 (footnote 21).

12. Ibid., 54–55.

13. Aurobindo, *A Greater Psychology,* 140.

14. Narmada Puri, personal communication 2013.

15. Amritanandamayi, *108 Quotes on Love,* 69, 71, 100.

16. Amritanandamayi, *Garland of Love,* 65.

17. Aurobindo, *The Life Divine,* 944–46.

18. Attributed to Tagore, as found on numerous online quotation sites; original source unknown.

19. Johari, *Chakras,* 149.

11. REMOVING OBSTACLES
TO COSMIC CONSCIOUSNESS

1. Johari, *Chakras,* 66.

2. Johari, personal communication.

12. WHAT NEXT?

1. Sharma, *Modern Saints and Mystics,* 80–82, 93, 119, 155, 160, 207.

2. Gandhi, *Gandhi,* 5, 23, 38, 50.

3. Johari, *Leela,* 112–113.

4. Amritanandamayi, *The Infinite Potential of Women,* Pamphlet.

5. Prabhavananda, *The Spiritual Heritage of India,* 149.

BIBLIOGRAPHY

Adiswarananda, Swami. *Sri Ramakrishna Biography.* www.ramakrishna.org/sa.htm.

Aiyar, K. Narayanasvami, trans. *Thirty Minor Upanishads.* Santa Cruz, Calif.: Evinity Publishing, Inc., 2009.

Amritanandamayi, Sri Mata (Amma). *The Infinite Potential of Women.* Amritapuri, Kerala, India: Mata Amrit-anandamayi Mission Trust. 2008.

———. *Garland of Love.* Amritapuri, Kerala, India: Mata Amritanandamayi Mission Trust, 2012.

———. *108 Quotes on Love.* Amritapuri, Kerala, India: Mata Amritanandamayi Mission Trust, 2014.

Anandamayi Ma, Sri. *As a Flower Sheds its Fragrance: Diary Leaves of a Devotee.* Edited by Richard Lannoy. Kankhal, Hardiwar, India: 1993, 2006.

———. *Sad Vani: A Collection of the Teaching of Sri Anandamayi Ma.* Translated by Atmananda Roy, 4th ed. Calcutta, India: Shree Shree Charitable Society, 1981.

Ansbacher, Hans and Rowena, eds. *The Individual Psychology of Alfred Adler.* New York: Harper/Basic Books, 1956.

Assagioli, Roberto. "Balancing and Synthesis of the Opposites." *The Esoteric Quarterly* 2004.

———. *Psychosynthesis.* New York: Viking, 1965.

Aurobindo Ghose, Sri. *A Greater Psychology: An Introduction to the Psychological Thought of Sri Aurobindo.* Edited by A. A. Dalal. New York: Jeremy P. Tarcher/Putnam, 2001.

———. *The Life Divine.* Pondichery, India: Sri Aurobindo Ashram, 1939.

———. *The Synthesis of Yoga.* Twin Lakes, Wisc.: Lotus Press, 1948, 1990.

Bettelheim, Bruno. *Freud and Man's Soul.* New York: Random House Vintage, 1984.

Bolen, Jean Shinoda. *The Ring of Power.* York Beach, Maine: Nicholas-Hays, 1999.

Canan, Janine. *Messages from Amma, in the Langauge of the Heart.* Berkeley, Calif.: Celestial Arts, 2004.

Chidvilasananda, Gurumayi. *The Yoga of Discipline.* Chennai, India: Chikshakti Publications, 1996.

Chinmoy, Sri. *The Wings of Joy: Finding Your Path to Inner Peace.* New York: Touchstone Books, 1997.

Dalai Lama. *How to Practice: The Way to a Meaningful Life.* Translated by Jeffrey Hopkins. New York: Atria Books, 2002.

Fitzgerald, Joseph A., ed. *The Essential Sri Anandamayi Ma: Life and Teachings of a 20th Century Indian Saint.* New Delhi: Motilal Banarsidass Publishers Pvt Ltd., 2007.

Frawley, David. *Vedic Yoga: The Path of the Rishi.* Twin Lakes, Wisc.: Lotus Press, 2014.

Fromm, Erich. *Man For Himself.* New York: Holt, Rhinehart & Winston, 1960.

Gandhi, Mahatma. *Gandhi.* Compiled and edited by Krishna Kripalani. Ahmedabad, India: Navajivan Publishing House, no date given.

Hall, Robert K. Personal communication, 1971.

Hari Dass, Baba. *Fire Without Fuel.* Santa Cruz, Calif.: Sri Rama Publishing, 1986.

———. *Silence Speaks.* Santa Cruz, Calif.: Sri Rama Publishing, 1997.

Iyengar, BKS. *Light on the Yoga Sutras of Patanjali.* New Delhi: HarperCollins India, 1993.

Jacobson, Edmund. *Progressive Relaxation.* Chicago: University of Chicago Press, 1929, 1938.

James, William. *The Varieties of Religious Experience: A Study in Human Nature.* Heraklion Press, 2014. Original publication 1902.

Johari, Harish. *Ayurvedic Massage: Traditional Indian Techniques for Balancing Body and Mind.* Rochester, Vt.: Healing Arts Press, 1996.

———. *Breath, Mind and Consciousness.* Rochester, Vt.: Destiny Books, 1989.

———. *Chakras: Energy Centers of Transformation*, 2nd ed. Rochester, Vt.: Destiny Books, 2000.

———. *Dhanwantari.* Calcutta: Rupa & Co., 1992.

———. *Leela: The Game of Self-Knowledge* (a book and board game). New York: Coward, McCann & Geogegan, 1975; Rochester, Vt.: Destiny Books, 1993.

———. Personal communication, 1985–1999.

———. *Tools for Tantra.* Rochester, Vt.: Destiny Books, 1986.

Johari, Harish and Will Geraets. *The Wisdom Teachings of Harish Johari on the Mahabharata.* Rochester, Vt.: Destiny Books, 2011.

Judith, Anodea. *Eastern Body, Western Mind: Psychology and the Chakra System as a Path to the Self.* New York: Celestial Arts, 1996, 2004.

———. *Wheels of Life: A User's Guide to the Chakra System.* St. Paul, Minn.: Llewellyn, 1994.

Jung, Carl. *Man and His Symbols.* New York: Dell, 1968.

Kedernath Swami. *An Introduction to Sri Anandamayi Ma's Philosophy of Absolute Cognition.* Indore, India: Om Ma Sri Sri Mata Anandamayi Peeth Trust, 2010.

Kempton, Sally. *Awakening Shakti: The Transformative Power of the Goddesses of Yoga.* Boulder, Colo.: Sounds True, 2013.

Keyes, Ken. *A Conscious Person's Guide to Relationships.* St. Mary, Ky.: Living Love Publications, 1979.

Korzybski, Alfred. *Science and Sanity: An Introduction to Non-Aristotelian Systems and General Semantics,* 4th ed. New York: Institute of General Semantics, 1958.

Marchand, Peter. *The Yoga of the Nine Emotions.* Rochester, Vt.: Destiny Books, 2006.

Maslow, Abraham H. *Motivation and Personality,* 3rd ed. New York: HarperCollins, 1987.

———. *Toward a Psychology of Being,* 2nd ed. New York: Van Nostrand, 1968.

Meher Baba. *Discourses.* 3 vols. San Francisco: Sufism Reoriented, 1973.

Milk Baba. Personal communication, 2012.

Mishra, Rammurti. *Fundamentals of Yoga.* New York: Lancer Books, 1959.

Muktananda, Swami. *Play of Consciousness.* San Francisco: Harper & Row, 1978.

Narmada Puri, Mataji. Personal communications, Haridwar, 2013.

———. *Tears of Bliss: A Guru-Disciple Mystery.* Santosh Puri Ashram/Cinnamonteal Print and Publishing, India: 2009.

Odier, Daniel. *Tantric Quest: An Encounter With Absolute Love.* Rochester, Vt.: Inner Traditions, 1997.

Perls, Fritz. *Ego, Hunger, and Aggression: The Beginning of Gestalt Therapy*. New York: Random House, 1947.

———. *In and Out of the Garbage Pail*. Moab, Utah: Real People Press, 1969.

Pilot Baba, Mahayogi. *Himalaya Unveils Mystery*. New Delhi: Mahayog Foundation, undated.

———. Personal communication, Haridwar, 2013.

Prabhavananda, Swami and Christopher Isherwood, trans. *The Song of God: Bhagavad-Gita*. Hollywood, Calif.: Vedanta Press, 1944, 1951.

Prabhavananda, Swami, with Frederick Manchester. *The Spiritual Heritage of India*. Madras, India: Sri Ramakrishna Math, 1977.

Prajnapad, Swami. In *Encyclopedia of Hinduism,* edited by Constance A. Jones and James D. Ryan. Encyclopedia of World Religions series, New York: Facts on File, 2007.

Ram Dass and Paul Gorman. *How Can I Help?* New York: Alfred A. Knopf, 1985, 1994, 2011.

Ram Dass with Rameswar Das. *Be Love Now.* Harper Collins E Pub Edition, 2010.

———. *Polishing the Mirror: How to Live from Your Spiritual Heart*. Boulder, Colo.: Sounds True, 2013.

Rama, Swami. *Living with the Himalayan Masters*. Honesdale, Pa.: Himalayan Institute Press, 1978.

Rao, B. Sanjiva, "Mother as Seen by Her Devotees." In Kedernath Swami. *An Introduction to Sri Anandamayi Ma's Philosophy of Absolute Cognition*. Indore, India: Om Ma Sri Sri Mata Anandamayi Peeth Trust, 2010.

Rogers, Carl. *On Becoming a Person: A Therapist's View of Psychotherapy*. Boston: Houghton Mifflin, 1961.

Sartre, Jean Paul. *Existentialism and Humanism*. Translated by Philip Mairet. London: Eyre Methuen, 1973.

Satchidananda, Swami. *The Yoga Sutras of Patanjali*. Integral Yoga Publications, 1950, 1990.

Satir, Virginia. *The New Peoplemaking, 2nd ed.* Mountain View, Calif.: Science & Behavior Books, 1988.

Satyananda Saraswati, Swami. *Kundalini Tantra*. Munger, Bihar, India: Yoga Publications Trust, 1984, 2013.

Shankara, Adi. *Shankara's Crest Jewel of Discrimination*. Edited by Swami Prabhavananda. Vedanta Society of Southern California, 1975.

Sivanand, Amritha, inter. "A Flood of Artistry: The Men and Methods behind a Stunning Rendering of Goddess Ganga's Mythic Tale." *Hinduism Today* January 1999: www.hinduismtoday.com/modules/smartsection/item.php?itemid=4423 .%20Magazine%20web%20edition,%20January%201999.

Sivananda, Sri Swami. *Kundalini Yoga, Tenth Edition*. Shivanandagar, India: The Divine Life Society, 1994.

Tagore, Rabindranath. Found on numerous online quotation sites, original source unknown.

Tulku, Tarthang. *Gesture of Balance: A Guide to Awareness, Self-Healing, and Meditation*. Berkeley, Calif.: Dharma Publishing, 1977.

Vivekananda, Swami. *Letters of Swami Vivekananda*. Edited by Swami Tapasyananda. Advaita Ashram, India: 1940.

———. *Raja Yoga*. New York: Vivekananda-Ramakrishna Center, 1955.

———. *Words of Wisdom: Swami Vivekananda*. Edited by Students Academy. Lulu Press www.lulu.com.

Wertheimer, Max. "Gestalt Theory." 1924. Reprinted by *Gestalt Journal Press* 1997, http://gestalttheory.net/archive/wert1.html.

Wilber, Ken. *No Boundary: Eastern and Western Approaches to Personal Growth*. Boston & London: Shambhala, New Science Library, 1985.

Wilhem, Richard and Cary F. Baynes. *The I Ching, or Book of Changes*. Princeton, N.J.: Princeton University Press, 1967.

Wynne, L. C., "Some Indications and Contraindications for Exploratory Family Therapy." In *Intensive Family Therapy*. Edited by Ivan Boszormenyi-Nagy and James Framo. New York: Harper and Row, 1965.

Yogananda, Paramahansa. *The Essence of Self Realization*. Los Angeles: Self-Realization Fellowship, 2009.

Yogananda, Paramahansa. Remarks found on numerous Internet quotation sites.

Yukteswar Sri Giri. *The Holy Science*. Amazon: Digital Edition 2014.

Index

BOOKS OF RELATED INTEREST

Matrix Meditations
A 16-week Program for Developing the Mind-Heart Connection
by Victor Daniels and Kooch N. Daniels

How Ganesh Got His Elephant Head
by Harish Johari and Vatsala Sperling
Illustrated by Pieter Weltevrede

The Magical Adventures of Krishna
How a Mischief Maker Saved the World
by Vatsala Sperling
Illustrated by Pieter Weltevrede

Chakras
Energy Centers of Transformation
by Harish Johari

Numerology
With Tantra, Ayurveda, and Astrology
by Harish Johari

Spiritual Traditions of India Coloring Book
by Harish Johari

Chakra Frequencies
Tantra of Sound
by Jonathan Goldman and Andi Goldman

Emotion and Healing in the Energy Body
A Handbook of Subtle Energies in Massage and Yoga
by Robert Henderson

INNER TRADITIONS • BEAR & COMPANY
P.O. Box 388
Rochester, VT 05767
1-800-246-8648
www.InnerTraditions.com

Or contact your local bookseller